Tammy

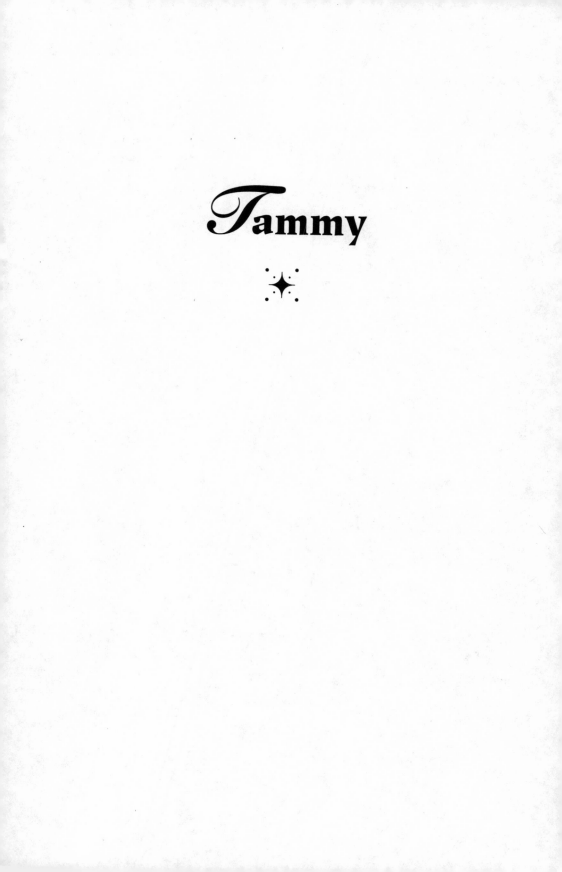

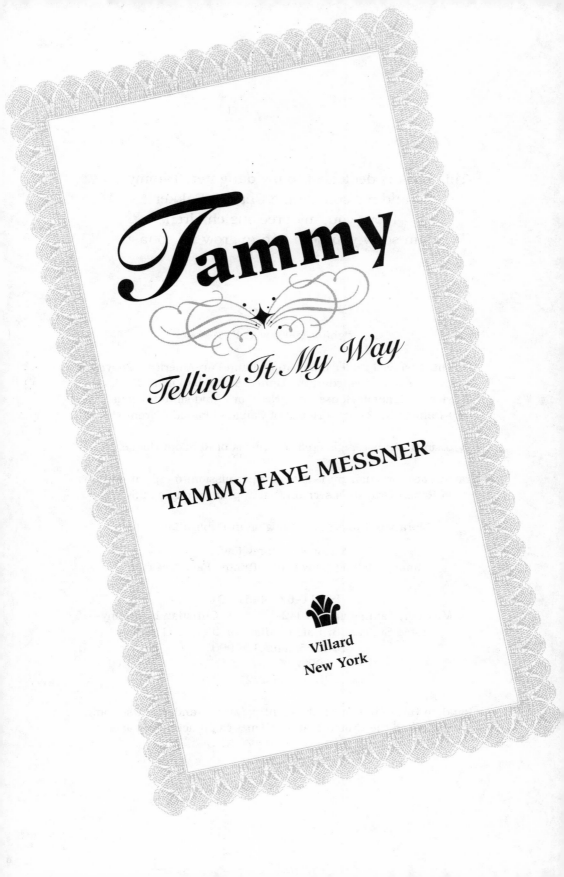

Tammy
Telling It My Way

TAMMY FAYE MESSNER

Villard
New York

This book is dedicated to my daughter, Tammy Sue,
and my son, Jamie Charles Bakker.
I love you, my precious children.
I am sorry you both had to grow up so fast.

Copyright © 1996 by T. F. Messner

All rights reserved under International and Pan-American Copyright
Conventions. Published in the United States by Villard Books, a
division of Random House, Inc., New York, and simultaneously in
Canada by Random House of Canada Limited, Toronto.

VILLARD BOOKS is a registered trademark of Random House, Inc.

Grateful acknowledgment is given for permission to reprint portions
of Robert Gray Jr.'s sermon that appear on pages 225–27.

Library of Congress Cataloging-in-Publication Data

Messner, Tammy Faye.
Tammy : telling it my way / Tammy Faye Messner
p.   cm.
ISBN 0-679-44515-3
1. Messner, Tammy Faye, 1942–   . 2. Christian biography—
United States. 3. Bakker, Jim, 1940–   . I. Title.
BR1725.M43A3 1996
269'.2'092—dc20
[B]   96-17274

Random House website address: http://www.randomhouse.com/
Printed in the United States of America on acid-free paper
2 4 6 8 9 7 5 3
First Edition

Acknowledgments

I want to acknowledge above all the Lord Jesus Christ. He has been my everything, through the good times and the bad times. Anything I am or ever hope to be, I owe it all to Him.

I respectfully acknowledge three women in my life: my mother, who brought me into the world, for her love and kindness to me; my grandmother, who taught me that no matter what happens in life, "Pick yourself up by your bootstraps and keep on going"; and my Aunt Gin (Virginia), who taught me how to be a lady and the importance of making my own decisions.

I want to acknowledge my many girlfriends who have been there for me through thick and thin. Thank you for believing in me. I wish that I could name each one of you, but I would feel terrible if I left out one name. You know who you are. Thank you, from the bottom of my heart, for being my support system.

I acknowledge my wonderful husband, Roe Messner, who gave me the courage to live again. He taught me that yesterday is gone, all we have for certain is today, and tomorrow is in the hands of God. He has taught me the importance of stopping for a moment every day to smell the roses. Thank you, sweetheart!

I acknowledge Tammy Sue Bakker Chapman and Jay Charles Bakker. You make my life worth living.

Contents

PART THREE: THE RISE OF PTL

PART FOUR: THE FALWELL OF PTL

PART FIVE: AFTERSHOCKS!

PART SIX: RESURRECTION

Closing One Chapter

The phone rang. It was my friend Deb Keener, who is like a sister to me. "Tam, quick, turn on Channel 6. Jim just got out of prison. Hurry!" My heart was beating so fast I could hardly catch my breath as I ran to the television and nervously tried to find the right channel.

After five long years, the day I had prayed for had finally arrived. Tears streamed down my face as I sat there watching the man I had been married to for over thirty years being escorted by our children, Jamie and Tammy Sue. I was so happy for him, happy in knowing that when he walked out those prison doors, he freed not only himself but our whole family. He looked good!

Jamie and Tammy Sue were so protective of him as the news media shouted their never-ending questions. But I felt guilty as I watched. *Mom should be there, too.* I knew that that's what everyone was thinking.

This is the story of Jim Bakker and Tammy Faye LaValley Bakker, better known as Jim and Tammy. It is the story of two people who set out to win the world to Jesus. You will follow them as they help to build America's first Christian TV network. You will go behind the scenes as victories turn to despair. You will share life with my two children, whose only wish was to live normal lives. But how can you be normal when people are watching you, wanting your autograph, pinching your cheeks, and wanting to take your picture when you are trying to play with your friends?

You will see what love can accomplish, but you will also see friends turn into enemies and enemies become friends. You will witness power, greed, and jealousy.

I did not want to write this book. I felt I *had* to—for the sake of my children and grandchildren and the millions of PTL partners who put their faith in Jim and Tammy. I have no axes to grind; I do not want to destroy anyone. I have no reason to lie. However, the truth is the truth. And I do not sugarcoat it.

I take full responsibility for any part I played in the eventual downfall and destruction of our beautiful Heritage USA and the PTL ministry that occupied it.

Millions of dollars have been made by people who write tell-all books. The news media told and retold the Jim and Tammy story over and over. I have seen Jim Bakker marched across television screens time and time again, handcuffed, his feet bound in shackles. The rag magazines have done their part in sensationalizing their "sources say" stories. And the *American Justice* TV series has written history their way. Now it's my turn.

I hope that in writing this book I can somehow change people's perceptions. I was there. I lived it every day. I knew all the participants. I was married to Jim Bakker. I've heard it said that there are two sides to every story. I want to tell my side.

And then allow you to be the judge.

Part One

In the

Beginning

Welcome to
International Falls

was born on March 7, 1942. My mom almost didn't make it to the hospital on time, as we were in the middle of a huge snowstorm. Welcome to International Falls, Minnesota. My name was supposed to be Sandra Kay—if I was a girl, that is. In those days you didn't know if you were having a boy or a girl. I think it was much more exciting that way. I don't know what name Mom had chosen if I had been a boy. She told me I came out kicking and screaming. And the thing she remembered most about me was that I had such beautifully shaped fingernails. She said it looked like I had been to the manicurist.

I was the first grandchild, so of course everyone thought I was the most wonderful baby that had ever been born. In fact, my Grandma Fairchild is the reason this book is not titled *Sandra Kay: Telling It My Way.* The day I was born she heard the name "Tamara" on a radio broadcast. It belonged to a Russian ballerina. She loved the name and convinced Mom to change Sandra Kay to Tamara Faye. I often wonder if my life would have been different as Sandra rather than Tammy. Probably not.

Only a few months after World War II ended, my mother,

Rachel, divorced my father, Carl LaValley. I was only three years old at the time, and I have no memory of what he looked like. A few years later my mom married Fred Grover, a wonderful man who had lost his wife to cancer, after which she became Rachel Minnie Fairchild Grover. But as far as I was concerned my stepfather was my real daddy, accepting me without question as his own daughter.

But out where we lived, in the tiny rural community of International Falls, Minnesota, being divorced was a dreadful and unforgivable sin; ours was a deeply religious township with a population of barely six thousand. Most of the people in my mother's church—the Assemblies of God—were heartless to her because of her divorce, mean and vindictive. It was as if a big scarlet *D* had been branded across her forehead.

I remember one night, when I was still quite young, a group of them came over to confront her. As soon as they started knocking, Mom sent all the kids upstairs and told us to shut our doors. But I kept mine open just a crack and listened. But open or closed, it wouldn't have made a difference. You could have heard them through solid stone.

"Please, please, just allow me to play the piano in church when the regular pianist can't be there," my mom was begging them. "It's better than no music at all. I just want to help. It's foolish to do without a pianist when I could so easily fill in for him. At least for Sunday service."

"Rachel, you will never play piano in our church. You have sinned a terrible sin!"

"God gave me a gift. Why shouldn't I be able to use it for Him? All I want to do is use the gift the Lord gave me."

"If you really believed in the Lord, you wouldn't have gotten a divorce! I don't see how you can hold your head up. You are an embarrassment to our church."

"You know I had to do what I did. Another woman was

having Carl's baby. What else could I do? He said he was in love with her. I couldn't stay married to a man who doesn't love me."

"Rachel, there's only one explanation. You must have driven Carl away. That's the real reason—face it! Not one of *our* husbands would ever dream of leaving us for another woman!" And on and on it went. I heard my mother pleading with them, but the delegation offered her no comfort, no compassion, no forgiveness; they said she deserved everything she got. Any hardship she was going through, any emotional problems . . . well, that's too bad, because that's what happens when you commit such a terrible crime against our faith.

"And your children, Rachel. You've given them such a heavy burden in the eyes of the Lord. To know their mother is a sinner and that she's going straight to—"

"But that's not right! God is love. God is not cruel. Please don't—"

I heard the door slam. The house was completely still, except for the forlorn sounds of my mother's sobs. The intolerance of those women made me so furious! I knew how good my mother's heart was, that she would never hurt a soul, and I swore I wasn't going to be ashamed of her—no matter what anyone said about her or my real father.

I ran down the stairs and threw my arms around her.

"Mom, I love you, I love you, I think you're wonderful just the way you are. Don't let anyone say anything bad about you!" And my mother just hugged me, wiping away my tears as her own streamed down her weary face.

What made it even more heartbreaking was that my mother was the finest singer and piano player you ever heard, always right on key and so pretty to listen to. As the years passed I came to realize these women were simply jealous of my mother's incredible talent.

Despite my mother's troubles with the church, we were still a very religious family, mostly because my mother wasn't going to allow what anyone said or did to interfere with her love of God. Therefore the church was really the focal point of our lives. During special gatherings or holidays you would find her in the church kitchen preparing dishes. She was always chock full of creative ideas and resources—the ultimate organizer.

Our family was like the Brady Bunch on TV, except there were *four* boys and *four* girls. Two of us, Donny and me, came from my mother's first marriage; the other six children, Larry, Judy, Danny, Johnny, Debbie, and Ruth, belonged to my stepfather. I was the oldest of the bunch and, as such, had to work extra hard in helping Mom raise the kids, consistently taking on loads of additional responsibilities.

I always washed the dishes. I was the one who took care of my brothers and sisters when Mom was busy doing a hundred different things. I took them to the playground; I did anything I could to entertain them and keep them out of Mom's hair for a little while. I was really like their second mother.

I used to try to help Mom with the washing. Washing in those days was quite a chore and took all day. Two days a week Mom would heat up water on the stove and then pour the hot water into an old wringer washing machine she would push into the middle of the kitchen. With eight children, you can just imagine the mounds of dirty clothes there were to be washed every week. She would separate them into piles of white and dark, washing the white things first. I could help her do that part.

But she would not allow me to get anywhere near the wringer that you used to squeeze the water out of the clothes after they had been rinsed in a big tub of cold water. After the clothes were run through the wringer, they were ready to be put in a big laundry basket and taken outside.

The next step was the clothesline. I can still see Mom in

twenty-below weather hanging clothes on that line, her mouth full of clothespins, her hands so cold she could hardly move them. I was too small to reach the clothesline, so I couldn't help her.

And I don't know what good it did to even hang up those clothes in the middle of those cold winter days. They would freeze and be as stiff as boards. When Mom finally brought them back into the house and they thawed out, they still weren't dry, and we would have to hang them all over the living room to finish drying. Afterward, I would spend hours ironing them for Mom. I was good at ironing and enjoyed the task.

As hard as winter was on our family it was also a time of immense pleasure. For this was the season Daddy would go out in the snowy backyard and clear a big circle. Then he would pile snow all around that circle, take out the garden hose, and spray water to make us our own ice-skating rink! Many times the weather was so freezing cold that you could go skating in less than an hour. So thanks to my dad, we were able to ice-skate to our hearts' content all winter long.

Also in the backyard was the outhouse, the outdoor bathroom we had to use rain or shine, year-round. Take it from me: On those cold wintry days in Minnesota when it used to hit twenty or thirty below zero, with the wind howling around outside and shooting right through the wooden slats, you didn't want to linger too long while doing whatever you were doing.

Whenever Halloween would roll around, my brothers would roam the neighborhood searching for outhouses that were occupied. When they found some poor, unsuspecting person relieving himself, they would push the outhouse over. Then they'd hightail it out of there at top speed, laughing their heads off hysterically as they jumped over bushes and fences.

In our house we also had an upstairs bathroom—of

sorts. Actually, it was a pail with a cover that the younger kids used when the weather was really awful. Once I remember my mom shouting up the stairs, "I want one of you boys to empty that potty this minute! It's practically overflowing!" It was my brothers' chore to empty the pail regularly, but nobody would be the first to volunteer. You can imagine why!

Anyhow, the boys quickly huddled together to decide who was going to lug that disgusting thing down. "As the oldest," proclaimed my brother Donny, "I elect Larry." But Larry didn't exactly relish the opportunity.

"It makes me nauseous! Since I'm older than Danny, I elect him."

"That's not fair!" protested Danny. "I did it last time." Instantly all eyes focused on Johnny, the youngest brother.

"No, not me," he said in his squeaky voice. "I'm not strong enough."

"The decision's been made," announced Donny. "The three of us elect you. And majority rules!"

Well, I could hear the pail scraping along the floor, and I peeked out of my room. Johnny was making a valiant effort, but halfway down the stairs he lost his footing and the pail went tumbling down the steps, its contents splattering all over the place. It landed at my mom's feet.

"Johnny!" she shouted. "Who made you carry that all by yourself?"

"I was elected by the majority."

That's when my mother really hit the roof. "This whole house is completely stunk up!" In a panic she ran over to the extra clothes closet under the stairs and threw open the door. The putrid mess had seeped in there as well. "I'm going to have to wash out everything all over again!"

Then she slammed the door and marched up the stairs. By this time the boys were all cowering in the corner. "Donny! Larry! Danny! Get yourselves over here this instant!" Suffice it to say, each one of my brothers got a good licking. We never had trouble finding a volunteer to empty that bucket again!

Besides not having a gas range or appliances like a clothes washer and dryer, we also didn't have a refrigerator. Accordingly the iceman would come calling on a regular basis, pulling out immense blocks of ice from the back of his truck with these huge menacing pincers and then carrying them straight into our icebox. I can still picture us kids during those scorching summer days of July and August, chasing down the block after that broken-down truck, scooping up all the broken chunks of ice that fell to the ground and greedily sucking on them to cool off.

The night we most looked forward to was Saturday, because that was the only time during the week when we got to take a real bath. We soaked ourselves in a great big galvanized tub that Daddy had gotten down at the paper mill where he worked. What a contraption! That thing must have weighed at least seventy-five pounds and was kept hanging outside in the garage. Daddy would hoist it up and then sling it over his back. Bent down under the load, he would struggle to haul it inside without giving himself a hernia; meanwhile, Mom would be outside pumping water from the well. As I recall, it would take more than two hours just to heat up enough water to fill that rusty old tub.

Naturally, the cleanest kid would go first; I have to admit that was always me. Everybody else would have to wait their turn. But to make the night really special, Mom would always set a large pot of fudge boiling on the stove. After our baths, each of us would receive a big piece of that delicious fudge. When we were all toweled dry and tuckered out, she would take us upstairs and then sing us softly to sleep. I'll never forget her sweet voice. It was like hearing a lullaby from an angel.

In the early 1950s there were no shopping malls, no

video games, no cineplexes with sixteen different movies playing at the same time, so you had to create your own form of happiness.

Back then owning a TV was beyond the means of most folks we knew. And even if someone did have one, they probably didn't get any kind of reception, since I don't think there was a television station located anywhere near us. Due to this our entire home life was centered around the radio, our link to what was happening in the outside world. Many a night we sat around and listened to the Grand Ole Opry.

I loved the Grand Ole Opry. It made me fantasize about singing professionally, maybe even on the radio someday, but I didn't believe that I would ever make it. For one thing, I never thought I was good enough, and for another, I just assumed I'd never get the opportunity, stuck all the way out in International Falls, right in the middle of northern Minnesota.

A Stormy Marriage

After my mom divorced my real dad, he married the woman he had gotten pregnant, and eventually they had eight more children. I found out when I was about eight that he was living only a few blocks away from us. I always used to hear about my brother Donny going to see Carl, but I was afraid to visit him myself. And deep inside I was hurt that he never came over to see me.

As I grew older, people began telling me what a nice man Carl was. My Aunt Gin, Mom's sister, told me that I would have loved my real daddy. She said that because Carl was dyslexic, he could never learn to read or write. Carl drove a truck, one of those big rigs that carried freight and crisscrossed the country. He was often away for long periods of time. The more I heard about him, the more I thought he was truly a remarkable man. Unfortunately he just loved women too much.

My mother had gotten divorced once, and many times it seemed like she might get divorced twice, because her second marriage was difficult as well. The truth was, Fred liked to drink and smoke, and my mother couldn't stand that. She couldn't tolerate alcohol and couldn't abide cigarettes. So Dad was always forced to smoke outside, even if it was twenty degrees below zero.

All the kids used to peek through the window and laugh at Daddy struggling to puff away while the winds whipped around something fierce. Dad smoked Camels or Lucky Strikes all his life.

Also, because Mom really believed in the church teachings, she didn't want her kids to see their daddy drinking. But my father's drinking never affected me. I never saw him what you would call drunk. Probably because I just didn't recognize the signs at the time. To me, he was always just happy.

I remember one time Daddy came in a little tipsy, and I could see Mom getting real red in the face. "Fred, you've been drinking again. I can tell it by your breath. What have I told you about drinking?"

"But, Rachel, I just had a couple of beers. All the guys were just having a couple of beers. I didn't think it would hurt nothing."

"I've told you a thousand times, I don't want you coming home drunk around these kids."

"Look, I got a headache. I'm getting some aspirins." And with that he started straight up the stairs—but tripped and fell to one knee.

"Fred, you're falling-down drunk. It's disgusting. You can't even make it up the stairs."

"What do you mean I can't make it up the stairs? Who are you to tell me I can't make it up the stairs?"

"I'm just trying to protect my children. I don't want my children to ever see—"

"Well, they're my children too. You think I don't protect my children?"

"I've told you time and time again," my mother said, pointing an accusing finger at him. "Don't come home from the mill if you're going to come home drunk."

"Hey, when you start paying the bills around here,

maybe that's when you can start telling me what to do. If you don't want me here, I'll just leave! You hear me, Rachel! I'll just leave!!"

"Then just leave," she screamed. "I'm not holding you here!"

Down at the mill—the paper mill down by the river—they constantly gambled and smoked and drank, so Dad didn't see anything wrong with it. Those kind of activities went with the territory—and besides, none of the other wives made a fuss over it, so what was the big deal? Sometimes when they would start arguing I would run upstairs and shut the bedroom door, burying myself beneath the sheets. Then I would press my hands over my ears.

But I could still hear my daddy's voice booming through the house. "If you don't want me around, I'll just leave!" And then I would hear the door slam—that sound was like a knife through my heart. And all I could do was just cry and cry, drowning in a pool of tears.

I'd get way down on my knees, clasp my hands together, and pray. "Oh please, God, oh please, dear Lord, please don't let my daddy leave my mom." Because if he left and she couldn't support us, then I didn't know what might happen. I was terrified that all my sisters and brothers would somehow be separated from one another. But I wasn't going to let anybody take them away from me—not even one.

Small wonder I took on so many extra chores around the house—anything to make it easier for my mother. Maybe if I just did a few more things, that would take the pressure off their marriage. Small wonder that early on I became a true caretaker, trained to fix things but still too young to know there are some things that can't be repaired.

My mother's life turned out very different from the way she thought it would. When she was just a young girl, she had been called by God to the mission field in Africa. She wanted to go and help care for the children in orphanages

and minister to the needs of the suffering. And she probably would have, had she not met my real father and fallen
in love.

At first my mother practically worshiped him, so much
so that she married outside her religion, since my real
daddy was Roman Catholic and she was Pentecostal. But
in this case love didn't wind up conquering all. My mother
didn't understand his religion, and he probably didn't understand her beliefs either. It's my theory that Mom had so
many disappointments in life that she decided to become a
perfectionist. If she couldn't bring the word of God to the
people in Africa, then she—and everyone else around her—
would lead a perfect Christian life at home.

Therefore I don't think it was Fred she was screaming at
as much as the whole situation. It was no doubt a cry for
help. How did I get into this? What happened? What went
wrong? She probably felt that she was digging a hole
deeper and deeper and that she couldn't get out, that there
was no hope for her dreams to come true. Here she was, so
cute, so intelligent, and so very charismatic, with so much
love and beauty to give the world. I guess she ended up
realizing that she was just going to have to give it all to her
children.

A Room of My Own

We were very poor, but I never considered us as being poor when I was growing up. I mean, that was just the way it was. You accepted life because you didn't know any other kind of existence. None of us kids could have our own rooms. All the boys had to sleep together; all the sisters shared a room. Four kids were crammed into a single small bed, something which most people today can't even begin to imagine. Most upsetting was when one of the young ones would wet the bed, because then we'd all have to get up and change the sheets in the middle of the night.

One day I came home from school and Mom was sitting in the rocking chair holding one of the babies. "Tammy Faye, I have something to show you. Come upstairs with me." As she carried the infant with her, we walked up to the second floor.

Upstairs there were three rooms: two bedrooms and a storage room. Therefore nothing looked unusual as we stepped into the bedroom where the four boys slept. But then Mom walked around the boys' bed and opened the door to the storage room. "Here's your new bedroom," she said. "It's all yours, honey!" Standing there I was just awe-struck. This had to be a dream.

I walked into the most beautiful room I have ever seen. The walls were all freshly painted white. Over the open window were beautiful white curtains softly blowing in the breeze. From somewhere Mom had found an extra bed and placed upon it a beautiful white bedspread. A little white rug lay on the floor, and against one wall was a small dresser with a mirror. And to my surprise I even had my own closet!

I couldn't believe my eyes! I thought I had died and gone to heaven. I nearly hugged my mom to death, I was so happy. My very own room, my very own bed, my very own closet—and a door I could shut. From then on, I sat in that room every hour of every day when I was not at school or helping Mom. Someone had given me a little plastic angel, and I hung it on the wall over my bed. It gathered the light during the day and then glowed a pretty blue all night long. I fell asleep every night dreamily looking up at that darling little angel.

The older I got, the prettier my room got. One day my dad brought home from the mill rolls and rolls of paper, the kind you wrap gifts with. As soon as I saw it, a wondrous idea struck me—wallpaper! The entire night I spent un-rolling that paper and sticking it on the walls of my bed-room with straight pins. When I was finished, I had the loveliest wallpaper in the world, pale white with little pink flowers. I was so proud of myself.

As you can see, even from my earliest years, I learned to make do with very little because we never really had that much.

But no matter how tight the household budget, Mom was always a wonderful cook. She had the great knack of being able to make something from nothing, knowing how to combine foods and season vegetables so that they tasted positively scrumptious. One of the dishes all the kids simply loved was hamburger and onions fried together; Mom would add whole-kernel corn and serve it with mashed potatoes. I still fix that today.

During the summer my father would bring home these huge cylinders of canvas from which he'd construct a giant Indian tepee in the backyard, usually towering over ten feet tall. When he finished, all eight of us would scamper inside and sit there all afternoon long—even though many times it was over 100 degrees outside. We would bang on paint cans, smear mud all over our faces, and then go on the warpath, as long as that path didn't cut through Mom's lilac bushes.

My mother's lilac bushes practically surrounded the house. In fact there were so many of them that in the early summer our whole place virtually smelled of lilacs, as if we were living inside some giant bottle of perfume. Also blossoming in the backyard were crab apple trees, which had been producing fresh fruit for generations. In the fall, Mom would gather those crab apples and can them to make her own sweet jelly, placing the jars way up in the cupboard. She canned all the fruits and vegetables in the garden, but I especially loved when she was busy canning tomatoes. It was the most delicious aroma you could possibly imagine.

There was a tremendous maple tree whose branches covered our entire backyard. From my window during the summer I could reach out and touch the branches. At night I would sit watching the leaves sway in the breeze as the moon lit up the whole backyard, eerily casting shadows this way and that. In wintertime the snow was often piled over two feet high. Everything seemed like a dream captured in a magic crystal, an enchanted fairyland ringed by icicles and created just for me.

Small wonder Christmas was the most special time of the year at our house. Mom would create for us an entire village on the dining-room table, a marvelous collection of miniature houses with tiny lights inside. She used cotton for snow and mirrors for an ice-skating rink. Then she had all kinds of little people dressed up in winter clothes with tiny earmuffs and mittens. Some had on ice skates, and she placed them inside the rink, as if they were racing around doing figure eights. The finishing touches were a pocket-sized Christmas tree and minuscule deer. Mom would then switch off all the lights in the room except for the ones in the tiny houses. For hours we kids would just sit and gaze at the little wonderland she created, fantasizing that we were living there.

We had a big old Model A Ford. Every year Daddy would paint it a different color, each one worse than the one before. One time it was this deep army green. The year after that he painted the Ford bright red. You'd swear that car belonged to the fire department. Before starting the car, he'd always say, "Giddyup there, Joe. Come on, now, let's go!" We kids loved hearing Daddy talk to that old car. He was so funny, and kept us laughing.

I can still recall driving out to see Aunt Tooty and Uncle Oscar, who lived on a farm about ten miles away. Ten miles was usually the farthest we ever ventured. Outside the ten-mile limit existed another world; there was Bemidji, Hibbing, and Virginia, and while I had visited all three of those towns, the truth was I was terribly sheltered. I had never seen a mountain. I had never seen an ocean.

But more than any mountain, more than any ocean, I wanted to see Minneapolis. Day and night I dreamed of that wondrous city. From what I had heard it seemed just like the Land of Oz, with wide avenues and huge buildings rising over ten stories tall. Ten stories! It was more than I could possibly imagine. Anything that tall must be able to just reach up and touch heaven itself!

The Language of the Lord

As a little girl, I attended a different church from the one my parents and brothers and sisters went to. On Sundays I went with my Aunt Gin to Mission Covenant, which was a different denomination from the Assemblies of God. Everyone asked me why I went to church with her instead of Mom and Dad, but I kept the secret to myself—that was the only time I felt special, like an only child, instead of merely being the oldest of eight.

But I thought about my mom's church a lot. Naturally, I had visited it, and I felt something different there, also something special. Everyone seemed so friendly and joyful as they prayed. At night I would lie in bed and wonder what it would feel like to be as ecstatic as they were. I knew it had something to do with God, but I wasn't sure exactly what. Even so, I couldn't give up my special days with Aunt Gin.

At Aunt Gin's church they talked about God as well, but it was on a whole other level. Somehow I never felt any different when I walked out of that Sunday service. I wasn't elated or overjoyed; it was just a pleasant experience.

One day my girlfriend Marion Kasara asked me if I wanted to visit my mom's church with her. I found the suggestion really exciting. Maybe I could find out the secret of what those people did, what they had that was so unique and inspiring.

Little did I know that my entire life would change that night.

The church service began, and my tiny ten-year-old heart was beating a hundred times a minute. The singing was exhilarating. The worshipers raised their hands up and told God they loved Him right out loud. Since I was a shy little girl, I could not figure out for the life of me why they did that, let alone how they had the nerve to carry on that way in front of everybody else. I had prayed to God many times, but it was always alone, down on my knees before going to bed at night.

I was fascinated by everything that was going on around me. But what I remember most vividly was actually sensing something powerful stirring deep inside me. I wished the feeling would never go away. There was such joy and peace and love inside me. I wanted to know what I could do to make it last.

Then the preacher said, "Everyone who wants God to touch them, come forward now. Everyone who wants to feel the power and the peace and the serenity that the Lord brings, come to the front. Now is the time to come forward. Now is the time to accept Him into your heart!" Well, I practically ran down the aisle, and I threw myself down on my knees by the front pew.

Almost immediately I started crying my little heart out, begging and pleading. "God, if what these people have is real, then please give it to me too! I want it more than anything in the whole wide world." What happened next will be etched in my memory forever, as if it were yesterday.

Speaking in tongues was something I had already heard

of. My grandmother did it sometimes when she was praying. I didn't know what to think about it; in fact I was rather scared by the whole notion. But I knew that if Grandma spoke in tongues, it couldn't be a bad thing, like some people were convinced it was. Still I didn't have a clue.

Now, no sooner had I said "God, please give it to me" than all of a sudden I just fell flat on my back. Raising my hands up in the air toward the Lord, I heard myself speaking in a language I had never heard before. As that language flowed from my innermost being I actually felt the presence of God within me. I have never in my whole life experienced such love. Liquid love pouring over my entire being!

I felt immeasurable joy. I wanted to burst out and just laugh and laugh, but I didn't. I just kept on speaking in the language God was giving me. In the blink of an eye I wasn't scared anymore. All the fear inside was gone, vanished, simply evaporated from every part of me. I felt immersed in peace, a sense of serenity that I cannot explain. For over two hours I didn't open my eyes. I just lay there speaking to God. It felt as if I were in heaven actually talking to God in person.

When I finally opened my eyes, it was like coming to. I sat up and looked around. Everyone in the congregation had gone, and the only people left were the pastor and my mom. Now, my mom had not gone to church that night, but when the pastor saw what was happening to me, he had called her immediately and said, "Rachel, there is something I want you to see. Tammy Faye found God tonight!"

Wherever my gaze fell, everything looked radiant. I never wanted to leave that spot—I wanted to stay there forever. But the pastor informed me that God would go with me, therefore I did not have to remain in church to keep feeling that way. From then on I could feel God at home, in the car, everywhere I went. I have never taken a drop of alcohol, but as I got up to be driven home by Mom, it was as if I were drunk. I was so relaxed and joyous and peaceful. The whole world changed for me that night. I would never be the same again.

My encounter with God would stay with me for the rest of my life. And from that moment onward I knew that God was with me, through whatever adversity or difficulty life threw my way. Beyond a shadow of a doubt I knew that God was real. For the next three weeks I felt that I was walking three feet off the ground. It felt as if a million pounds had been lifted off my shoulders. I wanted to tell everyone I met. I wanted to shout out loud and share my euphoria with the world!

Now I knew what I wanted to do with the rest of my life. It came to me as plain as day. As we got home and went into the kitchen, I hugged my mom with all the love in the world. "Mama, I'm going to do something for the Lord," I declared with dire urgency. "I want to sing, I want to preach the Gospel. I have to do something for God!"

As I told her everything that had happened, she held me to her breast and stroked my hair softly. Lord, I must have prattled on for at least ten minutes, but never once did she interrupt me. After I finally finished, she looked deeply into my eyes. "Honey," she said, "God is going to use you someday if you will always stay close to Him. Maybe you will have the chance to do for the Lord what I didn't." Kissing me tenderly on the forehead, she patted my rear and sent me on my way upstairs.

For years I had wondered how my mom could always be so kind to the people who treated her so badly. I had wondered how she could get up every Sunday morning and ready seven children for services. How could she give up her last few pennies to place in the church offering? And how could she stand the cruel rejection of her marvelous talent as a singer and piano player? Now it hit me like a ton of bricks.

My mom had received the Lord's message as well; she had undergone the same experience that I did. With this one realization I knew we would forever be joined spiritually—in a far closer way than even being mother and daughter.

I always loved school even though I was a shy little girl. It wasn't until high school that I realized that I didn't have as much as most of the other girls. They all seemed so well-dressed, so poised and confident all the time. Even though I worked at Woolworth's every night after school, I still could never afford clothes like they wore. So I stuck to straight black skirts and blouses. Because I was so tiny, everyone thought I was cute. The kids called me Shrimp or Squirt all the time, but I didn't mind. They also called me Sunshine. I guess that was because I was always so happy.

I kept waiting to grow tall like the other kids, but it never happened. I stopped growing heightwise in the seventh grade and never gained another inch. I have been 4'11" ever since. And not only was I short, but I was skinny. No matter how much I ate, I could never gain a pound. At age sixteen I still wore children's clothes. The smallest adult apparel at that time was size 8. They didn't have size 1 and size 3 in those days. So everything I wore had to be cut down to size by my Aunt Gin.

My most embarrassing moments always happened in

gym class. The girls all had to wear shorts, and my legs looked like two twigs hanging from my body. I would look at all the other girls and wish so bad that my legs would touch in the middle like theirs did. Then once a week we all had to be weighed, and I also dreaded that. Everyone weighed at least 100 pounds, and they would laugh when Miss Tripp, our teacher, weighed me in at 63 pounds.

Then came the time we had to take showers. I would constantly try to avoid taking a shower if I could, as the girls usually took showers together to save time, and I didn't want anyone to see that I had no breasts whatsoever. But it was then I realized that some of them were also stuffing their bras with Kleenex. So I was not the only late bloomer.

But at age seventeen I learned something wonderful. What I lacked in breasts I more than made up for in eyelashes. And thanks to my girlfriend Ada DeRaad, I discovered mascara. One day she summoned me into the bathroom, where she was putting some on her eyes from a little black tube.

"Tammy," she said. "You have really long eyelashes, but no one can see them. You would look just great if you put on some mascara." I had never even heard the word before, nor had I ever seen anything like that little black tube. Ada told me to hold still and open my eyes real wide. Then with a steady hand she began applying this black stuff to my eyes. When she finished I looked in the mirror. I couldn't believe it!

Now I really had eyelashes—long, dark eyelashes! I was completely exhilarated—for the first time in my life I felt pretty. "Wow!" I screamed, as seventeen-year-old girls will do. "I have eyes! Big, blue eyes!" But there was one problem. In our church, wearing makeup was strictly a sin. If you wore makeup you would go straight to hell, where you would burn forever and ever.

Making matters even worse, a woman would go straight

to hell if she wore pants or shorts or earrings. Now, that is one I could never figure out. You could wear a bracelet, a watch, a ring, or a necklace, but earrings were forbidden. But that one day in the bathroom changed my thinking for the rest of my life.

Ada had put makeup on me, and God had not struck me dead. I did not feel sinful, I only felt better about myself. Then Ada pulled out of her purse the biggest sin of all—lipstick! Beautiful red lipstick! Once again she told me to hold still, and she brushed that creamy, brilliant red across my lips. We hugged and laughed and screamed and jumped up and down, two typical teenagers discovering what life was about.

I felt absolutely beautiful. And once again God did not strike me down dead. But I was petrified of walking out of the bathroom. Afraid that if God didn't strike me dead, then one of those Assemblies of God women surely would!

The next day I couldn't wait to get down to my job at Woolworth's. They had the most wonderful makeup counter in the whole world. But how was I going to buy some without anyone seeing me? Ada said not to worry, and she secretly got it for me. By that afternoon I had a tube of black mascara and fabulous red lipstick hidden deep inside my purse. I couldn't wait to get home and try it out.

Although I never dared wear lipstick anywhere outside of my bedroom, I did start using the mascara. And if my mom or anyone else noticed, they never mentioned it. I was quite careful not to use too much. It was after I was married and began to do television that I discovered many other fantastic beauty aids such as eyelash curlers—and blush and eye shadow and red nail polish. Not to mention false eyelashes, which gave thickness to my long but somewhat sparse real eyelashes.

What has always stunned me is why people even care what you do to your face. For me, what I choose to do to my face is a very personal expression and should strictly be my own decision. Magazines and makeup artists all over the country have put me down. TV talk shows have made fun of me—thank you, Johnny Carson and Jay Leno. My makeup has been ridiculed on the Academy Awards and sung about by Bob Hope. While sometimes I laugh along, other times it hurts.

Makeup artists all over the country have tried to get me to take off my eyelashes or quit wearing so much mascara. And every time they make that suggestion, I just laugh and say, "That would be like Dolly Parton having a breast reduction and becoming a thirty-two B!"

So if you don't like how I look, look the other way. I plan on looking this way till I'm a hundred! I will be buried in my makeup and eyelashes.

Back in high school, beyond the superficial trimmings of mascara and lipstick, where I really made up for my insecurities was in speech class. I loved speech and anything to do with public speaking. It was a terrific confidence builder for me, and I had a real aptitude for it. I could get up and give a speech without even studying for it and get straight A's. I could just improvise. I was a natural performer.

After graduating, one of the hardest decisions I ever had to make was leaving home to attend North Central Bible College in Minneapolis. Luckily, I had the complete support of my parents. And even though my mother knew she was going to be left raising those children all by herself, she still encouraged me when I cried and wondered aloud whether I should go. My dad motivated me to go too. Both my parents loved God and really wanted me to continue along the path my heart had set for me.

The thought of leaving home was bittersweet. For down in my heart I knew that once I left nothing would ever be the same again. How I would miss lying out on the grass with my brother Donny searching for the Big Dipper. How I

would miss Dad's garden filled with corn, potatoes, cu-
cumbers, radishes, carrots, lettuce, tomatoes, peas, and
string beans. How I would miss stealing a tomato and hiding behind the lilac bushes to eat it. How I would miss the
smell of honeysuckle when I walked out the front gate; and
how I would miss sitting on the branches of the huge
weeping willow tree, swaying gently in the rustle of the
wind.

But these were small issues, for I was also hopelessly in
love. I was wearing the engagement ring of a young man I
had been going with for over two years. Stanley Kramer
and I were the same age and had graduated from high
school together. His father was the pastor of our family's
church, so naturally we had everything in common. Stanley and I were even going to be attending the same Bible
college, after which we had planned to get married—or so I
thought!

For some reason Stanley didn't want me going away to
college with him. We would argue day and night about that
until I thought it was the end of our relationship. I racked
my brain, but I just couldn't figure out his reasoning. "I
don't understand," I would tell him. "Should I wait for you
here in International Falls until you come back home?"

"Tammy, why is that such a bad idea? You mother really
needs you."

"But my mother is the one who wants me to go. It's you
who don't."

"Look, if you really loved me, you'd wait for me."

"What has one thing got to do with the other? Stan, why
don't you want me to go with you? We could be together,
we could study together."

"I said I don't think it's a great idea."

"Stan, you know I planned on attending Bible college
since way before I met you. Please don't force me to make a
choice between you and my calling. Please don't do that to

us. Because if you do, I will have to choose God. And, Stan, you know that!"

"I don't understand why you're being so stubborn."

It didn't make any sense whatsoever. I pleaded and pleaded, but he just wouldn't budge an inch. At this point I decided to take the chance of losing Stan and told him my final decision: I was going to Bible college—with or without his blessings—and that was that. I pulled back, and we both decided to let things cool down a little bit.

When it finally came time for me to leave, two weeks after Stanley had gone, I gathered up my suitcases and hugged everyone, feeling like I never wanted to let them go. I was scared and excited all at once. In my home we never let anyone see us cry. It was kind of an unwritten rule our family had. But as soon as the car drove out the driveway, I burst into sobs, looking back at all the people I ever loved. They were wiping their eyes too.

Part Two

The Fabulous
Bakker Boy

The Big City and Bible College

Stanley continued to occupy my thoughts until the moment I saw Minneapolis. It was like a dream come true. The minute I stepped off the Greyhound bus I was already staring up at the huge skyscrapers—well, at least to me they seemed like skyscrapers, although probably most of them weren't over twelve stories tall. Upon arriving at North Central Bible College I thought I was in heaven. It was a stately campus, shaded by majestic elms and maples, with ivy clinging to every building.

I opened the door to the dorm room that was to be my new home for the next four years. Although it was small and narrow, it was beautiful to me. There were two single beds, one on each side, two desks, two lamps, a huge window that overlooked the park across the street, plus a great closet. Just as I began putting away my clothes I heard this husky voice and in strutted the sexiest redhead I have ever seen—not to mention the biggest boobs! "Hi, I'm Aloha!" she exclaimed. She was not much taller than me and was thin except for those wondrous boobs. "Hey, looks like we'll be able to share clothes," she said.

The very thought of a double wardrobe was so exciting to

me. "I'd love that, Aloha." With that we hugged and danced around the room, deciding who got what bed and which desk, and whether we could afford to get matching bedspreads—of course, down at Woolworth's. Then I remembered I had to go job hunting.

"Don't worry, Tammy, I'll go with you. Maybe someone will hire us both!" I ended up getting a job the next day at a boutique called the Three Sisters. I don't recall if Aloha ever did get a job. I don't think she really needed to work.

Every night Aloha would tell me things that made my hair curl. For a girl her age, she was awfully experienced with boys, and she related in precise detail what went on during her dates. I would sit there at her feet, awestruck at her escapades.

As you might imagine, Aloha was not your typical Bible-college student. At first I couldn't figure out why she was there, because obviously she wasn't dedicated to studying the Holy Scripture like the rest of us. Later I found out she was forced to attend against her will—no doubt to change her ways. Well, I sure didn't see any change. In spite of this, we got along famously, and she taught me a lot of stuff that I might not have learned any other way.

I loved Aloha, I loved being part of a girl's dorm, and I loved taking two baths every day, just because it was so astonishing to have a private bathroom and be able to take two baths every day. I would sit in a real bathtub full of wonderful bubbles and think, "I'm the luckiest girl in the whole world." Still today, every time I get in a bathtub full of bubbles I thank God for hot water, bathtubs, and bubbles!

And also, to my amazement, down at the Three Sisters they carried sizes 1 and 2. I couldn't believe it. For the first time in my life I had clothes that actually fit me. It was thrilling. Finally I could look in the mirror and admire my style.

My only sadness was that things were not going well

with Stanley. It didn't take many brain cells to realize what was happening. There were so many beautiful girls attending North Central Bible College, and they loved Stanley and he loved them—and he didn't try to hide it, even though I was the one wearing the engagement ring he had given me just weeks before we left for school. My heart would break every time I saw him flirting with yet another pretty face.

I knew that I was not as sexy as they were, nor as streetwise.

And I had absolutely no idea how to fight them. One day I ran into Stanley in the hall making time with a raven-haired beauty, and I whispered to him, "Stan, I need to see you tonight. I have something I need to talk to you about."

He put his arm around me. "Sure, honey, I'll meet you after work, and we'll have a hamburger together."

That evening he picked me up in his car. I was waiting anxiously for him in front of the Three Sisters. My heart beat faster as I saw him drive up. He was dark-haired, with dark brown eyes that always had a mischievous twinkle in them. And like me, he was always ready for laughter. But there was to be no laughter that night.

We ate in silence—I think he knew what was coming—and then got into the car. "Let's drive somewhere." I said. "I have something I need to talk to you about." He put his arm around me, but I pulled away. "Stan, I don't think you're ready for marriage. I think you need to date some more." I don't even remember what he said as I took the striking diamond engagement ring off my finger and placed it in his hand. Maybe he was glad to be free, maybe he wished it could be different. I don't know. All I know was that at that moment, with tears streaming down my face, I felt utterly alone. My heart was aching so bad I wanted to die.

A Boy Named Jim

*E*ventually the pain of losing Stanley subsided, and then something amazing happened. I became popular practically overnight. I dated everyone in sight. Well, maybe I should rephrase that.

There was a group of guys at the school that ran around together, and they took a liking to me. So whenever they decided to do something special, they would come and get me and ask me to go with them. I never thought there was anything unusual about it—and certainly not wrong—as I had so many brothers and was used to being with boys all the time.

We'd go out bowling or just walk down to the candy store for a soda, things like that. I was simply the cute little girl who tagged along with them. I didn't go out with any one boy. I was like a kid sister, and not one of them ever made a pass at me. It was all innocent fun. Wherever that gang of boys went, I went too. It was a great way to forget Stanley.

One wintry evening as I was coming back to my dormitory just a few minutes after curfew, Jim Bakker was standing at the entrance, poised like a sentry. He was our hall monitor. "Tammy LaValley," he said sharply, pointing a warning finger in my direction and giving me a real stern look, "you are going to develop a reputation if you keep up this kind of behavior." I stared up at him blankly. I had no idea what kind of "behavior" he was referring to. "Remember, you've always got to protect your reputation. A girl's reputation is her most valuable asset." Then he sent me up to my room.

I was startled! I had never even thought of my reputation. We weren't doing anything wrong, but I did get Jim's point about being seen with so many boys at once and immediately decided not to do that anymore. From then on I went out with just one boy at a time, usually spending the entire evening dodging kisses and pushing away hands.

Later on I found out why Jim was overly concerned about my reputation. One evening he cornered a girlfriend of mine as she was getting back to the dorm. "Peg, I need to talk to you."

"What's up, Jim?"

"You know Tammy LaValley, don't you?"

"Sure, Jim, she lives on the same floor that I do."

"Is it true that she's no longer engaged to Stanley?"

"Yes," Peg answered. "And she's suffering real terribly from a broken heart. But under the circumstances I think she did the right thing."

"I want to ask her out," Jim said, shifting his weight nervously from one foot to the other. "Do you think she'll go? Peg, do you think she will? Ask her for me, will you? Please?"

"Sure, Jim, I'll talk to her about it and get back to you."

A few days later I walked into our room to hear Aloha's voice booming out of the bathroom from the shower. "Hey, Tammy, Peggy wants to talk to you. She says it's real urgent!" I always respected Peggy. She was a tall, no-nonsense type of gal. So I ran down to her room, which was just a few doors from mine.

"Hi, Peg, what d'ya want?"

"Sit down, Tammy. I have something real exciting to tell you." Her glee was absolutely contagious.

"Tell me, tell me," I said, already jumping out of my skin with anticipation. "Tell me!"

"You know the guy who's the hall monitor at night, his name is Jim Bakker. Anyway, he came to me the other day and asked me about you. He thinks you're really cute and would like to meet you."

"Me?" I screamed like a typical eighteen-year-old girl. "Jim Bakker wants to meet me? And he thinks I'm cute! Wow, Peg! Are you sure?"

"Of course I'm sure. Can I have him call you?"

I was so nervous I almost bit a whole strand of fake pearls I was wearing right in half. "Okay. Give him my number."

"I think he already has your number. Now, go back to your room, Tammy. Otherwise you might be missing an important phone call."

Back to my room I went. But my mind began to fill with doubts. What does this Jim really want? How do I know I can trust him? Maybe he's just like Stanley. After all, Jim was real good-looking, lean and athletic. He was a great dresser who had a relaxed, easy way about him. I knew lots of girls who had crushes on him. How could Jim possibly like a girl like me? The phone was on my lap. On the first ring I picked it up.

"Tammy, this is Jim Bakker. You know, the night monitor. Remember I talked to you the other night?"

"Yes, I—"

"Would you like to go out with me tonight?" he asked, without even stopping to catch his breath. "We can have dinner, and then I would like to take you to church with me. Now, we'll have to walk—as I don't have a car—but if you like, we could take a taxi." My heart was beating a hundred miles an hour. After all, I had just broken off with

Stan. Peggy said Jim really liked me a lot, but could I trust another man? "Tammy, are you still there?"

"Oh, yes, I'm still here." Then I took a deep breath. "Look, Jim, I don't think I should go out with you. I've just broken off an engagement, and I'm hurting really bad. I just would not make good company." With that I said good-bye and hung up the phone. I heard later that Jim told Peggy he would never ask me out again.

But he did. The very next day a dozen roses were lying on my bed when I walked into my room to answer the phone. "Tammy, at least go to church with me tonight," Jim said on the other end. I looked at the beautiful roses, and my heart melted. "Yes, Jim, I will."

Frankly, I don't know where he got the money for those roses, since students couldn't even afford to eat lunch in those days, let alone buy roses. Nevertheless, there they were: the largest, freshest, sweetest roses I had ever seen, and they smelled like heaven. When the other girls saw them, they all just swooned.

Aloha gave me a few last-minute pointers before I left.

Jim and I talked a lot on that first date. He told me he had not gone out very much since he had been at college. He had devoted almost all his time to studying for the ministry and working to pay off his college bills. Then he told me about the deep calling he had to work for God. It was such a miracle to find a man who had the same fire in his heart about serving the Lord as I did—something that Stanley never had.

We shared our dreams as we walked home from church. It was cold, but we didn't even notice, we were holding each other so tightly. The frozen snow crunched under our feet and sparkled like a million diamonds everywhere we looked. All of a sudden Jim stopped. We were right in the middle of the sidewalk. He put his arms around me and kissed me hard on the mouth.

"Tammy LaValley, I have loved you ever since the minute

I saw you walk into school. But you cannot imagine my disappointment when I saw the ring on your finger and realized you were engaged. I love you, Tammy! Will you marry me?"

With that he took off the bracelet he was wearing and handed it to me. I was overwhelmed. I didn't know how or what to think. Jim was well liked at school, he was a gentleman, and he had the same calling I had. This must be the man God was sending for me. Jim helped me put his bracelet around my wrist, and we walked the rest of the way back to school in silence.

After he kissed me good night I ran up the two flights of stairs to my dorm room and threw myself on the bed, screaming: "Aloha! Aloha! You will never believe what happened to me tonight!" Before I knew it our room was filled with envious girls all shouting at once, admiring my gorgeous bracelet. Suddenly a knock came on the door. "Girls! Girls!" It was the dorm mother. "It's time for lights out; everyone get to bed right now!" The girls melted away into the hallway, giggling and whispering.

All night long I dreamed about Jim Bakker. The next day I didn't do too well in my classes. It was like I was walking in a cloud. Often over the next few weeks I'd go back to my dorm and crawl into bed and there would be a big heart filled with candy or a beautiful vase filled to the brim with roses. Maybe I'd find a poodle—Jim would send these little stuffed white poodles to my room all the time. Aloha demanded to know my secret.

I think Jim came across as if he had more money than anybody, which I knew he didn't because we'd had to pool our resources to get a hamburger and share it. But Jim had a way of borrowing cash; it was hard to turn him down. Yet every time he'd always work hard and pay it back. As far back as I can remember he's been really great with money. I think that's the Jewish part of Jim. His grandmother was a German Jew, and I think he inherited this quality with her Jewish blood. In any event, he could always make it happen.

When Jim was growing up his family was very poor. They lived in a ramshackle old house that was painted this awful orange, which always embarrassed him. Because Jim was self-conscious about his modest background, he never asked about my home life until just before we got married. He thought I was an only child. And when I told him there were eight of us, he almost died. He couldn't believe it. He thought with my manners and breeding that I must be the only one.

Through the years of our marriage, I think what drove Jim was the memory of that little orange house. He wasn't going to be poor and live in a house like that ever again; he was going to have all the nicer things in life, no matter how hard he had to work to achieve them. And Jim was a hard worker. He sold shoes, he did every job he could do to make money. But I believe no matter what he accomplished, that little orange house was always haunting him in the back of his mind. There was just no getting rid of the image.

Two weeks after our first date, Jim gave me my engagement ring. And he did it in a most unusual way. Before we went to church he told his friends what he planned to do, so by the time we got inside practically everybody knew except me. We were sitting on the platform because Jim was a youth leader at Minneapolis Evangelistic Auditorium, the huge, gorgeous old theater where our congregation met.

Standing at the podium, Jim turned to one of his friends and asked him to come up and pray. While the friend was praying, Jim sat down next to me, grabbed my hand, and immediately stuck an engagement ring on my finger. But because he was so nervous he grabbed the wrong hand.

Meanwhile his cohorts in the audience were watching the whole scene, doing everything they could to stop themselves from laughing out loud.

But the ring was nothing to laugh at. It was quality.

Everything Jim did was quality. I couldn't take my eyes off the ring; it was the most magnificent little diamond ring you ever saw. I think Jim borrowed the money to make the down payment; we made payments on it for a long time after we got married.

Our sudden engagement didn't make everyone happy. Raleigh Bakker, Jim's father, flat out didn't want his son to marry me. He wanted Jim to make something of himself and pursue a career. He did everything he could to sabotage our wedding.

Jim's parents lived in Muskegon, Michigan, and we went out there to visit them. Their home was a palace compared to the place where I was brought up. By then his family had moved out of the orange house and were living in elegance, in a magnificent two-story Victorian-style home with a full basement.

Downstairs was a gracious music room complete with a baby grand electric player piano. It stood in front of a sweeping bay window framed by thick maroon drapery made of velvet. Plush oriental rugs covered the floor. Then there was the most beautiful dining room I had ever seen— the wallpaper alone was to die for! It must have been at least fifty years old. Around the ceiling, above the wallpaper, were hand-painted grapes and grape leaves. The house also contained a fascinating little library, all done in dark woods.

But what really knocked me out was the upstairs bathroom.

It was tremendous. Black-and-white marble adorned the floor, and it had a self-standing washbasin with a spectacular mirror overhead. Off to the side was one of those great old claw-foot tubs. I kept sneaking into that bathroom just to look at it.

When we first arrived, Jim's folks were very cordial to me. However, behind my back, Raleigh would say anything he could to discourage Jim from marrying me. "In my opinion, I don't think she's good enough for you. I don't think she comes from a good enough family."

"Dad, you don't even know her. You don't know anything about her."

"I know what I see. She's a poor nothing. If you marry her, it'll be like carrying a dead weight around."

"That's ridiculous, Dad. I love her, I adore her. She's the one I've been looking for."

"You don't know anything. You don't know what you're looking for. What do you know? You're just a kid."

"Tammy is going to be my wife."

"Listen to me. Marriage is for life. You make your bed, and then you sleep in it."

"Well, Tammy is the woman I want in my bed, and I want to sleep with her!"

"Look, if you're so all fired up to get yourself married, why don't you marry Sally? Now, there's a real woman, in my book!" Jim had been dating a young lady named Sally, the town beauty queen, who rode in the floats at the parades. After we were married, whenever Jim's dad knew we were coming to visit, he'd call Sally up and ask her to drop by. Thank the Lord Sally was woman enough to refuse.

So on and on went the barrage. Raleigh would say anything he could to change his son's mind, but all to no avail. Jim firmly stood his ground. He wasn't backing down no matter how much his father yelled. "I'm going to marry Tammy," he'd say. "I'm in love with her."

"Then go ahead!" his father screamed, all red in the face. "Marry that scrawny little thing! You don't know where she came from. You don't know, she may have some disease!"

Raleigh was hard as nails, a human steamroller determined to flatten anyone who disagreed with him. He worked at a steel piston-ring factory and never missed a day. A brash, hot-tempered man, Raleigh was always yelling at the top of his lungs—which is probably what made Jim so quiet and composed. Early on, Jim made up his mind that he wasn't going to be anything like his dad. Of course, Raleigh's constant bellowing most likely made Jim a nervous wreck too, for he never received the quiet comfort that you need from a parent once in a while.

All through our marriage Jim worked hard at pleasing his father. But unless he did something exactly the way Raleigh thought it should be done, Jim's endless quest to please his dad was futile. Raleigh would repeatedly criticize his efforts. And unfortunately, Jim's mother was a frail little lady who always did what Raleigh told her.

Jim had been the youngest of four brothers and sisters, born as a premature infant who would literally fit into a shoe box. I'm fairly positive that had some effect on his psyche. Jim was also born late in his parents' marriage, probably at a stage when they didn't want any more children. As a child he might have picked up on that, which would have driven him even harder to be loved and accepted by his parents, particularly his father.

It's my opinion that Jim was always looking for a father figure, a man who would offer him acceptance and approval, maybe even protect him from the world and make him feel secure. Through the years I've seen a number of men acting this paternal role in Jim's life, claiming they could fix everything but more often than not just taking advantage. If they just played Jim's daddy, they could win with him.

On the other hand, Jim's sister, Donna, was a real angel. After hearing we were getting married, she gave me her wedding gown. As we were leaving to return to Minneapolis, we placed it in the back of Jim's brother's car, since Norman was going to take us to the train. But his car broke down on the way, and Jim's folks had to come and pick us up. Jim's dad knew that wedding gown was in the back of Norman's car, so he put it in the trunk of his car. However, when we got to the station, he wouldn't give it back to me—and that was final!

Despite that incident and all the rest, Jim did everything he possibly could to get his folks to the wedding. He invited them several times, but Raleigh said they weren't coming to any wedding, that they would disown Jim if he got married. We just went ahead with our plans. Jim sent his folks a letter telling them about it. The stationery had "Mr. and Mrs. Jim Bakker" printed up in the corner. That's how they knew we were married.

My parents couldn't come to the wedding either, but for a much different reason. Since they were so poor, it was simply impossible for them to travel with seven children at home. When I called asking for my mother's permission, she said, "Tammy, that is your decision. I can't make it for you. If you've found someone you love, you have my blessing." Then my father got on the phone and essentially said the same thing. Both my parents were very, very kind to me.

Jim and I were married on April Fool's Day, April 1, 1967, down in the basement of the Minneapolis Evangelistic Auditorium, which had been renovated to make an absolutely gorgeous prayer room. The walls were hewn out of rock, carved with pictures of Jesus from different periods of His life. The floor was covered with plush carpeting, and in the middle was a round bench surrounding a rock sculpture of Jesus and Mary.

The wedding itself was a small, intimate affair—six people all together. I wore a mint-green dress, and my future husband wore a black suit. Bob Silky, Jim's roommate from Bible college, was the best man, and my matron of honor was Donna, Jim's sister. Pastor Olson and his wife, Fern, married us. They were very famous ministers, and we felt privileged to have them there. We were simply ecstatic, two young kids determined to "win the world to Jesus." And we meant it with all our hearts! Pastor Olson took pictures, but as it turned out, his camera didn't work, and we never got even one shot of the most special day in our lives.

I'll never forget that night after we came home, ready to be alone together as man and wife. I had just put on the sheer white negligee I had bought for our wedding night and was sitting there combing my hair when without warning there was a jarring knock at the door. Jim went to investigate. He pulled the door open and there was Stanley. For a few long moments he just stared at me in sheer silence. There was real hurt in his eyes. "I just wanted to check and see if you were all right," he finally said.

"She's fine, she's just fine," Jim replied sharply, impatiently shutting the door in Stanley's face. But just before it closed, I saw Stanley turning around and trudging down the corridor, looking totally crestfallen. Naturally I felt sorry for him, but my mind was occupied with more romantic matters.

A few days after getting married, Jim and I were asked to leave school. That hit us like a ton of bricks. No one had told us that you couldn't get married while you were students, so it came as a complete shock. Apparently the rule was that a man and a woman could enter college if they were already married, or they could marry once they graduated but not one moment before.

However, even if I had known about the rule, I was so crazy in love that I would have married Jim anyway. In fact

I thought it was a blessing in disguise. Both of us thought going to college was okay, but it sure wasn't doing the job that needed to be done. At that point we were pretty much convinced that we knew enough to go out and start a ministry of our own. Which is why getting asked to leave didn't really make any difference—at least not to me. I still believe Jim would have preferred to make the choice himself, rather than having it made for him.

We didn't have any money, but we were able to put together a darling apartment with furniture and stuff from the Goodwill. From day one I have never seen anyone stretch money as far as Jim Bakker could. He could do everything around the house—wallpaper, paint, fix the plumbing, you name it. We put together a superb little place, complete with wall-to-wall carpeting, which we sewed together from scraps. Boy, my fingers were sore for weeks after sewing together those pieces of tough, cheap carpet!

Jim was very enterprising right from the start. When he was just a little boy he sold pots and pans door-to-door. He would find all sorts of things that people threw away, fix them up, and then sell them for a few pennies on the street corner. Whatever he could do, he did, selling candy, newspapers, raffle tickets. There's no doubt Jim was a natural-born salesman, but driven by insecurity.

About a month after the ceremony we went to International Falls so that Jim could meet my family. I was kind of embarrassed about taking him home, since his parents had such an impressive residence. But he loved my family and my family loved him, and we had a marvelous time together. I couldn't believe I was a married lady. Here I was back home, all grown up and married. It was like a dream.

The first order of business was that Jim had to take a bath. "Well, Jim," I said. "We don't have a bathtub." And without thinking about it, I went out and got two big washbasins and filled both of them with warm water—one to wash in and the other for rinsing off. You should have seen what happened next! Jim sat with his butt in one and his feet in the other, never realizing that wasn't the way you did it. Well, that was some sight. Jim's butt stuck in the basin with all the steam rising up.

Just before leaving International Falls Jim said, "Tammy, your real daddy lives here, doesn't he?" I nodded. "Well, it's time you met him. Would you like that?" I nodded again. Actually, I was scared to death to meet my real father. I don't know why. Maybe it was the fact that Mom and I never talked about him, or that I thought he didn't love me. Maybe it was because I didn't want my stepfather to be hurt if he heard that I had gone visiting Carl.

But I was a married lady now. It was time to get brave and meet the man I simply called "my real daddy." Would he like me? Would he think I was pretty enough? Would he like my new husband? Would he be glad that I was his daughter? The thoughts tumbled around in my mind. Would I like him? Did I look like him? (I was told by Aunt Gin and Grandma Fairchild that I did.) Would Mom get mad at me if she found out that I went to see him? Would she be hurt?

We pulled up in front of my dad's twin sister's house, the place where we were supposed to meet. My heart was pounding in my ears. Getting out of the car I nearly tripped over my own feet. All of a sudden these men started walking from the house toward us. I didn't recognize any of them, but it was my dad and his brothers.

I looked at them standing there, and they stared back at me. One of the men stepped forward, and I will never forget his words as long as I live. "Tammy, I'm your daddy." Tears began streaming down my face as my father hugged me for the first time in fifteen years. Instantly I knew why I was only 4'11". And I knew why my eyes were so blue. And I knew why I had a square face and a funny nose. Yes, I did look like my dad.

A lot of questions were answered for me that day—except the one I needed to know the most. "Daddy, why did you leave me and Donny? Didn't you love us?" Many years later I was to learn that Carl did indeed love us. They said he would cry as he watched me every day on TV. But Fred will always be "my daddy." He raised me, and I love him with all my heart. As for Carl, I never got to know him any better than that.

Down in the Dumps

lmost immediately after getting back to Minneapolis, Jim showed me a side of himself that I would never in a million years have expected to see. Without reason he would suddenly become quiet and withdrawn, wouldn't bother speaking to a soul. At first I didn't know how to handle it. I had never been around such moody behavior before, and it disturbed me.

"Jim, what's wrong?" I would ask. "Please tell me, what's wrong?" Of course I never realized how many thousands of times I would repeat those words during our thirty years of marriage. "Is everything all right? Is there anything I can do? Did I do something? Did I say something? Jim, just talk to me—please, talk to me," I would cry out in anguish. "At least say something, Jim!" I just couldn't figure him out. Maybe he was unhappy that we had gotten married. Who could know? All I know is that inside I became absolutely frantic.

Eventually I came to accept that that was Jim's personality, simply the way he was. His method of coping was to shut the world out, and I was part of that world. I always felt deeply hurt by that. I soon learned that when Jim underwent one of his "quiet times," there was nothing I could do or say to bring him out of it. Sleep was his only solace. He would just take himself into the bedroom, remove his clothes, and pull the covers over his head.

"Jim," I would say, "you have this forlorn look on your face. You look so despondent, so out of it. It's driving me crazy. Tell me what's going on with you. I can't stand being in this house another minute. I'd have more conversation if I was in a mortuary. I could get more from a corpse!"

Sadly, all this disturbing moodiness was to recur again and again. Whenever Jim got discouraged, he would sink deep within himself, into some dark, cold place, like a snail withdrawn inside his shell; and each time he did this—I can't even count the times—it was all I could do to pull him out of it. "Come on," I'd say, trying to cheer Jim up, "everything's going to be all right. We can do it. We can *do* it!"

Of course, part of me understood very clearly what was going on. Jim was an ambitious young man, filled with hopes and dreams. But once we were out of college a healthy dose of reality hit us like a cold slap across the face. No one was breaking down our door to offer us a ministry. Instead of delivering sermons, Jim was delivering meals for a restaurant called Rothchild Young Quinlin, where he also worked as a dishwasher, scouring all the pots and pans and anything else that was greasy.

At seven the alarm would go off, but it was hard for him to get out of bed. Finally he would trudge out the door, wearing this miserable look on his face. His attitude would frustrate me, as I was working and helping out too. I felt that I was doing my part, and that we should be the two happiest people in the world.

Here we were newlyweds, and we were supposed to be up and going and being and doing, and he just didn't want to do it. Jim's mood swings made me tired, mentally and emotionally. I'm positive that bottling his emotions up, never expressing his real feelings, is what caused his physical problems. Throughout the building of our ministry Jim was plagued by really bad ulcers, and my heart would break every time he had an attack.

Soon after our marriage Jim decided he didn't want to go to services any longer, which was really unusual, because when we were dating church is where we always went. It didn't make a difference how hard I tried. There was simply no budging him. I decided to stop beating my head against the wall. One Sunday I issued an ultimatum. "Jim, if you won't go to church with me, then I'm going to start going by myself!" His answer was to curl up in bed, and I marched right out the door!

At church I was allowed to lead song service and minister to the congregation. But I was so lonely without Jim, and so confused. Finally I spoke to Sister Fern Olson. She had known Jim long before I did. "Tammy honey," she said, "let me make a call."

Promptly she picked up the telephone and dialed. "Jim Bakker," she said sternly, "if you don't get out of bed this minute and get back to church, your wife is going to be a better preacher than you are!" Well, that really turned the trick. The very next Sunday Jim was back in church and was reinstated as youth pastor.

Soon we both got the first of what would be several raises, and things started looking up. We began to comb the real estate section for a larger apartment. Maybe we could even find one with air conditioning. Now that he was preaching and involved in life again, Jim's dark moods subsided.

With the benefit of hindsight, I believe that part of Jim's moodiness was a way to control me. When I thought he wasn't happy with something, I'd work that much harder to make it right. You always work harder to try and please a moody person.

Several times the thought of leaving him crossed my mind. But there was simply no way I could have chosen to get out of this marriage. The memory of my mother being shunned and persecuted for being divorced was all too fresh in my mind. Well, that would never happen to me! Through thick and thin I was determined to stick with Jim. I was convinced that things would settle down and work out. I loved him so much I knew our love would conquer all.

Despite his moodiness, the first few years of our love life were remarkably tender and sharing. We always did lots of hugging and kissing, cozy cuddling up together. Jim didn't have a selfish bone in his body. He was always a very caring and concerned lover, gently making sure that my pleasure was every bit as satisfying as his. Our lovemaking was definitely addictive. There was a chemistry between us that couldn't be denied, and in that respect we were truly blessed.

Early on though, I discovered Jim was a hypochondriac. It was something our family and friends laughed about for years and years. If we ever wanted to get really hysterical, all we had to do was bring up Jim's hypochondria. He has always been "Mr. Clean," washing his hands a lot and smelling the milk before he poured it on his cereal.

We always tried to keep him away from hospital shows on TV or medical books of any kind. Because no matter what Jim read, heard, or saw, he always had a couple of symptoms. Whenever he wasn't feeling well, he would go get the doctor's dictionary, and before you knew it he had a couple of diseases. We would laugh until tears streamed down our faces.

One thing he constantly cautioned us was to never, ever, sit on a public toilet seat without first putting paper on it. He had all of us paranoid over that one. In fact, the kids and I were almost afraid to even walk into a public rest room, for fear that some disease would jump on us. As a result, the kids were always waiting too long before they would finally tell us, "Mom, Dad, I have to go to the bathroom quick!"

"Don't forget to put the paper on the seat!" Jim would yell as they were running toward some restaurant's rest room. One time I remember our daughter, Tammy Sue, didn't come back for a long time. She was about four years old and wanted to go by herself. I got concerned and went in to see what was taking her so long. I heard her crying inside one of the stalls.

"What's wrong?" I asked. She let me in, and there she stood, bathroom tissue all over the place and her panties dripping wet. "What happened?" I said, knowing full well what her answer would be.

"Mommy, the paper kept falling off, and by the time I got some to stay on it was too late."

"That's okay, honey," I said as I took some clean tissue and made a barrier between her and her wet panties. By the time I was finished, we were both laughing and promising we would never tell that she had wet her panties.

Hypochondriac or not, in front of church congregations Jim was always incredibly enthusiastic, an impressive figure who could not only rise to the occasion but dominate it. But no matter how inspiring or successful his sermons were, at home his moodiness would soon return and he would pull back, depressed, into a shell. I could never figure it out. Jim was the best preacher I've ever heard, a master showman with a genius IQ who transfixed audiences with his message. Whatever demons were lurking inside he kept locked up tight. I can't imagine what sort of mental technique Jim used to radiate such a positive public image while privately agonizing over such a negative view of himself.

But even though Jim was a natural performer, just before going into crowds he would hyperventilate, with his pulse racing a mile a minute from fear. Jim was fine once he was up in front of an audience, but as soon as he came down off the platform, once they switched off the microphones and shut off the stage lights, the anxiety returned. Even at parties he always had a hard time just mixing with folks. Nothing bothered him as long as he was in control. But once you placed him on the same level as everyone else, he became obsessed with finding ways to escape.

Jim showed almost no willingness to control his moods. It was a blind spot that he just couldn't see—or if he did see it, he didn't see anything wrong with it. We'd invite some friends over for dinner or coffee. If Jim got tired, he would just suddenly get up and go to bed and leave me alone with them—no explanations, no apologies, nothing. I always wound up having to make up excuses for him, doing all the talking, all the entertaining, all the everything.

That was really hard on me.

His insecurities came out in other ways. Through the years we were married, Jim and I lived in many little houses. But they didn't stay little for long. We would move into a cute little house, and before we had even been there a month Jim was already figuring out ways to add another room or two. It became a constant bone of contention between us.

"But, Tam, I'm doing it for you."

"Jim, you're not doing it for me," I would always reply. "I liked it just the way it was." And on and on we would go.

Jim and I were always moving. In the first years of our marriage, it was to make money. We would buy an old place, fix it up, and resell it for twice as much money as we had originally paid. That way we were able to move into bigger and better houses. I understood the common sense behind those moves, and they didn't bother me, but I got to the point where I wanted to settle down like other people and have a permanent home to raise children in. What really *did* bother me was when we finally got into just the right house—the right price, the right size, everything just the right way we always dreamed it would be—Jim would say, once again, "Tam, let's go look at houses."

"But, Jim," I'd say, "I really like this house. I love the den you added on. To me the house is cozy and just perfect for us." But still, the house would inevitably go on the market, a FOR SALE sign on the front lawn, and once again we were packing our things. The truth is that I liked all of our homes and would have been totally satisfied in any of them. However, I did like the smaller, more intimate ones the best.

Jim was a man of contradictions. On the one hand, when he was moody, he seemed indifferent to the feelings of others. On the other, Jim needed people's acceptance and their respect; he craved it like a drug. Jim had always gotten the leading roles in high school plays. He was very flamboyant and self-assured. Now I realize that he was looking for the love from his adherents that he couldn't give to himself. Deep down he never felt good enough. He had to go out and prove himself every single day. No matter how much he succeeded, nothing was ever enough.

You would have thought with all the years of overwhelming response from the congregations that Jim would have been content with himself and what he was doing. That he could finally put his father's influence behind him. But it was not that way. Jim never felt that he did well enough or that he was good enough. He was always convinced others did it better. And no amount of encouragement or praise from my mouth would convince him otherwise.

Whenever Jim was speaking to anyone he could never quite look that person in the eye. At first I thought he was just shy, but the problem turned out to be far more serious. Jim Bakker was incapable of looking at me—or at anybody—for any length of time. You always felt like you weren't there, as if there was something more important on his mind. Even worse, Jim would sometimes leave people right in the middle of a sentence—he would just walk away.

Years ago, during our marriage-counseling sessions, the therapist would often turn to him and say, "Look at Tammy. Look in her eyes. She's your wife. Learn to look at her when you talk to her." But either it was a skill he couldn't learn or he just didn't want to because that might have resulted in confrontation.

By avoiding all conflict, Jim lessened the chances of being criticized—something he couldn't stand. He interpreted all criticism as a personal attack, a horrendous failure on his part, the voice of his father belittling him. The bottom line was that I could never really communicate with Jim, or persuade him, and in the end that broke my heart. Couldn't he at least trust me?

The Long and Winding Road

About six months after Jim came back as a youth pastor, a preacher named Aubrey Sarah came through to lead a revival meeting at our church. Originally from Canada, Sarah was a leading evangelist of the time. His church was located in Burlington, North Carolina. He was a gentle, gracious little man who looked like the world's kindest grandfather behind his thick wire spectacles. After Jim and I had finished, Reverend Sarah came up onstage and started ministering. But out of the corner of his eye he kept glancing at us the entire time he was up there.

Later he came over and spoke to us. "Jim and Tammy, God has spoken to me. The Lord has a divine plan for the two of you. And I am His messenger!" Naturally, we were completely taken aback. But he spoke with such clarity and authority that we were mesmerized by his words. "I would like to invite you to come to my church in North Carolina and hold a revival meeting for me!" Jim and I looked at each other, then turned back to gaze into Reverend Sarah's eyes. This was the sign we had been waiting for.

Within days we moved out of our place and gave our furniture away. Without a penny in our pockets we began our journey to North Carolina. Aubrey's church was a white-framed building set on a rolling hillside, with poplars and sturdy oaks providing shade and comfort. Aubrey's congregation welcomed us warmly into their hearts. They were decent, God-fearing folks who worked hard to put food on their tables, meals they often shared with us.

Going out and meeting with folks invigorated Jim, and his self-confidence and drive returned full force. Much of our early joy came back as well. To me, our experience with Reverend Sarah represented nothing less than a miracle.

After a couple of weeks, we finished our work. Aubrey was so impressed that he called other Assemblies of God churches to recommend us. Before we knew it, our popularity mushroomed and we wound up being booked for a year ahead of time, preaching from one church meeting to the next without stopping.

At the end of our stays the local minister would take what he called a "love offering" for us. That would be our pay for the week. For the first two or three years, our average offering was about $50 to $100 a week. And we were so thankful for that. One time we stayed at the house of a very wealthy couple. As we left their home they put some extra money in Jim's hand. We needed those funds so desperately. But Jim gave it to the pastor of the church, saying that we had already received our love offering and he didn't want to be dishonest.

Every week or two we went to a different church and lived with the pastor there. Jim was doing all the preaching, and I sang. To accompany myself I had an instrument called a Cordavox. It was this huge accordion with an organ attached—bigger than me, almost—and it produced the loveliest music you ever heard in your life.

We traveled everywhere in an old Cadillac, which I have

to admit looked pretty good, considering the thousands of miles on its odometer. Now, an old Cadillac costs about the same as a new Ford or a Chevrolet. You see, Jim was taught that if you're going to be a success, you have to look like a success to begin with. The Lord must have been watching over us because that car always got us where we wanted to go. In those days we ventured throughout the Deep South, ministering in Virginia, North Carolina, South Carolina, all through the years of 1962, 1963, and 1964.

While we were driving along those dusty old back roads Jim was continually writing new sermons, working hard on every word. If a sermon worked well at one church, then he'd go to another church and preach the same sermon all over again, because it was a whole different congregation. You could do that because no one saw you on TV. In those days there was just no way to reach a mass audience—until we met an interesting man named Pat Robertson.

We Get on Pat's Wavelength

In 1965, while we were ministering in Portsmouth, Virginia, a man named Bill Garthwaite came to our service. He worked for someone called Pat Robertson, who was then trying to start a television station called the Christian Broadcasting Network. Well, CBN was some "network"! The station was way up on the UHF dial, and hardly anybody could tune in. And although his father was the senator from Virginia, nobody knew Pat Robertson or what his TV ministry was all about.

"I'm intrigued by your puppet ministry," said Garthwaite. "And so is Pat. Maybe we could do a children's show on TV." What he was referring to was a little program that we would put on for children after our Sunday services. I was the voice of Suzy Moppett and Allie the Alligator, and Jim talked to them. It was a Kukla, Fran & Ollie type of show. "Pat would really like you to drop by the station for a chat."

By this time Jim and I were ministering to the very largest Assemblies of God churches, so we were not exactly bowled over by this offer. However, we decided it could do no harm to meet this Pat Robertson and hear what he had to say.

Bill brought us over to Robertson's tiny studio. There was maybe one camera, a canvas backdrop, a few chairs, a table, and something that resembled a control booth. But Pat was right there to greet us, projecting amicability and warmth. "I'm really impressed with the work that the two of you have been doing. It's amazing how prominent you've become in such a short time." Robertson was very assured and well-spoken, obviously the product of good schools and an upper-class background.

"Jim and Tammy, you may not realize this, but television is the future of getting God's message to America." He let his words sink in. Pat had grand visions of what CBN could ultimately become, but frankly, sitting around in that dark, musty studio, it was hard for me to imagine. "Just try doing one live show to see how you like it. That's all I ask. I know how busy your schedule is, but I would truly appreciate your taking the time to grace our broadcast."

After the meeting Jim and I thought, why not? So we put together a special children's program for the station. It was fun because I'd always had a lot of child in me; I knew exactly what kids loved. Making up cute little cartoon voices was one of my favorite pastimes. To make Suzy Moppett we took a cartoon head off a Silky Bubble Bath bottle—it was a pig—and melted the ears off. Then we put a miniature blond wig on the critter, dotted on some freckles, painted a little mouth, and finally put the whole thing on a doll's body. It was sort of a cross between Miss Piggy and Barbie.

The show went off without a hitch, with just one camera steadily on Jim talking to the puppets. But packing up to leave that night, we got an urgent call from Pat. "Look, please listen. The station has been deluged with calls about your show. People said they just loved it! Would you please come back and do it . . ." And here Pat paused just a moment for effect. "Well, do it for good?" Jim and I were speechless. We never expected an incredible response like that. "Please, let me have your answer. You don't know how important this is!" Finally, to get him off the line, we told Robertson that we would speak to him in the morning, after we slept on it.

But there was no doubt Pat had touched a nerve—especially in Jim. This man of breeding and culture seemed to be affording him genuine respect and admiration. I believe Robertson represented yet another father figure to Jim, just like Aubrey had been. Of course I have to admit I was moved by Pat's pitch as well.

What we did then wasn't logical; in fact, it defied logic. After all, we were becoming a force in the Assemblies of God churches throughout the South, and then suddenly— one day in 1965—we gave it all away. Christian television was still something very new and experimental, and there was no guarantee that it would ultimately work. But we took the risk, because faith is spelled R-I-S-K. We canceled two years' worth of services. Following that, miraculous things started to happen.

At first when we started doing the children's show, we'd have to go into town and round up kids for our audience. Then more and more people began picking up this little signal, and before we knew it, we had hundreds of children streaming in every day to be part of our audience. It became a mob scene. After a while we were forced to give out tickets weeks in advance because otherwise the studio would have been overrun. The set was a barnyard, and all the kids would sit around on logs or fences or haystacks.

Our children's program began to build a solid TV audience, bringing in much needed finances so that Robertson could expand his operations. However, when we first made the commitment, one of the conditions was that someday Jim would be allowed to host a *Tonight Show*–type program for Christians. I remember the meeting we had.

"Pat, this idea will revolutionize what you're doing," Jim said. "It will change the face of Christian broadcasting."

"Sounds interesting, Jim," Robertson said evenly.

"Let's build a Johnny Carson–style set, with a desk and chairs for the guests. It will be an opportunity to give Christian performers a chance. We have wonderful speakers and singers in the Christian world, and they deserve a chance to be heard on TV. Mark my word, if you will allow me to do this, I guarantee you it will be a great success. It will change the face of Christian broadcasting. It will, Pat."

"You might be right, Jim," Pat answered.

By the time Jim finished even Pat had to admit it was a great idea, and eventually it went on the air with tremendous fanfare. The program was called *The 700 Club* because it needed seven hundred people to donate $100 each month to keep it up and running. Jim hosted the show.

The format was very much like *The Tonight Show*, except there wasn't really a band. An organ played background music. Jim sat behind a desk and interviewed guests on the couch. I was never really featured very much on *The 700 Club.* Once in a while I sang, but that was about it.

Anybody who was anybody in religious broadcasting, from Pat Boone to Mahalia Jackson, was on the program. Frequently appearing with Jim was Henry Harrison, another member of the CBN family. A heavyset, jolly man, Henry always had a yarn to spin, and his heartfelt laughter always made you smile. Everyone loved him and affectionately called him Uncle Henry. He was Christian TV's Uncle Miltie.

The 700 Club virtually skyrocketed to fame overnight and quickly brought in a fortune in donations to Robertson, who was immensely happy to receive them. The stacks of letters and accolades Jim and I received became overwhelming. It seemed as if we were working twenty-four hours a day, but we weren't complaining.

However, as Jim started getting busier, I noticed a definite change in our relationship. For the first few years of our marriage lovemaking had remained tender and wonderful, but now it was becoming just sex—and that was really disturbing. There was almost none of the hugging and holding that I had treasured so deeply.

I was especially vulnerable because these were the only moments we had a chance to be alone, the only time I could truly get close to Jim. When it became just sex, I felt terribly left out of his life and deeply lonely. The connection between us seemed to be weakening, but Jim never wanted to talk about it. Of course I tried to be an understanding wife. I knew both of us were exhausted when we laid down our weary heads at night; but it's hard to be understanding about times like that, particularly when they happen over and over again.

There was one thing that I wanted more than anything else, but Jim wouldn't give it to me. I wanted a child. But whenever I tried to talk to him about having a child, he would always say, "Tam, we don't need a baby. We are too busy and we have each other; that is all we need."

"But, Jim, I'm so desperately lonely. You're away doing *The 700 Club* and everything else for Pat, and I'm just at home waiting for you half the time."

"Tam, you always have your friends."

"What I want is a baby. I need a child to love, to hold in my arms. Someone to take care of."

"Be realistic. Both of us are just too busy to pay attention to a baby. As long as it's just the two of us, the late hours don't matter that much. Look, it wouldn't be fair to have a baby now, not fair to us, and certainly not fair to the child."

"Jim, I want a baby real bad. You know how much I love children." The truth was I would have had ten kids if I could have. But my words fell on deaf ears. I was perfectly able to bear children, but Jim didn't want any.

Still, every day I would pray, "Please, God, please give me a baby." And after all the long years I thought my prayers had finally been answered. We received an urgent call from a lady saying that her granddaughter was pregnant out of wedlock. They were looking for a good home for the baby when it arrived—and they had chosen us. I was ecstatic!

"Please, Jim," I implored. "Can we please take the baby when it gets here?" Jim listened to me calmly and claimed he understood.

But then he shot the whole idea down. "Listen, Tam, because we're on TV the mother would be able to see us and the baby all the time. That's why I don't think it's such a good idea. It would cause her too much pain." I naturally grasped the validity of what he was saying, but when he then called the people and asked them if his brother could take the baby instead of us, I was devastated. After the infant was born, a darling little girl, Jim and I went to the hospital and got her. We then drove to the airport where I had to place "my baby" into the arms of his brother.

I cried for days. My heart was broken. Finally Jim realized what he had done and said that we could finally have our own child. By this time I was twenty-eight years old and we had already been married nine years. We started trying, and I went from devastation to elation. Within six months I was the happiest pregnant woman in the world. The day I had Tammy Sue, March 2, 1970, was the most joyful day in my life.

And Jim was a changed man after she was born. Tammy Sue became his reason for living—at least for a while. Jim was the model daddy, doting on her, marveling at her every move. All of a sudden we were a family, a real family. It was a marvelous time for us. Until once again Jim got "too busy." But now that I had Tammy Sue, it didn't seem so bad. We had each other.

By the time of her birth we had been with Pat Robertson for nearly six years. Our programs were being syndicated across the country and were literally supporting the network. The people watching the programs would then support our efforts by sending their contributions to CBN, which in turn made it possible for Robertson to continue buying more airtime. It all worked out beautifully—up to a point.

A Rift Begins to Grow

The point being that everyone thought it was really Jim who owned the station. As a matter of fact, they thought he *was* the station, even though Jim always bent over backward to give Pat all the credit for everything he achieved. Jim had great respect for Robertson and sought his approval, and Pat always dispensed his approval in a fatherly way, which was just what Jim needed.

But in spite of Jim's generosity and the chummy scenes they played out in front of the camera, a great deal of maneuvering and personal politics were coming into play between Jim and Pat. Pretty soon a rivalry developed over power and influence—at least that's the way I believe Robertson saw it. I know Jim never saw it that way.

As Jim's charisma and rising popularity became more of a threat, Pat concluded he was going to have to get in there and take firmer control. And obviously the best way to do this was to become more visible, to get more time in front of the camera. He started the ball rolling by calling Jim into his office. "I've decided to take over one night a week on *The 700 Club*," he announced. "I think it will give the partners a little more variety."

Just a little stunned, Jim replied, "Well, that's your privilege, Pat. It's certainly your station and not mine."

"I'm glad you realize that, Jim. I wouldn't want any conflict."

But then Robertson would show up on the set and take over two nights, then three nights, until it became apparent to us that Pat wanted to do the show all by himself. Well, the handwriting was on the wall. It was pretty apparent that Robertson didn't need us as much as he used to. Thanks to the contributions our shows had brought in, he was able to build a new state-of-the-art TV facility for the network.

And to further broaden his financial base, Pat was also considering bringing in secular programs such as *I Love Lucy* and *Gunsmoke.* Now, that notion really rattled Jim. "Pat, you know I've promised our viewers this would never come about. I've sworn time and time again that the network would always remain one hundred percent Christian—without any commercials for deodorants or cars or pine toilet cleaners or anything."

But Robertson wasn't fazed by Jim's pleas. "Look, the decision has already been made. This makes perfect sense. Putting on these shows will give us a broader audience. Isn't that what we all want?"

"I want us to stay faithful to our principles," Jim shot back. "I want us to stay faithful to the people who contribute to keep our programs on the air. If you go ahead with this, it's going to look like I was lying to the partners." The breach between the two men was widening by the minute. But Robertson wasn't budging an inch. Finally Jim said, "If you're going to put in secular programming, then I'm going to have to leave because I made a promise to the people."

"Of course I don't want you to leave, Jim. But you have to do what you think is right." During this time Pat displayed no actual animosity, and neither did Jim; they were just two distinct people with different points of view, preparing to go their own separate ways. Indeed, just before we left the network Robertson offered us a raise—and a very hefty raise at that. But by this time it was too late. Jim felt that we just needed to move ahead and get on with our lives, so we didn't accept.

Nevertheless, separating from Pat's organization after seven years was very traumatic, like children leaving their parents' home for the first time. I felt disoriented. Part of me still couldn't believe we were saying farewell to Christian television. It was the fall of 1972, and we had no plan in mind. Nothing at all. On top of that we were exhausted, so tired that for all intents and purposes we had just about had it.

We had worked so horribly hard building Pat Robertson's empire. Jim had labored day and night for seven long years. There were many times when he would only get four hours of sleep. To further complicate the situation, Jim's health had been failing. Robertson's hectic production schedule wound up aggravating Jim's ulcers. His nerves also began to bother him, so the doctor prescribed Valium for him. The doctor told Jim that he was burning out, and that he needed desperately to get away and rest.

Through the years we had come a long way. The first three years we had just done the children's show. And over the next years came *The 700 Club,* too. In the beginning our salaries were virtually nothing, since almost all the donations were being plowed back into buying television time. But by the time we decided to leave, each of us was making $125 a week. If we had stayed, Robertson had offered to increase our salaries by another $25. I know it doesn't sound like much, but it was a lot in those days.

Over the years we had invested what little money we had in old houses that we bought for practically nothing. Then on the weekends we fixed them up and sold them. By the time we left CBN we owned a breathtaking place on a lake, filled with beautiful Italian provincial furniture. We sold the house furnished—just the way it was.

Now here we were, getting all ready to pull away from our dream home in a brand new Airstream trailer. Where we were going or how long we would be gone we didn't know. All we knew was that we were going to head toward California, a place we had never been. Luckily we had received enough money when we sold our house to live without working for a year.

Nobody could believe we had left Robertson's operation. Our kids' show was at the top of the ratings. CBN was syndicating it all over the country. But completely unknown to us, the moment we took off, there were people so jealous and wanting to take our place so bad that they took all of those years of shows and immediately erased them, destroying anything that had to do with Jim and Tammy Faye Bakker.

For instance, we had a giant Suzy Moppett doll that Coca-Cola had made to be used as part of a big float in a parade. That doll had been an award-winning entry, but someone literally smashed Suzy Moppett's head to bits. One young man took over our children's show, but it never did anything after we left. He was one of the main instigators against us. I guess the children watching saw him for what he was—and turned him off. Children are smart like that.

Tearing down everything we had built meant no reruns, no way for the public to be reminded of us, no way for us to come back. Although I thought we had parted on amicable terms, I was obviously wrong. I now believe Pat Robertson encouraged them to destroy our work because he was furious at us for leaving his domain. From what I've heard, Robertson never even spoke our names once we left. He was done with us. And when Pat is done with a person, he's done. Finished!

Jim and I weren't gods—and neither was Pat Robertson.

All of us were merely messengers trying to do God's work as best we could. We're only human, and our greatest redeeming quality is our ability to forgive—maybe not to forget, but to forgive. Even religious leaders as astute and educated as Pat Robertson can succumb to pent-up anger and jealousy. There's simply no avoiding it. You can't always reconcile what you're preaching with what you're feeling.

In any event, while cruising along the highways in our luxury trailer we tried as best we could to put the years at CBN behind us. We were journeying across the country toward a new life. We made it to California much sooner than we had expected.

Of California and Angels

After arriving in Southern California Jim decided to visit an old acquaintance, Paul Crouch, his former youth pastor from Muskegon. Paul lived in the city of Irvine and also worked for a Christian TV station that ran our syndicated children's program. After so many years Paul and Jim were thrilled to see each other, and the first thing Paul did was to invite us over to his house to meet his wife, Jan. They said, "Why don't you park the Airstream down on the beach? There's a lovely park there where you can stay for as long as you need to." So that is what we did. We lived in the Airstream on the beach for about three months. It was a fantastic time for me and Jim and Tammy Sue.

From the moment Jan and I met it was like we had known each other all our lives. Paul and Jan had two little boys, and Tammy Sue instantly took to them. Then during dinner it happened. "You know, I've been thinking about launching a station," Paul mentioned. "My own Christian television station."

"Well, that's a lot of work," Jim said.

"But I really want to leave the station where I am. There's no future in working for anyone else."

Jim laughed. "Tell me about it."

But at this point Paul got real serious and spoke plainly. "You know how to do it. You know how to do it better than anybody. Help me build this station." I looked at Jim. His interest was obviously piqued. This was a man he had always loved and trusted. "I've got a way to get the license and do all those things," Paul continued. "I know all of the business part of starting a television station, and you know the creative part. Let's pool our resources and get this show on the road!" There was no doubt about it. Jim got the bug again.

As the men continued their chat, Jan and I went off and explored her home. The views from the bedroom were breathtaking, since they were high on a hill overlooking a rolling canyon. Inside was all done with gold candlesticks, gold pillows—gold trim on everything. And what wasn't gold was red. I had never seen anything like Paul and Jan's house. I thought it was beautiful.

About an hour later, when we returned from our little tour, Jim and Paul were still talking a mile a minute. "Jim, you have to admit that we would make a great team," Paul said. "Come on, admit it!"

"I admit it, I admit it!" Jim replied enthusiastically. It felt good to see him so animated, so excited about something once more. Paul was older than Jim, someone he looked up to.

"Don't worry about the details. I'll take care of everything. This way you'll be insulated from all the day-to-day stuff. How does that sound?"

"So far, so good." Jim was beaming. After all, we were in a new place and Paul knew all the ropes. In a sense, he was playing a parental role for Jim. He would protect him, always be there for him.

"Okay, let's make this clear," Paul said. "You'll be the president of the station, and I'll be the business administrator. You'll be the power on-camera, and I'll be the power behind the camera."

Jim grinned broadly. "Sounds fine to me." With those words they shook hands. Needless to say, Jan and I were delighted. Within days Paul and Jim were planning their very own Christian TV station, setting up meetings with the right people who could help launch TBN, the Trinity Broadcasting Network, a nonprofit ministry.

Jim and Paul never signed any papers. What existed between them was an oral contract. Everything Jim ever did was an oral contract. Jim's handshake was his word. See, we were people of our word, and so we always took people at *their* word. Nevertheless, I take my share of the responsibility for not putting anything down on paper. In retrospect I'm appalled by the fact that we didn't. Jim and I weren't children. We certainly had been around long enough to know how business was conducted. Not signing an agreement with Paul was one of the biggest mistakes we ever made.

In any event, for three months we lived in our trailer on the scenic beach nearby. Then one day Jim announced we were going to sell the Airstream and buy a house. He felt it was a solid investment, money in the bank, as we had made so much money in real estate back in Virginia.

So we sold the trailer and used the money as a down payment on a charming house that was being built. Jan and Paul graciously asked us to move into their guesthouse until our home was completed. Not only did Jan and I become as sisters during this time, but Jim and Paul were as brothers. We were as close as any family could be.

Before we knew it the guys had located the perfect building in an old industrial complex. Outside was an immaculate lawn dotted by well-tended trees. Naturally it had to be renovated to fit the needs of a TV studio. Along with friends, we got down to work. We began constructing soundproof control booths. We took up the old tile floorboards and got ankle deep in tar. But once people found out what we were doing, miracles started to happen.

A beautiful Hammond organ was donated to us. And in six weeks the set was ready, the cameras were ready, and we even had a volunteer staff ready to go. As planned, Jim was the host of the new *PTL* (for "Praise the Lord") show, and I was the featured cohost and singer. We started at KBSA-TV, channel 46, and for about four or five months things ran smoothly.

Thanks to our teamwork the TV show began going great. The studio began to fill up every day until it virtually overflowed with people. We began to syndicate the show across the country, except this time it looked like there would be no stopping us.

After we moved in, our home was constantly filled with staff members and their children. But because we were putting everything back into the network, Jim and I were living on practically nothing. We were hardly making our house payments. People were giving us groceries, taking us out to eat, donating things to us—that's how bad it was. Even at the height of our popularity, we were essentially living hand-to-mouth.

Just after getting our home somewhat together, Jim and I were really rocked—by our first California earthquake. The next few days there were aftershocks, and each time my heart went straight into my mouth. At the time we never realized that these would be the least of the tremors to shake our lives.

The catastrophe started slowly. Paul decided to expand our board of directors, and because he was the business manager that was entirely his province. Since we knew nobody in the business world in California, there was no way we could stop him—not that we even wanted to at the time. Paul was filling up the board with prestigious people from the community. The justification was that TBN was swiftly growing by leaps and bounds and required the consultation of people with good business sense.

Over time, I noticed a certain competitiveness emerging between Paul and Jim. Paul observed how well Jim was being received. Concluding that California was really his domain, Paul started thinking he ought to be the man in front of the camera. Nevertheless, I truly believe that it was Jan calling the shots. One time I overheard her insisting in a very loud voice, "Paul, you ought to be the president. Jim shouldn't be the president. You ought to be on the air all the time!" It's my opinion that Jan goaded Paul—would not leave him alone and stayed on him until she finally forced him to do something. Looking back, I also now believe that Jan had a hidden agenda as well. She wanted to be featured on the air, but naturally she never said anything to us face-to-face.

Then, suddenly, we were let go. When we first got the news, we couldn't believe it. We had heard rumors that Paul was stacking the board of directors against us, but we refused to believe that Paul would do a thing like that. When we learned of the reports, we should have gone to Paul and demanded a written contract, but that just wasn't Jim's way. He never believed anything until it actually happened, and by then it was too late.

I was angry. I was hurt and felt terribly betrayed by Jan, my good friend. How could a friend do something like this to another friend, especially as close as we had been? We had lived together, raised our children together, we had prayed and cried together. We had shared the innermost secrets of our hearts with each other. This could not be happening, but it was. I begged Jim to fight.

"Jim, go to Paul and have a talk with him, work this thing out." Jim did make an attempt, but by this time Paul could see that his plan was going to work—if he remained strong, he'd end up having it all. So Jim decided not to fight Paul anymore and to just walk away. I didn't agree. "Jim," I pleaded, "God called us here. You and Paul are partners. You have just as much power as he does."

"Not anymore, Tam. Not since he put all his friends on the board of directors. I don't know those men, and they don't know me. They'll be on Paul's side no matter what. And in reality, it's now them, and not Paul Crouch, who decide whether we can or cannot stay. And the board will do whatever he asks. That's why he chose them."

I knew Jim had a point, but I couldn't face the fact that we had worked so hard, once again built up such a huge TV audience, and were going to leave yet another ministry. My heart was breaking. Our entire staff left with us. Paul and Jan had to hire all new people to take their places. The staff knew that Paul was wrong in forcing Jim out of a ministry that he had worked so hard to build. But maybe it was Paul's plan all along, to use Jim's expertise to build the TV ministry and then to get rid of him. I don't know.

I will never forget the tears and anguish I felt helping Jim pack up the things in his office. I was at my wit's end. Where would we go? What would we do? Where was God? Did He even care? Then something happened I shall never forget. I looked up, and standing in the doorway of Jim's office was a huge angel. He was dressed in a brilliant white robe that was covered halfway down by a glowing blue cape. On his head was a huge gold helmet, and in his hand he carried a large sword. He looked to be about eight feet tall.

I cannot remember seeing his face, but I do remember the words he spoke to me. "Fear not, for as of this moment I and my angels are going forward to do battle for you." With that, he disappeared. I have never seen an angel since, but I will never forget as long as I live seeing that one. A deep peace filled my entire being, and I knew that despite what Paul and Jan Crouch had done to us, every-thing was going to be all right. I told Jim and the staff about the angel, and it bought them peace also.

We left the building for the last time and went home to put a FOR SALE sign on our little house. We had no idea where we were going or what we were going to do, but we knew that God knew and that we could trust Him. Our staff had to make their preparations also, and I hurt for them. For a couple of weeks, we all got together every day at our house for prayer meetings and to ask God what we should do. Bills were coming due, and here we all were without paychecks.

Many people who had been supporters of our ministry heard of our plight, and they all came to our rescue. One wonderful lady, Herta Backlund, had a fantastic restau-rant, and we all ate there free, our entire staff, every day until we left California. I shall never forget Herta. No one ever missed a meal or a payment on their house or apart-ment. I still don't know how that happened except that it was a miracle from God. There is a verse in the Bible that says, "I've never seen the righteous forsaken, or His seed out begging bread." That scripture certainly came alive for us at that time.

We spent about a month more in California until one day, some friends in Charlotte, North Carolina, called to say that they had decided to start a Christian TV station, and they needed Jim's help. I assume word about our situ-ation had gotten out. "Jim, many of us have been praying for years that you and Tammy would come down here. This is where you belong. We know in our hearts that if you come, something wonderful will happen."

With that call, once more we uprooted ourselves, moving our whole staff and all of our belongings. A caravan of trucks brought everything to North Carolina. Jim flew ahead by plane, all fired up and raring to go. The staff soon followed, filled with Jim's contagious enthusiasm. With

Tammy Sue bundled up in my arms, I gathered the last of our belongings and closed up the house. I didn't know if I was tremendously at peace—or a little shell-shocked—as I said good-bye to California.

Paul and Jan Crouch have now been on the air for many years. They have successfully written us out of their history. But God knows the story, and after all, that is what really counts. I am glad that something we helped to build so many years ago is still going strong for the glory of God, and I really mean that with my whole heart. I hold nothing against Paul and Jan. When all is said and done, it won't make any difference who did anything in the kingdom of God, just that it got done!

Part Three

The Rise of PTL

Heritage Village and Heritage USA

The year was 1972, and we were starting all over again—in a small studio that only a few weeks before had been a store that sold adjustable easy chairs. It was a major job. The set was structured the same way as before, with Jim sitting behind a desk and his guests on a couch. Once again music was provided by a sole organist.

In spite of the modest surroundings, Jim always believed in making everything elegant, at least as beautiful as our limited funds would allow. We combed the thrift shops, back alleys, and flea markets.

It was a small, intimate set, but as word spread our audience started ballooning. In just a few months we were able to syndicate the new PTL program, called *The PTL Club.* People started writing and pledges began pouring in. With this financial support we were able to expand rapidly, buying more cameras and more equipment. Soon we moved to a brand-new facility. Every penny was spent on first-class production values and getting guests from every corner of the country.

Jim wasn't chintzy. He didn't hoard money trying to save every red cent. He put up our guests at good hotels, reimbursed them for their meals, and had them greeted at the airport and chauffeured over to the studio. We even offered them some modest compensation for their appearance, what was called an honorarium. To my knowledge, none of our guests demanded compensation for appearing, no matter how big they were. One of the secrets Jim knew about producing a successful show was making sure your guests are cheerful and relaxed. But he probably spent more money than he ever had to.

Thanks to Jim's savvy and marketing know-how, in just three months we started mushrooming. Virtually overnight *The PTL Club* became one of the most popular shows in every market across the country. Newspapers and magazines started paying closer attention to us. They wanted to know how such a miracle could be happening all over again. I'm not sure anyone, including Jim, was ever prepared for such colossal growth. If we had been, had we really taken the time to analyze what we could manage and what we could not, I'm certain that many of the problems we encountered later on could have been avoided.

Jim offered the position of cohost for the *PTL* show to Henry Harrison. And before you could blink an eye, Uncle Henry left Pat Robertson and CBN and came to work for Jim in Charlotte. The chemistry was great between them, just as before. Uncle Henry was always on the set, a close friend of everyone.

In less than two years Jim started laying the foundation for the Williamsburg complex in Charlotte, which would soon become Heritage Village. A series of adjoining TV studios, this venture would greatly broaden our production and audience capacity. It was a giant step but a much needed one. The property we located consisted of four classic buildings including a spacious home designed in eighteenth-century style. This building would provide not only ample office space but a place where we could start constructing a set to match our needs.

Jim patterned the inspiring new studio after a celebrated old church in Williamsburg, Virginia. The construction went along quickly, and I will never forget the dedication, complete with marching bands from the local high school and a bagpipe brigade. Heritage Village was the very first achievement of its kind in Christian television, elevating the entire field to a new level of professionalism and prestige. It was widely hailed as a stunning breakthrough. I thought this was absolutely the highest you could go, the most anyone could hope to achieve in a lifetime. I wanted to stay there forever.

But here and there people began to notice rising tension between Jim and me. You could feel it on the set, you could feel it when visiting our home. Jim became so preoccupied with the development of Heritage Village that there was little energy left over for deepening our relationship. While I encouraged his efforts, I began feeling more distant from him than ever.

I found myself reluctant to share moments of intimacy with him. And under the circumstances, it became increasingly unpleasant. More and more I found myself wanting to avoid relations altogether; but I didn't want to tell Jim this. I didn't want him to feel as if I was rejecting him. When you truly love someone, there are times when you have to put your own feelings aside.

During this time Tammy Sue turned six, and I missed not having a little baby to hug anymore. And I didn't want my daughter to be an only child. Coming from a large family, I knew how wonderful it was to have brothers and sisters. Consequently, once more I begged Jim for a child. And as usual, he came up with the same reasons all over again, but finally he gave in. Without much enthusiasm, he said, "Tam, if you want a baby, that's up to you."

In 1976 I was overjoyed: I was pregnant. Tammy Sue was so excited about having a new sister or brother coming to live with us. It was practically all she could talk about.

However, at the time I needed Jim most, he was never there.

During the entire nine months I was extremely ill. I couldn't keep a thing in my stomach and lost over thirty pounds, dropping down to under a hundred. Heritage Village required Jim's undivided attention. He would stay out until the wee hours of the morning with all the cameramen, stagehands, or the engineers who were building the complex. By the time he got home I was so worried and upset that I couldn't even speak to him. I was so lonely I wanted to die—and so sick I thought I was going to.

We had only one car, and of course Jim needed it. That made me feel very vulnerable. Outside my window was nothing but a deserted road. What if there was an emergency? What would I do? At that time I hardly knew anyone in Charlotte. I was never the type to ask for help. I never wanted to bother anyone, so I suffered by myself in silence.

I was nine months pregnant. I was sick, worried, scared, and lonely.

One night I heard the door open. It was 2:00 A.M., and I was frantic. Jim walked in smiling. "Why aren't you in bed, Tam?"

"Where have you been?" I screamed at the top of my lungs. "I have been trying to get ahold of you for hours. I thought you were dead along the road somewhere!"

But Jim just didn't seem to realize how upset I was. "Oh, I got to talking with the guys, and time just got away from us."

"The guys!" I couldn't believe he was saying this to me. "Why are the guys always more important than me and Tammy Sue? Why couldn't you just one time come home before midnight, Jim? Why couldn't you just one time come home at a decent hour and have supper with your family? Why is everyone else always more important than us?"

Before Jim could even respond, I did something I had never done in all our years of marriage. I walked into the spare bedroom and shut the door. Shut the door to his apologies and excuses, and shut the door of my heart as well.

"Tam, I'm sorry. I promise to try and get home earlier." But as far as I was concerned, he didn't exist. "Tam, I know the way you feel. Please, honey, please come out of there! Everything's going to be different. I swear it will! Do you hear me? I said I swear it will!" But I totally ignored his pleas. My water broke, and I didn't even bother to tell him.

However, in the middle of the night my pains forced me to call out, and Jim took me to the hospital in the morning. Jamie Charles—the precious little boy I had wanted so badly—was born the next day by C-section. I delivered two minutes before the *PTL* show went off the air. The doctor immediately called the TV station and told them that we had a beautiful baby boy, but Jim was the last to know. He was in the car en route to the hospital.

Why wasn't he at my side? Because once again work had been put first. "The show must go on" was Jim's credo. But it wasn't entirely his fault that he wasn't there for the birth of his child. After bringing me to the hospital, Jim asked, "Tam, should I stay or do the show?"

Of all the times to hear that question! "Jim, why don't you just go and do the show," I said finally.

"Are you sure that's all right?"

"I'm sure," I replied, hoping all the while that he would choose to stay with me instead. But he didn't. He kissed me good-bye and dashed off to get to the studio.

I guess all of us women are alike. We say one thing to our men and mean another, hoping they'll "catch on." If I could chart the time when I gave up the illusion of being first in Jim's life, I guess that would stand out as the straw that broke the camel's back. I became resigned to the fact that things were not going to change. The mom in me became more alive, while the wife in me began to die.

After my pregnancy I looked like a complete wreck. Even four weeks following delivering I was still having trouble getting down the stairs. My legs would buckle underneath me, and I felt faint all the time. Something was definitely wrong. I drove myself about twenty miles into town to see the doctor. He took one look and said, "Oh my God!"

It seemed the blood from the cesarean section had not dissolved back into my system as it was supposed to and instead had become clotted around the incision in my stomach. The doctor called his nurse and told her what to get. She came back with a package of razor blades and a pair of tiny surgical scissors and, much to my horror, started to reopen the wound in my tummy.

With that done, the old coagulated blood began to pour out of me. Towel after towel was needed to soak it up. Yet suddenly I felt tremendous relief for the first time in almost a year. Tears were streaming down my face. I don't know if they were from pain or peace of mind. I crawled back into my car (Jim had bought me a car after Jamie was born) and drove the twenty miles back home.

Wanting to raise my babies the right way, I just stopped performing on television altogether. I didn't care about doing the show anymore. Circumstances continued to improve a day at a time. I would hold Jamie Charles in my arms and thank God from the bottom of my heart for my precious daughter and son.

Jim continued to work long hours, but I was content now. I had my two children, a dog named Mandy, and my very own car. I no longer felt like a prisoner in my own home and even made a few TV appearances with Jamie and Tammy Sue. After years of being by Jim's side for hundreds of programs, I was now a housewife.

I cleaned my own house, shopped for my own groceries, and washed my own clothes. And Jim was happy as well.

The new TV studio was almost finished and more beautiful than anyone could have pictured. Jim even decided to move our family into town onto the grounds of the new Heritage Village. This was exciting because it meant we could now see more of one another and become a real family again.

All things considered, these times created some of my fondest memories, moments of wonderful fellowship. I did not have to entertain guests at home anymore. There was a beautiful old Colonial house on the property at Heritage Village that everyone called "the Mansion." That is where we would entertain all the show guests. From that immense kitchen all sorts of appetizing smells would continually emanate, from soft-shell crabs sauteed in butter to double-fudge chocolate brownies.

During the holiday season Heritage Village became a wonderland. Wherever you looked Christmas trees dotted the grounds, festooned with brightly shining lights and ornaments. Nativity scenes decorated the gardens. From large speakers hidden away behind bushes Christmas music permeated the air, gently echoing throughout the hillsides. Visitors would journey from thousands of miles away to see the spectacle.

About a year after Jamie was born, I started up my own program, called *Tammy's House Party*. I got permission from Art Linkletter to use the title *House Party*, since he had done a show by the same name. It was fun doing *Tammy's House Party* after being off the air for such a long time. In one aspect, the show was a significant step forward for me; but in another way it was just another symptom of the "going our separate ways and doing our own thing" problem.

My staff was mostly women, which was tons of fun. I had a fantastic woman director, women produced the show, and we even had a couple of women on the cameras. The show was extremely well conceived, provided lots of laughs, and quickly enjoyed prominent ratings. It ran on the same network as the *PTL* program.

When I went back in front of the cameras we hired a marvelous lady to take care of the children. Sometimes we had supper with them, when we came home; sometimes they were in bed. Jim would be planning more attractions, and I'd be recording albums or even traveling by myself. The tragedy was that a deep and profound separation of souls had begun to take place. We were two people living two different lives.

However, our personal difficulties had no effect on the growth of Heritage Village. Once again we were expanding so rapidly that we needed more space—for more employees, for partners coming to visit, for more parking, for more of everything. We were so crowded that we could hardly get the people inside. Cars would be lined up and down the street. The only reason Jim wanted to expand was so that we could accommodate more people. It was never seen as a way to provide cash flow, it was never a money issue. Because to Jim Bakker, money was always the means to an end, never the end itself.

Per his instructions, our people searched for land to build on. Although I knew all the reasons why Jim wanted to do this, my heart sank right down to my feet when I heard that they had found over two thousand acres of land right on the border between the Carolinas.

Jim would build again. And in my heart I already knew the price our family would pay for this expansion. Instead of being delighted, I grieved. I got this sickening feeling down in my stomach.

Soon plans went into rapid-fire development for an enormous new expansion, a Disney-like theme park that would be called Heritage USA. Jim had to hire a builder and an architect, and he thought of Roe Messner, who had earned a national reputation for his work on churches. Roe was a tall and athletic man, reserved in his manner but with the confidence and can-do attitude that Jim needed to fulfill his dream.

"Roe, nothing like this has ever been done before."

"I know that."

"You know how big it could be."

"I know that too."

"But you know what my problem is." The truth was everyone in the financial community of North Carolina knew what Jim's problem was. In his incredible rush to get Heritage Village off the ground, the ministry had developed a terrible credit rating. There were always cash shortfalls.

"Jim, I know that you can't get anyone to even bring a plank up here unless they pay cash," said Roe jokingly, but Jim brushed the remark aside.

"What I need is someone who sees the big picture. Someone who understands the potential of what this could mean." Jim knew that at this point Roe had millions of dollars. As an extremely successful designer and builder of churches across the country, Roe had immediate access to huge lines of credit.

"Just what do you want, Jim?"

"I can't raise the money to get this off the ground, not until I can first show people what it's going to be."

"I'm still listening."

"With your vision, Roe, with your talent and ability, you could make the people see what I see. Do you understand what I'm saying?" Roe knew exactly what Jim was saying.

"As I see it, you want me to help advertise what you're intending for all that land you bought." Even though he was playing it cool, Roe knew this was the greatest opportunity he'd ever had. The construction of Heritage USA would be a tremendous shot in the arm for his church-building business.

"I need beautiful pictures and renderings," remarked Jim, "to give people the idea. But more than that I need your bulldozers and machines and men working and digging on that land. I need to put cameras on all that activity and get the people excited. Let them feel that something is really happening down there."

"I'm following you, Jim. Let me get this right. What you want is for me to carry you till the people start coming through. You want me to put up all the money."

"You're the only man who can do it, Roe. And I trust you."

"Well, Jim, I'll be straight with you. I think it's a great idea. I don't think it can miss."

That's all Jim needed to get it going. The actual nuts and bolts of erecting the gigantic theme park fell squarely upon the shoulders of Roe Messner, chief architect and contractor. Pretty soon the donations started pouring in. Excitement about Heritage USA spread like a fever.

It Takes Two to Tango

But with all this dramatic new expansion, I was feeling increasingly alienated from Jim's life, left out of what was going on in the ministry. My problems seemed like a snowball that had gotten away from me, rolling down the mountain and picking up speed until I felt buried under an avalanche. In all my frustration, hurt, and anger with Jim, I allowed something disastrous to happen. I fell in love with another man.

His name was Gary S. Paxton. He had written "Monster Mash" and "Alley Oop," plus many other famous funny songs of the sixties. He was also a very popular on-air personality on *PTL*, appearing many times. What's more, Gary had produced six or seven of my albums, so we had worked very closely together for years. But during all the sessions Gary and I never even flirted once—until, I don't recall exactly when, one day we just looked at each other and realized there was a lot there.

As the attraction grew, we began to say things like "Oh, we can't let this happen, we've got to be careful, we're too good friends for this to take place." It began by talking on the phone much more than was necessary.

Gary lived in Nashville. But every time he came to be on television with Jim, he and I would figure out a way to be together. That was easy, as Jim never seemed to know or care what I was doing during the day.

Even though I don't think Jim believes it to this day, the relationship between Gary and me never went any further than hugging and kissing. Gary did not believe in sex outside of marriage and knew that I didn't either. It was Gary's feelings about sex that made me feel comfortable with him. He always told me that sex ruined friendship, and that he valued our friendship. He knew that I felt the same way. And more important to both of us was the fact that we were Christians and that our walk with God meant more to us than anything in the world. What I needed was a feeling of closeness, of tenderness, and somebody who would listen to me. Gary talked to me, and he let me talk. He treated me like an intelligent person, not just some little giggly girl. Gary made me feel like a woman.

Our meetings had been going on for about a year before Jim found out. Someone went to him and said, "Open your eyes, buddy. Can't you see what's happening between Paxton and your wife?" But Jim was always so preoccupied with his own doings that he never had any idea his wife could be turning to another man. "Well, if you don't believe it, why don't you just go home and ask her?" Which is exactly what he did.

"What's the thing with Paxton, Tammy?" he asked, barely able to keep his voice from cracking. "I hear you've been seeing him. Is that true? Have you been slipping around with someone behind my back?"

I didn't want to beat around the bush. The time had come to tell Jim just how I felt. "What you've heard is right."

"I don't believe it!" he said, trembling like a leaf. "Have you lost your mind? Do you want to ruin everything we have?"

"Only blame yourself, Jim. Maybe if you had ever shown me some kindness, some feeling, I wouldn't have to go to another man to get the love and attention that I should be getting from you!"

"I'm not hearing this." Jim was fighting back tears. "I've given you everything, Tam. Tell me one thing I haven't given you!"

"You haven't given me your respect. You've shut me out of your life. I've been out there by myself, raising two children by myself, and they don't even know you. They don't even know their own father."

"That's not true, Tammy. You don't know what you're saying."

"Gary tells me how intelligent I am. He listens to my opinions. When was the last time you paid attention to anything I had to say?"

"I always listen to you."

"That's the problem. You listen but you never twitch an eyelash. You just don't hear me. It all goes in one ear and out the other!"

At that point Jim calmed himself down. He paused to collect his thoughts and then pointed his finger straight at me. "Tam, this thing with Paxton is over. Do you understand me? You're never going to see him again!" With those words Jim turned his back on me and stormed out of the room. I broke down sobbing on the couch. I didn't know which way to go or what to do.

First thing the next day Gary was called into Jim's office. Right off the bat Jim accused him of treachery, but Gary stood his ground. Jim wasn't buying into any of this and banished Gary on the spot. Bluntly Jim told him that he could never show his face around PTL anymore, never sing on the air again. That was so sad, because Gary wrote such beautiful Christian music and everyone loved him.

Gary called me after meeting with Jim and told me that he would never be back. He said that he had been forbidden by Jim to ever set foot on the grounds again. We knew that the time had come for us to face reality. We had to quit living in a dreamworld. I had to stop trying to escape. I had to make my marriage work, for my children's sake and for the sake of God's work. I cried until there were no more tears to cry.

I will always be grateful to Gary for not pushing our relationship over the line. I will always be grateful that he did not beg me to go with him, and that he did not make me feel guilty about his losing his place at PTL. Many years later, long after he and his wife, Karen, divorced, she went to the rag magazines and told them about Gary and me. For months, pictures of him and me were all over the supermarket racks. Gary was offered thousands of dollars to "kiss and tell," but he refused. He refused—even though he desperately needed the money they wanted to pay him. I respect Gary for that more than he will ever know. Gary did remarry, to a beautiful girl, and they have a son.

Was my relationship with Gary what eventually drove Jim into the arms of Jessica Hahn? Well, I'm sure it didn't help. Although I swore that Gary and I never slept together, never had sex, I'm certain that Jim didn't believe me. Was Jessica Hahn his idea of getting even? No doubt it contributed. If I share some part of the responsibility in the chain of circumstances that led to Jessica Hahn, the scandal that eventually brought down PTL, then I am truly sorry. Unfortunately, in retrospect everything becomes clearer.

By 1979 the fact that we were having difficulties was no secret from our audience. They knew our marriage was in trouble. But I don't think they suspected another man as much as they figured we just weren't getting along. The situation had gotten so bad that I couldn't even bear to look at Jim. I was severely tempted to get back in touch with Gary, but I never did.

It was then I decided to separate from Jim. I needed time

to be by myself and think about where our lives were going. I remember informing Jim that I was leaving him. We were just about to leave for Honolulu to do a week of shows called "With Love to Hawaii." How ironic!

First Jim tried to talk me out of it. "It won't look good if you desert me before this Hawaiian trip. It's crucial that you come along. You know hundreds of PTL partners have bought tickets to join us for the whole week." But I was crying so hard that anything he said sounded distant and faraway, as if echoing faintly through a dense mist. "Tam, you can't leave me now. It will be a disaster! Just come to Hawaii with me—just for this one week. Then afterward if you still want to leave, you can just leave." As usual, Jim was very persuasive. Once more I capitulated.

It turned out to be a fantastic week—from the show's point of view, certainly not mine. Here we were in this tropical paradise, where people should be romantic and in love, and we were totally miserable. If you're a complete masochist, I suggest going to the most beautiful place on the face of the earth with someone you're about to strangle.

Picture the closing shot of these shows: flickering torches reflected in the dark waters of the Pacific, dissolving to Jim and Tammy meeting the audience. Trouble was, after shaking hands and signing autographs, we couldn't wait to get away from each other. The only joy was in having my children along. But not even Tammy Sue and Jamie could help offset the sense of foreboding. Though Jim and I were sharing the same hotel room, I doubt if two people ever felt more lonely in their lives. When the last show was over, I told Jim I wasn't going home with him. He didn't even try to talk me out of it. He knew my mind was made up.

As I was packing, Jim came over to me. "Just do me one favor," he said. "When you leave, move to Palmdale, California. There's a nice apartment complex next to the hospital. That way you'll be near Vi in case you need any advice." Vi Azvedo, the leader of PTL's counseling staff, knew about our troubles because we had consulted her on several occasions. Exhausted and emotionally shattered, I couldn't think of a better place to go. Jim took the children back to North Carolina, and I went to Palmdale, carrying only my suitcases, to try and piece my life together in the middle of the California desert.

Jim did not make me fly to Palmdale alone. He sent my secretary, Joyce Cordell, with me, and David Taggart, who was Jim's right-hand man and handled much of our personal finances. Only in his early twenties, David went on all the trips, kept all the receipts, and made sure everything was documented. We had every faith in him; he always appeared to be doing everything correctly. When he was first hired, David disclosed that he soon would be receiving an inheritance of over a million dollars from his grandmother. We had no reason to doubt that. David was a very well dressed young man, always wearing the finest Armani suits and presenting a very classy demeanor. He would often mention that his father owned a Cadillac dealership, so we naturally assumed that he had his own money. Those suits certainly didn't come from the salary *we* paid him!

With Joyce's and David's assistance, I moved into a pretty little place next to the hospital where Vi Azvedo worked. I felt safe there. Joyce and I were such close girlfriends. I'll never forget the day she had to leave me alone in that apartment.

"Tam, are you sure you're going to be all right? Are you sure you want to do this?"

"I'll be fine, Joyce," I said, with much more confidence than I felt. But Joyce could see right through my brave front. I could never fool her. We both started to cry as if our hearts would break. "Joyce, please make sure that my babies are taken good care of. Please tell them how much I love them and how much I miss them." I was in agony!

Across the country, the PTL partners knew something was wrong because they didn't see me on their television screens anymore.

But it's just as well they didn't. I was a sight to behold, with the pallor of a ghost and dark circles under my eyes. Even though the gorgeous sun was streaming down brightly every day, I just wanted to lock my door and push the world away. Outside of a few people at PTL and the counselors in Palmdale, no one knew where I was. Because if my whereabouts had ever become known, the press would have come swarming all over me.

I felt miserable and guilty, the lowest of the low. I didn't know what was going to happen to me. I had run away and shut myself off from the millions of viewers who had always been so generous and supportive. My marriage had failed. How could I possibly reconcile that with who I was or what I stood for? I missed my children. I had let down everybody in the world and was on the brink of a nervous breakdown. Soon they would be coming with a stretcher and carting me off in a straitjacket.

I knew no one in Palmdale except Vi Azvedo and Dr. Fred Gross, who was also a part of the PTL counseling team and worked at the hospital with Vi. I was so lonely that often I would just walk to the hospital and sit and talk with them. One day Dr. Gross came over to me with a bunch of papers. "Tammy," he said, "come into my office. I have something I want you to do. I want you to fill out these papers for me." After I finished, he collected the papers, left me alone, and came back in about fifteen minutes, looking at me with utter amazement. "Tammy, you just completed an IQ test. Do you know how intelligent you are?"

"No. I have no idea. And I'm not sure I want to know."

"I didn't think so, otherwise you wouldn't be acting so

nervous." Dr. Gross grinned and stated a number. He was looking for a reaction, but I stared at him blankly because I had no idea what the number meant. It could have been my weight—or even my temperature, for all I knew.

"Tammy, I think it will help you to know this. You are extremely intelligent. Which means no one can ever make you feel dumb or inferior ever again."

"You mean I'm as smart as everyone else?"

To which he started laughing. "Tammy, you're probably smarter than everyone else."

"Including Jim?"

"Don't push your luck!"

Well, I was really impressed with my IQ. For the first time in months my mood brightened. I wasn't a genius, but I was way above average, and that gave me a genuine dose of self-confidence. Maybe I am worthwhile; maybe all those people who are so talented and confident aren't any better than me. Maybe I'm as smart as they are—maybe even smarter! I wasn't just this giggly little thing running around with an empty head.

Stepping outside, I felt glorious sunshine warm my shoulders. Instead of going back to sleep, I decided to take a stroll along a secluded path I knew lined by desert cacti in bloom. And with each breath I filled my lungs with the fragrant scent blossoming all around me. I felt better about myself, stronger and more confident. I was alive, really alive, for the first time in years. It was around this time that Jim started making a powerful effort to get me back.

He would fly all night long and sleep on the plane so that he could visit me. Then one day he asked if I would like to come to the inauguration of President Reagan. And that was the beginning of our cementing things back together again. The swearing-in of the new chief executive was truly an inspiring and momentous event.

Jim and I attended all sorts of Washington parties. But he was always careful never to get political. Jim never publicly supported any candidate. Right after the inauguration I decided to travel back home to my children. I knew they were missing me. I'd gotten myself rested. I had gotten my head back together again. And I felt like I needed to go home and be the woman of God that I had claimed to be.

Returning to PTL was one of the most incredibly joyous days of my life. Viewers by the thousands had written us, telling Jim and me that they prayed for our reconciliation. I was welcomed by our partners with open arms of forgiveness. Just before I came back Jim had sold our house, and I agreed that that was the right move. We were determined to start our lives all over again.

"Tam," he said. "I promise I won't be so moody. I'll really try to control that. I don't want to hurt you anymore. I don't want us to be apart ever again!" Then for the first time in months we made love. It was tender beyond belief. One moment we laughed; the next moment we cried in each other's arms. Jim began to talk to me: "I was a fool, a complete idiot. The truth is I didn't know what I had until I didn't have it anymore. There's not one single thing I would change. I love the Tammy I married! And I hope in her heart that she still loves me!" The euphoria was short-lived.

A Woman Called Jessica

Our situation improved for a while. Jim and I were determined to share our experience, consequently we devoted hours of TV time to discussing our problems. The PTL partners knew about our misery, our frustration, and our determination to recapture the magic between us. We started the marriage-workshop program as a result. It was a sizable undertaking. But because people saw that we were hanging in, maybe they could hang in there too. Unfortunately, Jim's old patterns were starting up again.

Throughout his life he was torn between the spiritual and the secular part of himself. Jim admired what the secular world did but knew he could never be a part of it, therefore he wanted to bring the Christian world up to that level. Jim loved Disneyland and decided that the new Heritage USA should be just as exciting and impressive. He felt that the Christian population deserved to have something with just as much quality as Disney.

Jim wanted to forever do away with sawdust tabernacles and crude dormitories, creating a safe haven for people of faith to vacation without being afraid or intimidated. But more than a site for family recreation, it would serve as a spiritual mecca for millions of visitors. It would be unsurpassed, like nothing the world had ever seen before—that was Jim's dream, his vision.

Heritage USA would be the size of a small city. The huge facility would contain a large TV studio, hotels and motels, shops and restaurants, pools and tennis courts, and a subdivision of homes. When the main buildings were completed, Jim planned to add many features that people would enjoy, such as a petting zoo, trams, a water park, and man-made lakes. He wanted Heritage USA to be *the* dream vacation spot for families.

There was a tremendous amount of excitement within the Christian world about Heritage USA. Folks everywhere thought it was a remarkable achievement. In what seemed to be a genuine spirit of reconciliation, Pat Robertson telegrammed to congratulate us. Hundreds of church leaders called to lend us their support, including an enthusiastic reverend named Jerry Falwell.

Falwell was the president of a small Christian college in Lynchburg, Virginia. A minor religious leader who had managed to rise rapidly to national prominence after forming the Moral Majority, Jerry had cleverly hitched his wagon to the rising star of conservatism and Ronald Reagan.

In the midst of all the accolades, once again I was shunted aside. It was very frustrating. To avoid the fiasco of publicly separating again, and all the negative press that would bring, Jim and I unofficially stopped living together as man and wife. This time we wanted to be discreet. Who knows? Along with everything else, maybe deep down Jim never really forgave me for Gary. Maybe he dreamed of getting even—a fantasy that would soon become a reality, eventually destroying everything he ever built.

It was telethon time for one of the affiliate stations down in Clearwater, Florida. Jim was asked to help them raise funds to stay on the air. Consequently he and the PTL staff went to help them. Jim brought Tammy Sue, and they stayed in a hotel on the ocean so that Tammy Sue could play in the water with some of the staff children while their dads worked. I kept Jamie, then still a baby, at home.

One of Jim's friends, a reverend named John Wesley Fletcher, knew that we were having a lot of problems. I don't know why Fletcher decided to act when he did, but at that telethon he told Jim, "I think it's time you put Tammy in her place. You need to show her, prove to her that you're the boss and that you're a desirable man. Jim, you can have anyone you want. You have power, money, and fame. Any girl would be glad to have you." Fletcher looked around and bent a little closer toward Jim. "In fact I know one who is just dying to meet you. I just talked to her, and she says that she will fly in from New York and meet with you while you're here. Trust me, she's very discreet."

Jim mulled the proposition over. "John, I don't know. It would be wrong before God. And I have my daughter here. And a telethon to worry about. And I haven't been with another woman in twenty years."

"Well, maybe it's about time you were."

"What would happen if Tam found out? She would divorce me."

"Oh come on, Jim, she isn't going to find out. And this girl is good, really good. I've had her myself. She's like a steel trap—know what I mean? She hasn't had two kids." By this time Fletcher had the little wheels in Jim's mind spinning. "Why don't you let me fly her down. I'll pay for the trip myself. She can be here by this evening. In fact, I've already talked to her. She's packed and ready to go to the airport at a moment's notice. Come on, Jim, prove that you're a man."

Fletcher continued to goad him and chide him until finally Jim said, "John, I won't promise you anything, but I will meet her and at least say hello." That was all Fletcher needed to hear. Instantly he was on the phone, and in less than an hour Jessica Hahn was on her way. When she arrived Jim was strolling on the beach with Tammy Sue.

Fletcher's voice rang out from the hotel balcony. "Jim, come on in. I have someone I want you to meet." Jim's heart was beating out of his chest as he ventured toward the hotel, knowing full well who awaited him. Would he like this girl? What would she look like? What would he say to her? Jim almost turned around and went back to the beach when John's words came to him again, "Jim, prove that you're a man!" He continued to walk toward the hotel.

"Hey, Dad!" It was Tammy Sue. "Will you be coming right back?"

Jim's face paled. "I'll be back in a little while, honey. You have fun with your friends."

Before he knew what was happening, Jim was standing there in the hotel lobby in his swimming trunks, meeting the girl who would forever change his life. "Jim Bakker, meet Jessica Hahn," crowed Fletcher. When the introduction was completed, Hahn followed Jim back to his room. Her first words upon entering were "And what can I do for you?"

Hahn was wearing a short black dress, black nylons, a black garter belt, and black panties. Jim stood there frozen. "Come on, let me rub your back," she said. With that, Jim went over to the bed and lay facedown as she began to rub him all over. "I heard from John that you and Tammy are having marriage problems. I bet I can make you forget her. . . . Oh, Jim, I have always wanted to meet you. I have always thought you were so fantastic. . . . I couldn't wait to get here. You have such a wonderful body, Jim. You are such a sexy man. . . . I know how to do things to your body that you will never forget. . . . Tammy doesn't satisfy you, does she, Jim? She has never satisfied you, has she? When I am finished with you, you will never want her again!" But even with all her expert kneading, Jim was very tense. His body wasn't responding the way she wanted, at least not yet. "Come on, Jim, loosen up. I came all the way from New York to see you. You aren't going to disappoint me now, are you?"

Years later Jim told me that nothing would have happened between him and Jessica had she not been so skillful. He said that he was not drawn to her physically in any way, nor did he remember her to be even good-looking. What took place that day was only sex. And not very satisfying sex at that. Jim confessed that he didn't even know how he was able to have relations at all, he was in such a troubled state of mind. But Jessica was a professional. She knew what she was doing. She knew what to wear, what to say, and all the right moves. She was no virgin. Jim can attest to that.

After they finished, Jim said, "Jessica, I have to go. I have a telethon to do, and Tammy Sue is waiting for me to go eat with her."

"Well, Jim, just remember," Jessica cooed, "I will always be here for you. If you ever need me, all you have to do is call me in New York and I'll fly anywhere to meet you." Jim told me that afterward he felt filthy and couldn't wait to take a shower. Determined to wash this experience away from his body and mind forever, Jim got beneath the hot, steady stream of water. He scrubbed himself over and over, not missing a single inch, until his flesh was raw. Jim never saw Hahn again.

However, he did hear from her again. About a week after arriving back home he was back at his office. "Jim, there is a woman on the phone for you," announced Shirley Fulbright, his secretary. "Her name is Jessica Hahn, and she absolutely insists on talking to you. She says you know her and that you had better take her call." Of course he took the call.

"Jim, I loved our time together, and I want to see you again. When can we see each other again, Jim?"

The lump in Jim's throat swelled to the size of a grape-fruit. "Jessica, I want to apologize to you for what happened in Florida. It was so wrong and I feel terrible about it. I have dishonored God and my wife. I never want to see you again. Please don't call me again." With that he hung up the phone and spoke emphatically to his secretary. "Shirley, if that girl ever calls here again, I will not take it. I simply will not take it!" But Shirley was going to have to deal with Jessica many more times before it was all said and done. To my knowledge Jim never spoke personally to Hahn again.

The news media proclaimed time and time again that Jim had a tryst with a secretary in his church. That's simply not true. In reality Hahn was a secretary for a church in Massapequa, Long Island, pastored by a Reverend Eugene Profeta. John Wesley Fletcher was a friend of Profeta's and had ministered in his church many times. That is where Fletcher met Jessica Hahn.

Years later, when the scandal broke, at least two ministers came forward and told us that Hahn had also come on to them while they were preaching at Profeta's church. Both claimed she blatantly offered herself to them but that they had turned her down. Then they informed Jim that Hahn had a strange fixation for preachers; in fact she was known for it.

Following his one-night stand, Jim was inconsolable. Within days of the episode he went to see Dr. Fred Gross. The doctor reported that Jim was severely agitated, drenched in his own sweat, trembling like a leaf from the moment he walked into the office. Jim sat for hours and poured out the agony of his soul. Dr. Gross prayed with him and counseled him. "Jim, you can't possibly undo what has happened. You have to get on with your life."

"But what do I tell Tammy?"

"In my professional opinion, don't ever tell her. I don't think she would be able to take it." It was just the kind of doctor's advice that Jim found easy to take. It was not until nine years later that I found out, together with the rest of the world, about Jessica Hahn.

A Father Figure Comes to PTL

After our second separation, I returned to Jim and we tried again. With the Hahn affair dead and buried, Jim returned with new passion to building Heritage USA. Often I said to myself out of sheer frustration, "Oh no, here comes Roe Messner again. That means something else is going up." And with each new building there was less and less time for our marriage. It was as if a sharp wedge was being driven between us. The rift soon became wider and wider, the size of the Grand Canyon.

Plans were constantly sprawled across our bed, and Jim spent hour after hour poring over them. He would move a wall here, change a door there, add more square feet in another place. It never ended. As the construction progressed, other materials would take their place on our blankets: piles of wallpaper samples, carpet swatches, drapery fabrics, furniture catalogs, and on and on it would go.

Every day Jim would make checklists, some as long as twelve pages. He had an eye like a microscope. No detail could escape his scrutiny. The smallest things had to be attended to immediately. A burned-out light in the sign over the campgrounds would catch his eye. If there was a single candy wrapper caught against the front gate, the head of groundskeeping would immediately be informed. Should there be a small crack in a sidewalk or grass uncut along the parking lot, Jim would make a special note of it. Rest rooms had to be kept spotless; Jim could spot a tiny fray in a carpet, chipped paint on a building, brass railings that required polishing, minute stains on furniture. And the landscapers were always trying to figure out where he'd want the next bush or tree to go.

It was as if Jim were ten people rolled into one. Whether it was discussing crowd control for the Fourth of July, adjusting the angles of the water slides, selecting the kinds of Hawaiian music being played at Heritage Island, designing new exhibits, laying out an organizational chart, or merely deciding where people could park their cars, Jim was a stream of creative energy. At times he almost seemed superhuman, accomplishing more in one week than most people do in a lifetime.

But Jim was never satisfied. He could never finish Heritage USA, just like he could never finish Heritage Village. From the beginning Jim seemed incapable of experiencing any sense of completeness, nor would he allow himself to just sit back and enjoy his achievements. Nothing was ever enough. There was always something else to be built, a new goal to reach, a new mountain to climb, something more impressive on the horizon.

Whatever the case, the reality was that the ministry was growing so rapidly that Jim badly needed help running it— an older, seasoned, wise man—so that he could fully concentrate on doing television and raising the money needed to support such an immense organization. With my encouragement, he hired the Reverend Richard Dortch in April 1983. Reverend Dortch's position was general manager, making him second in command.

From the very first, Jim and I loved Reverend Dortch. As

a legendary force in the Assemblies of God, he was very visible and much admired. A man of impeccable credentials, he was well known for his wise counsel to hurting ministers. And he enjoyed a considerable reputation as a church problem solver.

Reverend Dortch impressed me as a father figure. Whenever I would see him and Mrs. Dortch at church conventions, I would always feel so proud that such quality people were part of our leadership. A smallish man with beautiful gray hair, Reverend Dortch always seemed to manage the kindest expression, exuding warmth and sincerity. Without his even uttering a word, his demeanor put you completely at ease.

Reverend Dortch seemed the kind of person to whom you could reveal your deepest secrets—which is exactly what Jim did. Even before Dortch was hired, Jim confided in him about the one-night stand with Jessica Hahn. And true to his word, Dortch kept the entire matter strictly confidential—at least from me.

After the celebration party commemorating Dortch's arrival, it felt as if a million pounds had been lifted off my back. Jim was finally going to have someone to shoulder part of the load, and maybe—just maybe—he would have the opportunity to spend a little more time at home with me and the children. Maybe now we could all have supper together around the table next to the fireplace in our cozy kitchen. Maybe now he could tuck Jamie in bed some nights. Maybe now we wouldn't have to attend all those nightly functions held for the PTL partners.

And in the beginning, Dortch was precisely what we hoped he would be. He and his wife began to make some appearances in our place. I was ecstatic. Because Dortch was there to occasionally host the daily TV show for us, our family was finally able to take a vacation together. Dortch proved to be a solid on-the-air personality, and the people responded to him.

A few weeks after his arrival, Dortch summoned Roe Messner up to his office. "Roe, I just wanted to let you know that I'm in charge. Everything that gets done around here now has to be run through me. I'm the one responsible for making all the decisions." Roe listened respectfully to every word Dortch was saying. "Where Jim is concerned, it is acceptable for you to meet privately with him and discuss any building projects, but I want one thing made clear. You have to keep me advised and send me copies of all your correspondence."

At that point Dortch turned around and gazed out the window, surveying the grounds beneath him. "Roe, I just wanted to tell you that I'm bringing in my own people. There are going to be lots of changes around here—lots of changes." Assuming he was finished, Roe was about to leave. "Oh, yes, just one more thing," Reverend Dortch added, smiling ever so slightly. "I can't be fired."

The PTL Show

O nce operations moved to Heritage USA, Jim's remarkable foresight engineered an unprecedented broadcasting coup. We acquired the satellite network. Jim leased an entire communications satellite, and this provided a space-age link to hundreds of cable systems around the country and around the world, twenty-four hours a day. Virtually overnight the total number of stations carrying *PTL* mushroomed. The show could now be carried live, seen simultaneously all across the nation, just like the news on ABC or CNN. Jim had negotiated an exclusive multiyear contract. It couldn't be broken. That was the valuable thing that PTL possessed.

The satellite network meant the *PTL* show no longer needed to be distributed separately on videotape to hundreds of stations. This saved considerable money as well. Because it was a live telecast, we suddenly had much more freedom. Without the constraints that naturally come from being prerecorded, our shows could now be instantly updated and we could go over our allotted time, staying on as long as we wanted.

The satellite network opened up our programs to more

than fourteen million homes, domestically representing a potential audience of more than thirty-five million people. And with media outlets across six continents, *PTL* instantly became a major international force, a broadcast of great power and influence.

Anytime someone is on the airwaves as much as we were, there's always an issue of power. With tens of millions of people watching Jim every day, of course he was bound to be influential.

Jim wasn't sexist. He didn't believe that a woman's place was just in the home. Jim was absolutely committed to women being in the workplace, particularly in the higher-paying technical end of the business such as working the cameras or doing lighting design. He offered many women their first prominent positions, and all this at the same time women's liberation was just beginning to break down the barriers of "The Boys Club" at the three major TV networks.

Our whole production was built around the home, featuring one of the most breathtaking sets you've ever seen. It had a working kitchen, a spacious living room with a fireplace, and an imposing dining room. Outside the house there was a tremendous patio with fresh flowers and bushes all around. All the different parts of the set were cleverly connected so that we could easily glide from one to the other without jarring the viewers or the audience.

Off to one side was our incredible band, as talented as you would see on *The Tonight Show* or anywhere else. There were ten musicians, including a piano player and organist, two guitarists, a drummer, and a horn section, in addition to eight singers.

The studio itself was completely air-conditioned and state-of-the-art, with enormous seating room. Every day of the year more than a thousand people would line up to get in to see the program. Sometimes the crowd was so overwhelming that it would spill over into the other studios.

Whenever that happened we'd entertain them by having the *PTL* broadcast fed live onto oversized television monitors.

All over America Jim reached out to the forgotten people, those who had practically given up on life, people in pain, those without a reason to go on. Jim understood their hurt, their years of suffering, their disillusionment with life, and he offered them hope, a way out of the quicksand sucking them down. Whatever the tragedy, whatever the source of conflict, Jim Bakker was always there for them.

The whole world of PTL centered around our live broadcasts. They were the glue that held the network together. When it came to mixing the key ingredients of a serious spiritual message and lighthearted Christian entertainment, Jim was a master. No one could touch him. Jim made all the complexities of TV seem so effortless. Every element of the format flowed seamlessly.

Jim could take a TV director aside and tell him shot-by-shot exactly how a program should be produced, how long each segment should be, and what should follow what. He devised fund-raising campaigns that were second to none. He was truly a Renaissance man, with the incredible ability to work on many areas at once. The *PTL* show attracted actors and singers, pastors and politicians. Familiar faces included Billy Graham, Oral Roberts, Robert Schuller, and countless others.

Jim was equally comfortable with Hollywood stars and powerful evangelists. Through the portals of our show came a glittering array of entertainers. Living legends such as Pearl Bailey and Mickey Rooney graced our stage on several occasions, as well as stars such as Carol Lawrence, Gavin MacLeod, and Colonel Sanders. Those who tuned in also got to witness the miraculous testimonies of timeless personalities like Roy Rogers, Dale Evans, and of course Pat Boone.

More than anything we loved to discover fresh talent.

The ever popular Mike Murdock, a minister as well as a gifted gospel singer and songwriter, was a regular on the program. Thanks to his appearances the membership of his own ministry shot up. Other discoveries included Dr. Evelyn Carter Spencer as well as BeBe and CeCe Winans. It didn't make a difference who it was: An outing on the *PTL* show would instantly cause a performer's or preacher's career to blast off like a skyrocket.

Of course, this included Dortch too. Thanks to *PTL*, the reverend got a taste of fame, and soon he hungered for more. All of a sudden he wanted to be on the show every day with Jim. As a result he started spending less time in his office and more time in front of the camera—every single opportunity he could. We would inform the producers that Dortch wasn't needed on the set that day, and they would come back and tell us that he insisted on being there. With that a warning signal went off in my head, a feeling of déjà vu, just like when Pat Robertson had wanted more airtime on *The 700 Club.* I began speaking to Jim about it.

"Why isn't Dortch in his office doing what we hired him to do anymore? Why is he always in front of the cameras with you? Why are you paying him a quarter of a million dollars every year?" But Jim would always defend Dortch, and our conversations would turn into arguments.

"Tam, he's doing exactly the job he's supposed to do."

But I wasn't convinced that Jim was being truthful with me. Down deep I could tell that he was having second thoughts as well. "You know that's not true. All he wants to do is be on television. Jim, can't you control him? You didn't hire him to be on the show, you hired him to manage the ministry. You hired him to keep a cap on spending, to guard the finances, to make sure that everything was done right."

"Well, he's doing that, isn't he?"

"No, Jim, he is not doing that. Take a look. He is busy

with his own agenda. There must be something you can do, anything."

"I can't interfere with what Dortch is doing. We have an agreement. I have to stick by that agreement."

"But he's not sticking by it. Open your eyes, Jim.

"Look, Tam, I already told you. I can't do anything. I have to allow Dortch to continue with his operations."

"What do you mean, you 'have to'? You're the president of PTL! If you want Dortch spending more time working in his office, then it's your call. Your decision. Because you're the boss."

"Can we just drop it?" Jim said. "I have a show to do."

And he would just walk away from me, the man in charge seemingly powerless. Had I known about Jessica Hahn at the time, I could have easily understood how Dortch might be using Jim's infidelity as a club over his head. I can't see how he could have wielded so much influence otherwise.

As best I could—even beyond the matter of Dortch—I would always try to assist Jim. I would take him aside and say that person doesn't belong here. There's something wrong. But Jim wouldn't listen to me. He would listen to camerapeople. He would listen to directors. He would listen to anybody. But he wouldn't listen to me.

Of course I always realized that *PTL* was "Jim's program," not mine. Even though I was his wife, I always felt like one of the guests on the show. And what's more, if I never came back, I felt I wouldn't be missed. Jim never quite treated me the way he treated others. True, he would pay me lip service and thank me for my opinions. But at the time I suspected there was a part of him that just didn't want me to grow up. Nonetheless, there may have been altogether another reason for Jim's attitude toward me.

A friend of mine named Bob, who knows both of us quite well, recently revealed something that fascinated me but made me sad. He mentioned that Jim always felt that I was in competition with him. I looked at Bob in shock and dismay and said, "I would have never dreamed that in a million years. How in the world can a husband and wife be in competition with each other when they're a team? The only thing I ever competed with Jim for was his time. I wanted part of him. I certainly never competed for the ministry or anything else because I didn't think I had to. I thought we were a team and automatically we did everything together. What he had I had, and what I had he had."

But as I thought about what Bob said, it gave me an insight into why Jim treated me the way he did, shunting me off all along. Maybe he felt that I was getting too big for my britches. But I sure wasn't aware of that. I recall people always told Jim how much they loved it when Tammy did *The PTL Club,* how they never knew what I was going to say or do next.

Jim would always laugh when he told me about it, and I thought he was glad that the people liked me. It sure made things easier for him when he knew that I could do the show by myself. Though I didn't realize it at the time, however, maybe this threatened him. Who knows? But even today it hurts to find out Jim thought that way.

Conflicts Behind the Scenes

Despite all his confidence on camera, Jim never seemed to have enough faith in himself. I have always felt that if he had just trusted his gut instincts, everything at PTL would have turned out differently. Jim is an exceptionally intelligent man but has never felt that way about himself. I think the fact that he never finished college always made him feel a "little less than." Jim always believed that everyone else was more capable than he was and somehow knew better how things should be.

In spite of this, it is my opinion that Jim was smarter than any of them, and I always told him that. But in times of crisis he always wound up listening to the wrong people, trusting them because they were college graduates or had a "Dr." in front of their name or boasted Ph.D.'s. If only Jim Bakker would have trusted Jim Bakker instead of the people with their own agendas at heart.

Because of its phenomenal growth, PTL was a magnet for all sorts of individuals, an umbrella that provided spiritual shelter for those trying to discover the path God had set for them. But it also attracted people who did not have the calling. To many of our two thousand employees this was just another job. And I understood that. PTL was not just a ministry, it was also a major business enterprise. Which meant that professional managers and administrators had to be brought in for various positions. This resulted in two factions: the people devoted to working for God, and those who viewed it strictly as a professional career.

Locked away from public view, behind the cameras, the spotlights, and the impressive sets, there were frequent conflicts. Clashes over attitudes, goals, rules, and procedures often clouded the bigger picture. In other instances long-standing jealousies among particular individuals would explode to the surface. But this was only natural. We were only human beings with human frailties.

It showed up more when we had to hire performers. The policy was that they were hired because of their expertise. If the music department needed an extremely high voice, for instance, to complete a singing group, of course they hired the best that applied. Sometimes, though, the best person who applied was not always in agreement with our way of worship. But because of the possibility of national exposure, however, that singer would try his or her best to act the part. And for a while it would work. But only for a while. Eventually you'd sense the feelings and hear the disapproval.

This would cause great dissension among the ones who really believed the way we believed; consequently, our on-the-air performers changed frequently. That was hard for me to get used to. And it was also hard on the TV audience, who would get used to seeing a person and then demand to know why that person was no longer there. But we could not allow anyone to remain who was simply looking at a PTL job as a way of being discovered or as a way of becoming a star. We all had to be in one accord, and that meant *everyone*—the band, the singers, and the guests. And getting that many people together with the same vision and keeping them together was not an easy task.

What was disturbing was that *PTL* was at risk of becoming just a highly polished show rather than a true place for spiritual guidance and comfort. And I always knew that if we allowed this to happen we would lose the whole reason of why we were there, which was to win souls. But sometimes this was hard for Jim to see. He had a constant fight within his soul. He wanted everything to look and sound professional. He wanted the world to watch and be impressed enough to continue watching. He didn't want audiences to be turned off. And people did watch, by the millions. I am still hearing today of people from all walks of life, both Christian and non-Christian, who watched the show every day.

Over the years, Jim and I had many disagreements about the content of the *PTL* program. I loved worship and praise. I always wanted the show to be more like a church program. Jim favored the talk-show format, which I'll admit was certainly more professional.

Still, I would warn Jim when people were something less than he thought he had hired—but to no avail. His favorite words to me were "Tam, don't come to me with hearsay. I want proof. If you don't have a solution for the problem, I don't want to hear about it." Therefore I felt my hands were tied. I didn't want to be a nagging wife or get in a big fight. So I would just forget it.

Jim would be polite and listen to people who disagreed with him or warned him about something that might be going wrong, but in the end he always ended up going with what his buddies said. People invariably convinced Jim they had his best interests at heart, but usually "his best interests" coincided with the interests of their pocketbooks. Rather than listening to the one woman who really cared about him and cared about the ministry, he got taken in time and time again.

Jim tried to stay above petty disagreements. He avoided conflict at all costs. Jim always got his people to handle anything that would be even the least confrontational. As a matter of fact, his favorite song was "Don't Nobody Bring Me No Bad News."

Richard Dortch, bolstered by his ever-increasing presence on the *PTL* show and Jim's unwillingness to check his authority, started bringing in his own people by the droves and putting them in key management positions. I wasn't the only one disturbed by this; many people shared my concerns.

Once again, the only real time I ever got to speak to my husband was in the privacy of our bedroom, and he was usually exhausted by then. "Jim, there's a lot of resentment going around. Dortch is hiring his friends and paying them better salaries than people who have worked at PTL for years."

"Tam, Dortch is the head of business operations. That's his decision to make. I can't second-guess him."

"We don't need all his friends. We're way overstaffed now. He should be cutting down on staff, not putting new ones on the payroll."

"I can't see what you're worried about. PTL is going stronger than ever. And if Dortch needs a few people around him, I don't see what the problem is. We've had this discussion before."

"And we're going to keep on having it! I don't care for these people he's bringing in, Jim. I think they're up to something. They're all devoted to Dortch—not to you or the PTL ministry. And that's not good. You know that's not good."

"Well, if you think he's up to something, prove it. Bring me proof."

"Jim, it's just a feeling I have. Call it my woman's intuition. I get a cold feeling around Dortch. Something is just not right with the man. Something that you know that you know, even if you don't know how you know."

"Look, I can't run PTL on your intuition. You can't con-demn Dortch on just a feeling. You need facts."

"How much more do I have to tell you? Simply check out the people he's bringing in. That's all I'm asking you to do."

"Tam, let's talk about this tomorrow. Can't you see I'm bushed?"

The light would be switched off, and I would be left in the dark. Of course, as it turned out, it was Jim who was really in the dark. Rumors began circulating among the staff. The people Dortch hired were being called "Dortchites." A crack was beginning to appear on the smooth surface of PTL. I saw everything that was hap-pening, but I honestly don't believe that Jim did. Jim had a way of blocking out anything unpleasant or un-happy, so he refused to believe it.

As I've said, Jim avoided conflict at any cost. I have actu-ally watched him stare down at the floor rather than risk a confrontation. Under the circumstances it was easier for him to trust Dortch and not attempt to look any further. For the life of me, I still couldn't fathom why Jim couldn't see what was happening all around him. It was plain as day. I thought my skin would crawl off my body every time he mentioned how much he trusted Dortch.

Morale grew worse and worse. And before we knew it the staff that had loved us and worked with us for years were beginning to take sides. It was the Bakkerites versus the Dortchites. This was well known to everyone. You were lined up either on one side or on the other. A red flag of danger waved constantly across my mind. Again and again I begged Jim to do something.

Every day I could see Dortch building his own kingdom, securing a loyal following among his employees. Adding insult to injury, he began insisting that the producers of the *PTL* show use the guests he wanted. Naturally these guests were all his friends and he paid them much higher honorariums than our regular guests were getting. And believe me, we paid our guests well! Dortch lured his guests into the organization this way, then before you knew it they would be working in one of the top management positions of the company.

By this time Jim was finally beginning to see that something was not right, but he still refused to admit—or didn't dare to admit—that Dortch was doing anything wrong.

Dortch ran the board meetings of the corporation, and since Jim proclaimed his trust in him all the board members were motivated to comply with Dortch's suggestions and vote them in without much debate.

I could see repeating all over again the same familiar pattern: Jim giving his power away to another man. Was this Jim's way of escaping responsibility, his need to seek the approval of a father figure, or the seeds of a self-destructive compulsion rooted in his feelings of unworthiness? I can't say for sure. Maybe it was a combination of all three.

Where Did All the Money Go?

im and I were the trailblazers in Christian television, and we did a lot of things wrong. We regret those mistakes, but we learned from them. However, there's no other way we could have learned, because nobody had been there before us. Nobody had ever tried to mix the business of a TV ministry with a Christian theme park. To this day, every other televangelist has learned from Jim's mistakes.

Nevertheless, as I've said before, both of us were adults. Whatever character flaws and weaknesses we had were no excuse for poor judgment, and I don't offer them as such. Plenty of mistakes were made at PTL, and I am ashamed and appalled by them. But they were honest mistakes of judgment. They were not criminal!

Today I'm convinced Jim suffered from a terrible inferiority complex, only he overcompensated for it. Maybe Heritage USA was his ultimate vindication, proof that he was as good as everyone else, that he could be loved. I wish that I had somehow found the strength or the way to have more influence over Jim. If I had, he would not have let matters get so out of hand. But now that's wishful thinking.

"So where did the money go?" Over and over I'm asked that question. To those of you who have already condemned me, I'm afraid no answer will suffice. I can't account for every single dime that went in and out of PTL, nor would I ever attempt to. All I can recount is what we achieved, what we delivered, and where we fell short. I hope you will judge me on my words, not on any preconceptions.

From 1983 through 1986 PTL underwent its greatest period of expansion, often referred to as "The Glory Years." During Christmas, tens of thousands of visitors would make their pilgrimage to Heritage USA, and they would never be disappointed. Ringing the grounds was a dazzling spectacle of lights, a breathtaking extravaganza of more than a million colored bulbs. It took almost a year to plan and execute this display, the grandest celebration of the year. Long lines of cars trying to enter the grounds would stretch for more than twelve miles.

Every Fourth of July, Jim would organize an immense pageant to commemorate our country's day of independence. A colorful parade of marching bands and patriotic floats was the central highlight of the festivities. In 1985 more than sixty thousand people streamed into Heritage USA for that single occasion. With over six million visitors in 1986, the theme park was the third-biggest tourist destination in America, second only to Disneyland and Disney World.

During this three-year period the number of employees swelled from just under seven hundred to over two thousand. Contributions quadrupled, rising from $40 million to $160 million annually.

Jim Bakker was a human locomotive barreling down the rails at breakneck speed; there was no way to keep up with him. He wasn't slowing down for anybody. Because of this

Jim frequently appeared impulsive, sometimes bordering on obsessive. The urgency of his vision seemed to transcend all rhyme and reason. Once he got a plan into his mind, there was no talking him out of it, or slowing him down. Many people thought he should slow down, even Roe Messner. "What's your rush, Jim?" Roe used to ask him. I too begged Jim to please slow down, but it was no use.

Jim had to have everything finished yesterday. He wanted to give the partners everything they deserved as quickly as possible. As a result, construction costs often doubled and occasionally tripled. There seemed to be no end in sight. As the erection of more buildings got under way, we had to hire more people.

Add in the hotels and restaurants, entertainment such as water parks, and colossal productions such as the Passion Play and other extravaganzas, and you can just imagine the number of men and women needed to bring it off. And all these people needed to make a living, they needed to be paid. Therefore salaries siphoned off a huge chunk of our income. But the more salaries we paid out, the more airtime we had to buy to keep contributions coming in. It became a vicious circle.

Nevertheless, Jim was very good to his employees, and PTL was a great place to work. He gave them benefits comparable to what any large corporation offered, and salaries matched anything they could earn in the secular world. Jim had no intention of having his best staff members snatched away from him.

Unfortunately, he also was incapable of firing his worst staff members. There were some individuals whose hearts may have been in the right place but whose heads simply weren't up to the task. Some of these people simply fell apart under the pressure of Jim's full-steam-ahead attitude.

I tried to remind Jim of this problem many times.

"Honey," I'd say, "I know that we are working for God, but when you have two thousand people working with you, that's a business! We're in business for God, but we're still in business. You really need to let the people go who are not doing their jobs. In business you don't keep people working for you just because you feel sorry for them, Jim."

Jim had such a big heart that sometimes it got in the way of him using his head. This is one of the things I loved about him, yet one of the things that frustrated me constantly. I would name a few of the people I felt he ought to let go, and he'd have great excuses for each one of them. "Then cut the salaries of some of the executives," I'd suggest. "That will help to make up for those that you feel you need to keep. Maybe we could balance it all out that way."

I was desperate to help Jim find answers to our ever-growing staff problem. I felt that we could have done twice as much work with half the staff. I mean, even secretaries had secretaries. There had to be a better way of controlling things. Sometimes I felt as if we were on a merry-go-round spinning faster and faster and faster and no one knew how to stop it.

One day Jim told me he wanted to bring his parents to PTL and that he was going to hire his sister and his brother and his sister-in-law. I was happy that Jim wanted his parents close by, but I hated for him to uproot them from their home in Michigan, plus uproot the rest of his family from their jobs in Chicago and Portsmouth, Virginia. I felt that once we hired one family member we would be duty-bound to hire *more* family and *more* family, and I didn't think that was a good idea. I was afraid it would cause friction and jealousy. I could just imagine what might happen: "You gave *his* side of the family a better job than you gave *our* side of the family."

But Jim went ahead and hired his family members anyway. Many people resented Jim doing that, and it caused much friction. Even though Jim's relatives were well-qualified and hard workers, people always accused Jim of giving family members preferential treatment.

Eventually, Jim also hired my mom and my dad and several of my brothers and sisters. My mom had wanted a job outside the home all of her life, but couldn't do that and raise eight children too. So when Jim gave her a position in the mailroom, he made Mom the happiest lady in the whole USA. She was so proud of her job, and everyone adored Rachel. My dad worked in the kitchen of one of the restaurants. He worked hard and loved it so much. Dad was retired from the mill by this time, and the kitchen filled the many hours that would have otherwise been empty for him.

We bought our parents small houses on the grounds. My mom lived in her house until she died two years ago. Jim's folks still live in their place. I was always so happy that we could do that for our parents. I think it is something most kids dream about doing but are never able to. (By the way, Jim did not get any special deals on the homes. We paid the *same price* as anyone else buying property at Heritage.)

There were other practices that, over the course of time, I've had deep regrets about, areas where we could have simply cut back and not gone overboard. For instance, when coming to work for the ministry, some people in key positions were provided with PTL-owned homes as part of their salary. In other words, PTL paid the mortgage. If they stayed with us a certain number of years, usually about fifteen or twenty, then the home became theirs. But if they left the ministry beforehand, the home just reverted to PTL ownership. The homes were obviously a perk by which we could draw the best people—a perk that I felt then and still feel we could have done without.

The ministry provided us a parsonage; it also provided Reverend Dortch and his wife with one. Now, this is not unusual. There are many thousands of congregations across the country that freely provide their ministers a place to live. But considering that we were earning more than your typical minister, today I'm remorseful about this as well. In view of the fact that the vast majority of people don't get houses along with their jobs, I think this practice with our employees became excessive and unnecessary. While the ministry surely wasn't giving the homes away, in retrospect I regret how this all must appear.

Such was the case with two of our dearest friends, Doug and Laura Lee Oldham. Doug was a very famous gospel singer who had formerly been working for Jerry Falwell. But due to poor health Doug hadn't been singing anymore. When he showed up at PTL, Jim had mercy on him, compassion for his well-being, viewing him as a good man. He realized Doug needed to get back on his feet, so Jim decided to give him a break. Doug was hired at a very good salary to be a regular on the show.

Jim provided Doug and his family with a beautiful home on the same hill as ours. Their house was on the top, and ours was at the bottom. We instantly became great friends. They were lots of fun, and our personalities just clicked. Almost every day thereafter we were either at their house or they were at ours. We ate together, went to the movies together, our kids were the best of friends. All of us loved the great relationship we had.

We also hired Laura Lee to be my personal secretary. She and I became virtually inseparable. We couldn't have been closer if we were sisters. After Jim put Doug on the air, he made a miraculous comeback.

Hiring couples was nothing unusual at PTL. To maintain that special feeling of family, Jim tried to bring onto the payroll both husbands and wives whenever feasible. However, since we were already overstaffed, it's my feeling there were quite a few instances where just one spouse working for PTL would have been enough. But Jim's generosity often exceeded rhyme or reason.

I will never forget the time he gave away our car. It was

the only car I ever fell in love with, a brand-new red Cadillac, fully equipped, with a luscious white leather interior. I cried when Jim gave it away even though I loved the people he gave it to, a visiting country pastor and his family who were driving a beat-up old wreck. Jim knew they needed it more than we did. There was no stopping him. Whenever he got an impulse he immediately gave in to it—not exactly the best trait for a chief executive of a large organization.

Consequently the financial pressure on us was enormous. Day to day it seemed as if we lived in a constant cash-flow crisis. Jim had a hard time seeing the forest for the trees. He was blowing up a balloon that was getting too big for us. As PTL grew, the national news organizations were having a field day, trying to exploit the myth that we never paid any taxes or that we profited from our tax-exempt status.

The truth is, PTL *did* pay taxes! Only four small pieces of property attached to the ministry actually qualified for a tax exemption, and these counted for less than thirty acres out of a total of more than twenty-three hundred. The separate commercial areas such as the restaurants, the gift shops, and the various amusements comprised a for-profit corporation. Millions of dollars were paid out over the years in property, sales, state, and federal taxes. By the way, the ministry even paid income taxes. Twice a year we were audited at our own request. The IRS even maintained an office at PTL.

I understood where Jim was coming from. Our Bible speaks many times of the word *faith*. It speaks of great men of faith who trusted God for everything. It speaks of moving mountains by faith, of the sick being healed by faith, of God's great provision for people because of their faith in him. Jim was taught faith all of his life and he believed that anything could be accomplished *by faith*. Jim was a man of great faith, and his faith worked. He saw miracle after miracle happen at PTL.

He believed that if the money was not there to do the job, then God would provide. And God did. He spoke to the hearts of millions of His people to give to the building of Heritage USA. The people were not coerced into giving; they gave because they wanted to. They gave because they wanted to be a part of what was happening at Heritage USA.

Therefore I felt our first and foremost obligation was to do quality programs every day, since our primary focus should be on the millions of viewers watching from their homes rather than the thousands who were able to come and visit Heritage. I repeatedly told Jim that our entire television production was in danger of becoming the sacrificial lamb for financing the construction of the theme park. We had the same argument over and over.

"Jim, we've got to slow down, we're moving too fast," I pleaded. "Honey, the show is suffering. You are losing sight of your first calling. That calling was to preach the gospel, not build. I don't care if you build, just slow down and take your time. All we do anymore is raise finances to pay for more and more buildings. You are trying too much too fast. Please, Jim! I'm afraid this is all going to come crashing down on us."

But as usual my words fell on deaf ears.

"Tam, I have to build."

"Jim, the strain on you is beginning to show. You are wearing yourself down to nothing. Just stop for a little while. Stop and smell the roses and enjoy what you have already done. Stop building, just for a year. Then let's see where we are. The people will understand. Millions are watching you on TV who will never be able to come to Heritage USA. You need to think about them, Jim."

Naturally the phone would then ring or there would be some other distraction, and once again we'd be left at an impasse, with nothing ever resolved. I would be upset, and he would be more determined than ever to steer the course he had laid out for himself. Then a few days or a few weeks later we'd pick up the argument all over again.

"Tam, don't you see? We need more room for the thousands of people who are coming every month. If we don't have the space for them, they won't come."

"But, Jim, they can just stay in hotels over in Charlotte. There are hundreds of hotels, really good hotels in town."

"That's not the same. You know that's not the same."

I tried reasoning with him every way I could. "Jim, I understand how much you love people. What I don't understand is your willingness to sacrifice everything for them. I love them as much as you do. But I know they do not expect as much of you as you expect of yourself. If you could just ask them, I think they would tell you the same thing: Jim, take your time, slow down a little."

The partners were always first, always number one in Jim's eyes. He couldn't do enough for them. His desperate need to please them, to make everything perfect for them, ended up destroying his life and everything dear to him.

As time wore on, my worst fears materialized. Because the building was draining so much emotional energy, effort, and time, the programming was getting dragged down. I didn't feel we were giving the best because Jim was tired all the time. It got to the point where he had to spend more and more air time on each show raising money to pay for the building he was busy building at the time. I felt sorry for him, as he was constantly under the gun. But I felt that he had put himself in that position.

Then, one bright and sunny day, Richard Dortch came to Jim and proclaimed, "What PTL needs is our own airplane. We would save thousands of dollars in valuable time if we just had our own airplane." Well, that seemed feasible to Jim, a reasonable suggestion, since we all had to travel a lot for PTL. Accordingly Jim took it to the board of directors for a vote, and the motion passed without a single dissent. Before we knew it, PTL had its own little jet. Most of the large ministries had a plane, therefore it was nothing new for a ministry to own one. I recall using the plane maybe four times altogether in the years PTL owned it.

But it was in constant use by Dortch, not to mention the legions of people he had hired. I wondered about that. But like a broken record Jim defended Dortch, until one day he began to study the flight schedules and the air miles and the gas bills for the plane. Suddenly he realized that something wasn't right.

Dortch had been using the plane to go everywhere. When Jim found that out he stormed into the board of directors and—in one of the only moments I can ever remember where he defied Dortch—demanded they sell the plane. Dortch was livid. Yet despite his protests the plane was finally sold and we all went back to flying commercial. Dortch's trips were cut in half. Well, at least that problem was solved.

But in another instance, clearly exorbitant spending by Dortch was not. At the time the Dortches were living in a spacious retreat provided for them by PTL. It was located on the same lake we lived on. Since we had a houseboat, they wound up purchasing one as well.

One morning we were out in our boat and decided to cruise by the Dortches' and see if they were home. To our utter amazement, there, right in front of their house, was the biggest boat dock I had ever seen. It had a covered roof and resembled a house. We were flabbergasted. Our boat just sat out in the open.

Jim went to Roe Messner. "Roe, what in the world is going on over at Dortch's house? Who gave him permission to build that huge boathouse?"

"Well, Jim," Roe replied, "I just did what he ordered me to do. He told me to bill it as part of the house renovation. I thought that was strange—but, Jim, I don't have any business questioning Dortch. After all, he *is* the general manager, and I'm expected to do what he says. He made that clear to me the day after he was hired."

Jim was terribly upset, but what was done was done. I don't know if Jim ever confronted Dortch about the dock or not, but I do know that it really made him furious. He simply could not believe that Dortch would mishandle PTL funds like that. He felt that Dortch was taking advantage of the position with which he had entrusted him.

For the last several pages I've focused on the downside; but there's an also incredible upside, one that I believe far exceeds the excesses and errors that were made along the way. Jim Bakker was a visionary; and even during the brief period of time that Heritage USA existed, he left a lasting legacy. I'd like to share that legacy with you, because that's truly where the vast majority of the money went.

Despite his problems, the majority of partners I've encountered still believe in Jim and still stand up for PTL. Ask them and they will tell you that they gave because they wanted to. People gave because they enjoyed the huge hotels, the water park for their children. They gave because they enjoyed the church services and the plays and the all-night singing. They gave because they enjoyed taking their kids to the swimming pools and tennis courts and to the beautiful petting zoo filled with wonderful animals that people had donated.

I feel the people who contributed to PTL loved the programs and sent in checks just as people who give to public television do. Every day, 365 days a year, we featured twenty-four-hour Christian programming for the family—and it wasn't junk. There were no violence, swear words, or pornographic rock videos. We always gave our viewers the cream of the crop. So they weren't paying for Jim or Tammy. They were paying for the programming they wanted, the programming they weren't getting anyplace else. It was that plain and simple. By the way, the average donation to PTL was about ten dollars a month, less than half your average cable TV bill.

The partners loved Heritage USA. They shared Jim's extraordinary dream. They loved to ride the little trains that circled the park. They rejoiced in being able to attend live TV shows every day. This is what donations were for. Our ministry was an unlimited partnership. Everyone loved the feeling of being part of this extended family. Millions of people were drawn together by a common denominator.

Of course now and then, for whatever reason, someone would want his money back. And Jim would always give it back—no questions asked. If someone called and said, "My husband got angry because I sent a hundred dollars to you and we really need it back," Jim's staff would immediately have a check written out and mailed directly. He gave back every bit of money that anyone ever asked for. I think that's very important to realize. There were literally thousands of checks written out to people who gave and then had second thoughts. We understood that, and that was perfectly fine. PTL always came with a money-back guarantee.

Today what many people forget is that Jim Bakker donated millions of dollars to charitable causes both here and overseas. Those whose bodies and minds were ravaged by addictions came to Heritage USA. The New Wine Fellowship provided rehabilitation for drug abusers and addicts, in addition to treating chronic alcoholics. The program combined medical treatment with spiritual counseling, producing a success rate surpassing many more secular approaches.

Jim constructed a beautiful home for unwed mothers called the Heritage House. He built it so that women who were planning to have abortions would go ahead and have their babies instead. Counseling was provided for those who wanted to keep their babies, and adoption services for those who chose not to. The women lived there throughout their pregnancy and were given jobs at Heritage USA that provided them with spending money. I thought it was a remarkable plan. Many, many babies were saved from death as a result of Heritage House.

Jim also built a wonderful place called Fort Hope. It was a self-contained village where homeless men could come and live if they were serious about getting their lives back together. Men who had been living under bridges in Charlotte and sleeping on the streets in front of doorways now had a place to stay and receive counseling and learn a trade. Men who had no hope began to live again. Many got jobs, returned to their families, and became responsible citizens again. I will never forget something that happened one day on our TV show: Jim announced that we were going to have a group of special singers on the program that day. Out walked about thirty men. Some of them were dressed in ill-fitting suits, some of them in slacks and shirts. They walked straight and tall, and all of them were smiling from ear to ear. It was then that Jim said, "Meet the men who are graduating from Fort Hope."

The studio audience of over a thousand people rose to their feet, and as those men sang there was not a dry eye in the place. After the men finished singing, one by one they stepped out and told their stories, with tears of gratitude streaming down their faces. I don't think anyone who saw that show will ever forget it.

Besides Fort Hope, Jim constructed more than six hundred "People That Love" centers around the country. These were places where the destitute and downtrodden could find work, hot meals, and warm garments. Jim founded and supported Kevin's House, a home for physically challenged children so that they wouldn't have to lie around in institutions. He made large donations to the Boys Ranch in North Carolina, where troubled teenagers could get away from their broken homes and learn the values of teamwork.

I believe that PTL gave away more money to charities than any ministry I know of. Millions went to the Salvation Army and the Red Cross and the Goodwill organization in Charlotte. Within Heritage USA there was a round-the-clock telephone counseling center called the Upper Room, where staff members ministered to thousands of hurting people twenty-four hours a day. Many called in on the verge of suicide and were helped by our faithful counselors.

Marriage workshops were created. Each year thousands of husbands and wives enrolled in these workshops to learn how to save their relationships. They were offered spiritual guidance as well as psychological techniques to aid in their communication and their commitment to each other. The program had a phenomenal rate of success, and as a result hundreds of marriages were saved from divorce. I still meet couples today who tell me they would not be together if it had not been for the marriage workshops at PTL.

PTL offered the finest conference facilities so that famous pastors and nationally acclaimed Christian authors could conduct seminars there. Participants in these events often numbered in the thousands.

Generally overlooked by the media was the fact that Jim was a fighter against injustice. I remember once sitting at the breakfast table while he was browsing through the morning paper. All of a sudden his face flushed red with outrage and he practically choked on what he was eating. Jim was reading about a lovely old church in South Carolina, a historic wooden-frame building with a mostly black congregation, that had been bombed by racists and burned to the ground. Before even catching his breath Jim raced to the phone and called the office. Within a week PTL wired money, and just six months later that marvelous church was rebuilt.

Jim never hoarded funds. He donated millions of dollars

to other ministries that were in financial difficulty. In fact I've seen preacher after preacher leave PTL with large checks in their hands. Jim contributed to Oral Roberts and his special school. To Mark Buntane, an Assemblies of God missionary, Jim gave millions of dollars for equipment and supplies for his hospital in India. He gave generously to Franklin Graham, the son of Billy Graham. He gave $100,000 to Tom Trask for his church, and today Trask is the head of the Assemblies of God ministries. Another $100,000 went to pastor Don George, a member of our board of directors, for his new church, since he ministered to one of the largest congregations. This is just to name a few. The partners loved the fact that their money was going to help keep these ministries alive.

No area was off-limits when it came to expanding the message of hope. Hundreds of penitentiaries across all fifty states were given free satellite dishes, allowing inmates immediate access to the PTL network whenever they wanted. Thousands of prisoners and ex-convicts called to tell us of the profound effect our programming had on their lives.

Bible-study courses were provided to thousands of inmates, and we sent people across the nation to sing and minister to them. To provide help for their families, PTL gave out Christmas trees and toys for the children, clothing for the adults, and meals during Thanksgiving and Easter.

Jim believed in education and in training young people for the future in Christian television. That's why he organized a grade school as well as a college for broadcasting. Through this program students got hands-on training, working right alongside our TV crew and learning the trade from the ground up. Today there are young people in stations all over the world who graduated from the Heritage USA college. This too was very costly, but again the PTL partners were kept well informed about where their money was going.

Unlike many other family amusement centers, Heritage USA has not seen a single person mugged on its grounds. No one was ever attacked or beaten there, nor was there ever a fistfight. When you consider all the years we were in operation and the fact that more than thirty million people came to visit us, that's an amazing statistic. I take that back—that's a *miraculous* statistic!

Jim Bakker embraced the entire human race; I never heard him utter one prejudicial word against any group or religion. Never once did he portray the Pentecostal movement as being the sole avenue for achieving divine grace. Since Jim was a strong proponent of spreading the faith as far and wide as he could, he invited people from different countries to produce programming at our facilities in their native tongues. Until Jim came along, religious broadcasters had merely used voice-overs in their overseas markets.

But Jim also realized that religious leaders, especially those in the Third World, couldn't afford the tremendous expense of producing their programs at home. Consequently he decided that as part of Heritage Village's missionary effort he would produce and pay for those programs. He flew in the hosts, built sets for them, and paid for the airtime in several different countries.

Just as important, we traveled across the globe to spread the Word. We did a special program called "With Love to Israel" from the Holy Land. Israel was the only place I'd ever been—and I've been all over the world—that I never wanted to leave. I remember feeling its spirituality. I visited the Western Wall, where in every corner there were people reciting their prayers and praising God in their different languages. And it moved my heart to think that the world could be united despite all these diverse cultures, all these distinct types of human beings.

But of all the places we saw, none moved me as much as Yad Vashem, the Holocaust memorial to the six million Jews who were murdered in Nazi concentration camps.

Shivers went up and down my spine when I went inside and witnessed what people are capable of doing—the most unspeakable atrocities. I think if every man, woman, and child went to Yad Vashem, maybe this type of thing could never happen again to anybody anywhere. They have a powerful saying in Israel: "Never again!" I will never forget the day I stood outside that memorial and sang "I Wonder If God Cries." Israel is dear to me and always will be.

Our "Extravagant" Lifestyle

Another part of the "Where did the money go?" controversy revolves around our lifestyle. I would be lying to you if I said that Jim and I didn't live well. We did have a very comfortable standard of living. Over the years this has fueled an extraordinary amount of criticism. In the tabloids, stories circulated about us having gold-plated faucets and air-conditioned doghouses, about the big cars and mansions we lived in. The media constantly accused us of taking money from "little old ladies" so that we could live in extravagant luxury.

Later on I will deal with where many of these exaggerations came from. But the funny thing is that our partners knew exactly how we lived, where we lived, what kind of cars we drove. They knew everything about us because we shared our lives with them on television. On many occasions we did programs directly from our homes in Charlotte and California. We took them for rides via special mobile cameras in our cars. If there was going to be outrage over our "extravagant" lifestyle, it would seem apparent to me that it would have arisen at the grass-roots level. But it never did.

Another issue brought up by our detractors was that they thought we were being paid too much money for the work we did at PTL. Yes, Jim and I were paid salaries totaling well into six figures. This is a matter of public record. But if I could do it all over again, I know that we could have gotten along on much less. I don't need a lot of extras anymore, because I'm older and I realize it's not mere things that bring happiness.

Looking back, I think that one of the most devastating errors in judgment we made was to accept the bonuses originally engineered by Richard Dortch and voted on by our board of directors. Dortch himself presented me with my first bonus, and I have to admit I was thrilled. I hugged him and thanked him. I was so naïve!

The board of directors also voted Jim a bonus, saying how much they appreciated his tireless work. Neither of us thought a thing about the fact that Dortch himself had also arranged to receive a bonus, the same amount as Jim. One of the reasons no red flags went up was because the board of directors were not being paid any salaries, so they had no financial stake in these bonuses at all. There was no financial pressure anyone could put on them. As successful businesspeople and pastors, they could quit anytime they wanted to.

As the years have gone by, I've come to realize that these bonuses were clearly excessive and unnecessary. But at the time we thought it was merely a show of appreciation, rewarding the corporate side of what we were doing. We never dreamed that anyone could think of it as greed. For example, Jim paid income taxes on more than he had to; he didn't take anywhere near all the deductions to which he was entitled—and that's a fact. If Jim were really greedy, he would have looked to protect every cent he could from the government. And let me remind you, he was never once accused of income tax evasion.

Anyway, after that first one, the bonuses started coming

more frequently, about twice a year, usually after a period of particularly hard work. Dortch assured us that since the bonuses were always approved according to corporate standards, they were fully proper and within the scope of the law. The bonuses were legal. It was just a poor decision on our part to accept them when we were receiving sufficient salary to live well on. But no matter how much money you receive in your paycheck, it's always exciting to get something unexpected. And Jim and I were just like anyone else. There is always something you can do with extra money.

Later on, the government did consider the bonuses, and although they found them perfectly legal, I believe that the appearance of impropriety became one of the major reasons Jim was indicted.

I wish so much that we had not accepted those bonuses. In fact, I wish that we hadn't taken a salary from PTL and that we'd taken as our salary just the royalties from the books we'd written and the albums I recorded. That is what the government said we should have done. But we gave all our royalties to the ministry. They amounted to much more than we ever received in salary, but still, it would have looked better to forgo a salary. And looking back—hindsight is always 20/20, they say—it would have been a more acceptable way to pay us.

The Assemblies of God church has always preached prosperity. They based it upon the scripture in the Bible that says, "Give and it shall be given unto you, pressed down, shaken together, and running over." There are so many scriptures in the Bible that speak about prosperity. That is the essence of our faith.

Much of the criticism directed at us strikes me as somewhat hypocritical. Jim and I certainly lived no differently from Pat Robertson, Oral Roberts, Robert Schuller, Paul Crouch, or other popular ministers of our time. And I also guarantee that no religious leaders have been as open with their lifestyle as we have. Has anyone ever seen Jerry Falwell's home?

It all boils down to this: How much is too much when it comes to paying spiritual leaders? I suppose this all depends on your point of view. I have never once heard complaints about the millions of dollars paid each year to Oprah Winfrey or Paul McCartney or Kareem Abdul-Jabbar for the work they do. What is the difference? It seems to be one word. We were *ministers*. And in people's minds ministers are not supposed to live well—no matter how hard they work.

People have this romantic image of how a preacher should live, but that's all it is—a romantic image. It has nothing to do with reality. I have often wondered where this came from. People say Jesus was born in a manger, that he had no place to lay his head. They give me scripture after scripture about how Christians are supposed to not care about possessions or money.

But for every scripture they quote I can find just as many or more that say the opposite. That God wants us to prosper. That God wants us to have life and have it more abundantly. That if we give to Him, He will give back to us pressed down, shaken together, and running over. To me that does not speak of living meagerly. And it certainly does not say "except for ministers."

I think this theory got started in the Catholic church when their priests were commanded to take the vow of poverty. And I must say, I admire them for that. I think it is noble to be able to live on the barest subsistence, without earthly possessions. It takes special people with a special calling to be able to do that. And I believe that God is pleased with such sacrifice. But I don't think the fact that you have money and possessions has any bearing on how much you love God.

After all, I loved God with all my heart when I was very poor and had no money or possessions to speak of. And my love for God did not change when money and possessions came into my life. My number one goal in life was still to serve God and minister the gospel. I never felt that my prospering displeased God in any way. If I'm preaching about a God who gives freely to all and I'm going around in rags, who is going to believe what I say? Who's going to want what I have?

I'm often asked, "What's the fine line between spirituality and materialism?" Well, I don't think anyone has a right to decide where that line is for anyone else. If you have a diamond ring, that diamond ring isn't going to keep you from loving God. If you drive a Cadillac, that Cadillac isn't going to keep you from giving to the poor and working hard for God. Being material and being spiritual can work hand in hand. Just because you acquire material things doesn't mean you are less spiritual.

The Bible says that in itself money is not sinful. It's the love of money that becomes a sin: accumulating more and more of it just for the sake of having it, rather than taking the money and using it for good things like helping people. The danger is when it becomes a passion in our life and begins to possess us, rather than us possessing it.

I have often heard snide remarks about my substantial wardrobe. When you are on television every day there are many people, especially the gals, who tune in just to see what you're wearing. Like Oprah or Leeza Gibbons, I was always creating different looks and putting myself together for my viewers. So I never ventured out without my makeup on, without my hair looking good, without great clothes. That was the least I could do for all the partners who watched me and supported me and cared about me. But again, this somehow became "extravagant."

After the fall of PTL, one of the items the media took aim at was our houseboat on the lake. I can understand that. A houseboat certainly looks like an extravagance. However, one thing forgotten about famous people is that they need

My great-grandmother
Hale and me in
International Falls,
Minnesota, 1943.
AUTHOR'S COLLECTION

Our house in International Falls wasn't very large, but ten
of us lived happily there. AUTHOR'S COLLECTION

As the oldest of the bunch of eight kids, I was more like a second mother to my brothers and sisters. Here's Danny, me (at age thirteen), and Donny in our living room in International Falls, in 1956.

Look, Mom, no makeup! Here I am in 1960, at age seventeen, before I discovered eyelashes and Maybelline!

My mom, a wonderful and talented lady. This picture is from 1976. Happy fifty-seventh birthday, Mom!
AUTHOR'S COLLECTION

The wonderful man I call Daddy: my stepfather, Fred Grover, in 1979.
AUTHOR'S COLLECTION

My mom and dad, Fred and Rachel Grover, in 1979.
AUTHOR'S COLLECTION

Our messenger from God, Reverend Aubrey Sarah, allowed us to hold our first revival meeting at his church in North Carolina. AUTHOR'S COLLECTION

F. W. Woolworth is where I worked from the day I turned fifteen. Here's me and my daughter, Tammy Sue, back in International Falls. AUTHOR'S COLLECTION

Making an album for PTL: Here's me, Jim, and Cliff Dudley, who worked on two of my books, *I Gotta Be Me* and *Run to the Roar*.

AUTHOR'S COLLECTION

I waited nine years for this little girl: Here's Tammy Sue Bakker in 1975, at age five.

AUTHOR'S COLLECTION

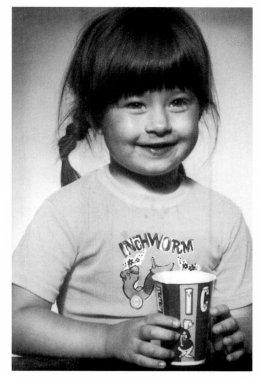

The PTL musicians were among the nation's best. Here, the band and singers from *Tammy's House Party,* my own show on PTL.
PUBLICITY SHOT

Here we are on the set: Jamie Charles, me, Tammy Sue, and Jim.
PUBLICITY SHOT

Tens of thousands of visitors made their pilgrimage to
Heritage USA during Christmas each year. Here's one of our
Christmas photos. PUBLICITY SHOT

Here are two of our dearest friends: Doug Oldham, who sang on PTL, and Laura Lee Oldham, my personal secretary.
AUTHOR'S COLLECTION

Heritage USA went up at lightning speed. Here's Roe, who designed and built everything, with the Heritage USA building permit.
AUTHOR'S COLLECTION

The Grand Hotel, and it was grand! AUTHOR'S COLLECTION

Here's Jim and me with Pat Robertson. We worked for Pat for nine years. AUTHOR'S COLLECTION

The Reverend Richard Dortch, in 1986.
AP/WIDE WORLD PHOTOS

Jamie and
I visited Jim
in prison,
1990.
AUTHOR'S
COLLECTION

Being a great-grandmother made
Mom so happy. Here's Rachel
Grover and James Charles, 1990.
AUTHOR'S COLLECTION

James Charles, age three.
AUTHOR'S COLLECTION

I love being called "Mama Faye" by these two. Here are Tammy Sue's sons: James Charles, sitting on the floor, and Jonothan, in my arms.

Roe, me, and Alan Dershowitz entering court, 1991.

Here's me and my best friend, Tuppins. She licked my tears away when I was hurting. AUTHOR'S COLLECTION

My mom's funeral was the first time in many years that all eight of us kids and Dad were together. Here's Donny, Larry, Judy, Dad, me, Ruth, Danny, Debbie, and John. AUTHOR'S COLLECTION

Starting over again: Here's Roe and me on our wedding day, October 3, 1993. SCOTT MCKIERNAN/ZUMA

Roe and me honeymooning in Hawaii, 1993. AUTHOR'S COLLECTION

My wild, crazy, and lovable
friend Jim J. Bullock and me
in a picture taken for
The Jim J. & Tammy Faye Show.
PUBLICITY SHOT

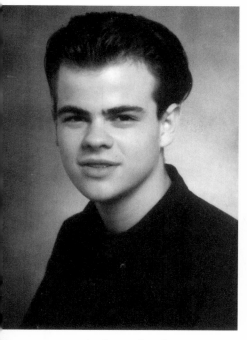

My son, now studying for the ministry.
AUTHOR'S COLLECTION

Tammy Sue Bakker Chapman, a singer and minister and the mother of two sons. AUTHOR'S COLLECTION

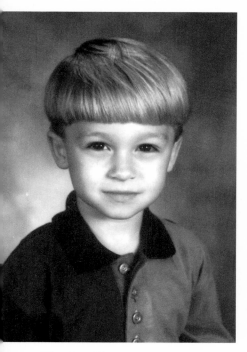

James Charles Chapman, age seven.
AUTHOR'S COLLECTION

Jonothan Chapman, age five.
AUTHOR'S COLLECTION

Roe and me today, at home in Palm Desert, California.

their privacy—just like all people do. The fact was that Jim and I weren't able to even see a movie without being instantly recognized and then mobbed. We couldn't venture anywhere near a public swimming pool like ordinary folks. (The *Enquirer* would have loved snapping pictures of that!) So our only form of relaxation was a simple safe haven where we could escape media scrutiny and just relax like a normal American family.

For that reason we purchased a beautiful houseboat. It was about thirty feet long and moored on a lake behind our house. The houseboat was the only way we had of getting away from everything and everyone. The only quality time we ever got to spend together as a family was when we were aboard. I loved that old houseboat—it was heaven to us. There we were safe, free of any need to be surrounded by guards or other security.

We would sail out into the middle of the lake and put down the anchor, and I would cook simple meals. Jim and I actually had a chance to talk and play with our kids without distractions, uninterrupted by the glare of lights and television people. Thank goodness there were no cellular phones around at that time. The houseboat offered us many opportunities to take people away from PTL for a few hours and have normal conversations.

I remember sometimes simply slipping away without anyone seeing me. I would run down to the dock and just sit in the houseboat while it still was moored. Locking all the doors, I would just enjoy the peace and tranquillity, the serenade of crickets and the gentle lapping of the water against the shore. No headaches, no hassles. It was about the only place I could go to hide out, and I loved it so much.

The lake house itself was old, and we bought it as a fixer-upper. Boy, did it need fixing up! When we first moved in, the refrigerator was falling through the kitchen floor. But we loved that house and decided to get in there and do it right.

Yes, we were situated on a beautiful lake, we had a boat and a swimming pool. And after we lost PTL the media vilified us for that. From these times I know exactly how Elvis felt. He was a prisoner of his own fame, as indeed were we. And although you still love people with all your heart, there is only so much of yourself you can give back.

If we had decided to pursue more private lives, I think that Jim and I would still be married today. But living in front of the cameras put pressures on our marriage that were impossible to surmount.

Unfortunately, fame sometimes brings out the worst in other people. There are those who don't agree with what you're doing and become extremely vehement in their outbursts.

Threats came in to PTL all the time, via mail and the telephone. And you never knew if you should take them seriously or not. But our security force did. They would always make sure that the proper authorities were notified and that the threats were checked out as thoroughly as possible.

If we had paid too much attention to some of the terrible threats we used to get, we'd never have left the house. We'd have bought a castle, ringed it with barbed wire, filled the moat with piranhas, and raised the drawbridge. We'd be safe that way.

The trouble is, you can never really be safe, if that's your view of being safe. To me, safety is in knowing God is always with you, no matter what happens. Therefore I was never really afraid, because I knew that God loved me and my family. When all is said and done, if God can't take care of you, then nobody can. Both Jim and I felt that way.

However, the insurance company didn't. Jim's life was insured by PTL for millions of dollars, which is not unusual for presidents of large corporations. Therefore the insurance company demanded a lot of security for us.

They insisted that we be well guarded twenty-four hours a day.

Our guards went everywhere we did. There was a small guardhouse in our backyard, which was manned day and night by expertly trained watchmen. Surrounding our house was the most advanced alarm system money could buy. Of course, even with all the faith in the world, this tended to make you more paranoid. Because when you've got all that security, you're afraid that you really have something to be afraid of.

Looking back, I believe we would have been better off without it. I feel we wouldn't have lived in such fear. And when you live as if you are inside a prison, you can't possibly have a normal marriage, no matter how hard you try. *That* is what I remember most about our "extravagant" lifestyle!

The Beginning of the End

John Wesley Fletcher, the man who arranged for Jim to meet Jessica Hahn, was a regular guest on the *PTL* program. He was very charismatic and was well liked by our audience. But John had a problem that we did not at first know about. We began hearing rumors that he was being seen in nearby bars. Jim approached John about these allegations, but John denied them vehemently. And with Jim's always wanting to believe the best of everyone, time and time again he would let the issue drop.

But one day he couldn't deny it any longer. One of our limousine drivers, who regularly drove our show's guests while they were in town, came to Jim and said, "I don't want to bother you, but I'm having to take John Wesley Fletcher to places you would not approve of."

Jim questioned him. "Where exactly?"

"To bars in downtown Charlotte. He has me park the car a couple of blocks away and tells me to wait for him. Jim, he comes back to the car very drunk and hardly able to function. I'm afraid that the partners are going to find out, and that it will hurt the ministry."

The next day, Jim called John into his office. "John, I have something to talk to you about," he began. With that, he informed John that he could no longer minister at Heritage USA.

John was livid!

"Just what are you saying?"

"I'm taking you off the air. Your drinking is an embarrassment to the network. John, you need help. Serious help. You've got major problems. I can't allow you to be a detriment to the ministry anymore. My hands are tied." And with that, Jim cut him off from PTL. Fletcher was absolutely stunned.

Just before leaving, he turned to Jim. "Don't worry," he said. "You'll be hearing from me."

"Good-bye, John."

I never saw Fletcher again. Little did I know that he would eventually be responsible for nearly destroying our family.

Only a few months after Fletcher was forced out, a series of bizarre phone calls started burning up the switchboards at PTL. The woman on the other end of the line sounded distressed as she ranted and raved about a supposed encounter she once had with Jim Bakker.

I can't say for certain why after all that time Jessica Hahn decided to threaten Jim. But I've reached the conclusion that someone put the idea into her head. Someone suggested there was a blackmail gold mine out there in the form of Jim Bakker and PTL, and that she could get hundreds of thousands of dollars—if she played her cards right.

"I haven't been able to eat or sleep!" Hahn screamed into the phone. "I've lost over thirty pounds, and I look like I'm dying. I take that back. I *am* dying. I'm dying of a broken heart! I'm dying of disappointment! I'm dying because Jim Bakker went back on his promise to me! He swore that he loved me! Do you hear me?"

Our phone counselors were all too familiar with crank calls, sick people who had delusions or even fantasies about us or our guests. But this woman called so frequently and her voice was so shrill and panicked that it was particularly disturbing.

"I can't take it anymore! I can't go on living like this! Jim Bakker ruined my life. Jim Bakker is forcing me to kill myself. Jim Bakker is going to have my blood on his hands. I'm going to slash my wrists, do you hear me? I'm going to swallow a bottle of sleeping pills. And when they find my body, they're going to find the note that Jim Bakker drove me to suicide! He's the one putting the knife through my heart. They'll read all about it right in that note next to my body. Get what I'm telling you?"

Jessica was becoming so convincing that she was finally put through to the executive offices, where Richard Dortch fielded the call. It didn't take him long to put two and two together. This Hahn was the same woman Jim had told him about, the same woman he confessed to having sex with.

"I've been humiliated, I've been scorned by the man I love. How am I supposed to endure the mental suffering? How can I possibly go on?" Weeping pathetically over the phone, Hahn confided to Dortch, "I need help. Lots and lots of professional help. All kinds of treatment. Medical and psychological. I'm all screwed up!"

As Jessica continued her tirade, perhaps a plan was being hatched in Dortch's mind. Maybe he could make greater use of a secret that he had carried for years and, have even more ammunition to work with, a way to further tighten his grip on PTL. One afternoon Dortch brought the entire matter to Jim.

"Hahn wants a payoff to keep her mouth shut."

"Why is she calling again after all these years?"

"Who knows? Maybe because you're worth a lot more

now. Maybe she was just biding her time. Look, it's your call." Jim got up and circled the office, deep in thought. "It's still your call," Dortch added. "What are you going to do?" Jim took a big breath and exhaled.

"Anyone who understands human nature knows that you can never pay off a blackmailer, because they'll always be coming back for more. There has to be another way."

"Well, did you have one in mind?"

"I don't care what kind of threats she's making. Never, ever pay her blackmail," Jim declared. "There must be another way to handle it. You know I respect your judgment."

"Don't worry," Dortch said, projecting his most fatherly expression of trustworthiness. "Everything is going to be okay. I'll protect you."

Now, I was not in the room when that conversation took place, and I also know that Dortch tells a different story of what was said that day. But what I *do* know is that Jim had a rule that was strictly enforced at PTL: No matter what, never, *ever* pay blackmail. With my own ears, I heard him say that time and time again. So I cannot imagine how all of a sudden that rule would change. He had been blackmailed before and never given in to the threats. So in this instance, it's Jim's word against Dortch's word. I believe Jim. However, I feel sure that he did leave the final decision of what to do in Dortch's hands.

I have no reason to lie for Jim, not even for my children's sake. We are no longer married or even in touch, so I have no vested interest in perpetrating a fraud. Knowing how much Jim avoided confrontation, I can well imagine him leaving the entire matter in Dortch's hands. Clearly, he should have dealt with Jessica Hahn himself. Not doing so was a huge mistake.

In my heart I know that if Jim would have faced it, told the *PTL* audience everything and been honest with them, none of what happened would have happened. Side by side we could have appeared on TV, told the partners what had happened so many years ago, and asked their forgiveness. They had so willingly forgiven me when I left Jim, and I knew in my heart they would have forgiven him as well. But that didn't happen.

Following his meeting with Jim, Dortch took it upon himself to fly to New York City to meet with Hahn. The meeting was held at the Holiday Inn across the highway from La Guardia Airport. Also in attendance were another pastor Dortch had brought along and a woman who referred to herself as Jessica Hahn's "paralegal." Dortch gave $2,000 to this second pastor and instructed that it be dispensed to Jessica to cover her needs. I suppose by not forking the money over directly, Dortch kept his hands clean.

Hahn's phone calls stopped for a while but soon started up again, this time with a vengeance. Now the ante was upped. Jessica required $10,000 for her "medical condition." Obviously this was more than pocket money, so Dortch enlisted the aid of Pastor Sam Johnson. After years of service in Spain and Portugal, Sam headed up the missionary division of PTL.

Dortch cut a deal with Johnson to borrow the $10,000, assuring him that he would be reimbursed from PTL funds. So again through an intermediary the money was given over to Hahn.

For a while it seemed Jessica was finally satisfied. There was a definite lull, and then it started all over again. Hahn harassed the phone counselors day and night with the same threats and allegations. It is my opinion that this was a brilliantly orchestrated tactic, an ever-escalating performance designed to wear the ministry down. Dortch fielded many of these calls himself.

Finally Richard Dortch received a certified correspondence from Hahn's "paralegal." The entire letter is much too long to reprint here, but I would like to share some excerpts. I think you'll get the gist of it:

> I represent Jessica Hahn. . . . We have to discuss a matter of mutual importance and I'm afraid we cannot put it off any longer. To be more to the point, this conversation is in reference to the events of the afternoon of December 6th, 1980, in Clearwater Beach, Florida. . . . Numerous effects and ramifications this has caused this young lady . . . who has never been married, who lives with her parents . . . and her father is a police officer for the County of Nassau in the State of New York. . . .
>
> I contend that he [Jim Bakker] enticed her and coerced her into making a wrong decision to act against her better judgment. . . . I charge this because he helped arrange and finance her flight to Clearwater Beach. . . . She was led to believe that she would join him socially in the company of others for a luncheon and to observe a television show being taped on location from the hotel or nearby studio. I must discuss with you the damages and suffering incurred by Miss Hahn.
>
> She's been through a tremendous shock. . . . She has to be compensated for her injuries of being socially disgraced. . . . You must also know she has suffered spiritual damages as well. . . . She has sustained permanent psychological and emotional damage. Her job may be at stake. . . . It has cost her in her womanhood. She is unable to respond to and sustain any romantic attachments. This all has the potential of ruining her chances to enjoy a full and normal life. . . . She was left broken-hearted. It is unrealistic, unjust, and unwise of him to presume she will walk away empty-handed as well. . . .
>
> You all seemingly have survived most of this. You all appear to be managing quite well down there. . . . You are fortunate this never did blow up sky high. . . . You're blessed that you are building up instead of tearing down. In view of all these facts, it is my belief Miss Hahn has the right

to be duly compensated for this series of emotional set-backs. . . . We're giving you the opportunity to settle this matter justly and privately. . . . $100,000 is not excessive in view of what happened here. . . .

You may as well know she is despondent. . . . Nothing else matters to her anymore. . . . You people have a lot more to lose than she has. . . . The very last thing Miss Hahn wants is a scandal, but if Mr. Bakker chooses to ignore her requests, she will have no recourse. . . .

Dortch claims that he tossed this document into a desk drawer, forgetting all about it. He never informed Jim of its contents or the seriousness of the implied threats. Again, we have to wonder how his mind was working at the time. Did he actually believe that Jessica Hahn and her so-called paralegal would simply go away? Or did he intend to provoke some kind of greater legal action? If Jim had been kept informed, could this tempest have been kept in the teapot? We'll never know. That letter stayed locked in Dortch's drawer, a bomb all set to go off.

After the letter arrived, Jessica's calls stopped coming for a time. The phone counselors were very relieved they didn't have to handle her hysterical shrieking anymore. But this was only the quiet before the storm. In the middle of January 1985, PTL was hit with a lawsuit brought by Hahn. Named as defendants were James Bakker, Richard Dortch, the Assemblies of God, Inc., and the Sheraton Key Hotel in Clearwater. The plaintiff was requesting damages of over $12 million.

Apparently this legal maneuvering wasn't conceived by Jessica alone. Certain evidence points to the fact that some parts of the scenario may have been suggested by Hahn's former pastor, Eugene Profeta. Profeta and John Wesley Fletcher were acquaintances, and perhaps even good friends, given the fact that Fletcher had ministered several times at Profeta's church. When Profeta started calling PTL on Jessica's behalf, Dortch felt the situation was serious enough to warrant a call to Hahn's lawyer.

But the man who referred to himself as Jessica Hahn's "attorney-in-fact" was not a lawyer. Paul Roper, a self-serving guardian of the public trust operating out of California, was a muckraker, and his passion was raking religious leaders over the coals. After appointing himself a one-man vigilante group, he had gained considerable clout within the media. Roper passed judgment on pastors and preachers alike, and his power was widely feared, since he had the ability to ruin reputations overnight, much like a latter-day Joe McCarthy.

According to Dortch's memory, Roper demanded that an attorney representing PTL come out to California on the double. Heeding his request, Dortch flew out a few days later, accompanied by his wife and Dr. Fred Gross. But first they met with the lawyer who had been hired to handle the case for PTL, none other than the famous Howard Weitsman.

It was determined that an out-of-court settlement would be the best bet. Soon afterward Paul Roper and Weitsman sat down, and in a couple of hours they came up with a figure to buy the silence of Jessica Hahn—a figure that exceeded a quarter of a million dollars. Jim claims the terms of the negotiations and the transfer of funds were done without his knowledge or his express consent.

In any event, after the settlement was reached, $265,000 was approved by Dortch as payment to Hahn. To avoid any internal scrutiny at PTL or setting off any other fiscal alarms, Dortch concluded that the logical choice to front the money would be the person who had the most to lose if Heritage USA was shut down—someone who was already owed a huge amount of money by PTL, but most of all, someone who knew how to keep his mouth shut.

That someone turned out to be Roe Messner. As primary contractor on many projects including the Heritage Grand

Hotel, he already had over $45 million in building construction under way when the deal with Jessica Hahn was concluded.

Dortch called and asked Roe to lunch. At Bentley's restaurant in the Heritage Grand Hotel Dortch proceeded to tell Roe about a woman in New York who was going to blackmail Jim and PTL.

"What's her name?" Roe asked.

"Cynthia Jobour," responded Dortch, not wanting to reveal her true identity. "But that's not important. What is important is that we've got the best attorney to handle the details."

"Which are?"

"She'll get a hundred thousand cash up front, and the other hundred sixty-five thousand will be put away in a trust fund. From this she can collect interest for twenty years, but she can't withdraw the principal. After twenty years is up, she can close the account and get the rest of her money."

"So you're buying her silence?"

"Let's simply say we're giving her impetus to be discreet."

"I don't like the way this sounds."

"Take it from me. The deal is solid. If she breathes a word, the money instantly reverts to the PTL attorney back in California, who makes arrangements to give it back to us." Roe mused over this.

"Well, what's this all got to do with me?"

Dortch looked around cautiously and bent closer toward Roe. "I want you to loan us the money."

"Come again?"

"I've got the whole thing worked out," Dortch said confidently. "You'll get paid back next month. No problem."

"I don't think paying off anybody is a good idea, no matter where the money is coming from," Roe replied sharply. But Dortch brushed aside whatever considerations Roe had.

"It's simple. Just add it to next month's billing on the amphitheater project." Roe listened and shook his head.

"Why do you need me? Why don't you just write the check?"

"You know why, Roe. It would be impossible to cover up that much." Then Dortch's eyes turned dark and deadly serious. "Listen, we're already paying you large sums of money every month. You're doing a lot of work for us, and we're very happy with that work. I would like that relationship to continue."

"Which means what?"

At that point Dortch turned on his grandfatherly smile again. "It simply means no one will notice if you add that amount to the construction draws we're already paying. Look, just view it as insurance." Roe was still dubious about the entire proposition.

"Does Jim know what's going on here?"

"I'm authorized to act on my own. You know my position. I don't have to answer to anybody. Listen, my friend, give me either a yes or no." His back against the wall, Roe finally agreed, and they shook hands.

"Does Tammy know about this?" Roe asked, just before leaving.

"Don't worry. She doesn't know a thing."

So reluctantly the money was wired to Weitsman, who presumably sent it along to Paul Roper and Jessica Hahn. And right on schedule Roe was repaid on the next month's billing, and that was the end of it—or so he thought. Later, when word got out that Jessica Hahn had been paid off, Dortch pleaded with Roe to make up a phony invoice for some so-called extra work that was never billed, such as lumber, brick, or labor.

But Roe refused. "You asked me to bill it to the amphitheater back in 1985, and that's the way it's going to stay."

How Roper and Hahn actually split the money I can't say for certain, although I've heard Roper made out a lot better than Jessica did. But we do know that Jessica Hahn eventually broke her agreement, probably because there was much more cash to be made from the scandal. Consequently over $150,000 of the hush money paid to her was returned to PTL.

Months later, Jim and I were taping shows in Hawaii. He looked wearier and more ragged than I had ever seen him, and he was mentally run-down too. Just before leaving, he had promised the partners that $6 million had been banked with which he was going to pay off the Heritage Grand Hotel. Jim was so proud of being able to put that $6 million into savings. He felt as if at last we would be able to get a little ahead. He had worked so hard to save that money. But while Jim was gone, completely unbeknown to him, Dortch took all the money out of savings and spent it as he saw fit, paying off other outstanding debts, trying once more to look like the Big Man in Town. I don't really know if there was anything improper in the way Dortch distributed those funds.

I feel this was the real turning point for Jim. I think that for the first time he realized he could not control Dortch. I will never forget Jim coming to me with tears streaming down his face. "You will never believe what Dortch has done. You know the six million dollars I promised the partners I would pay off the hotel with? Well, Tam, he took it out of savings and spent it."

"What in the world did he spend it on?" I asked in disbelief.

"I don't know. We didn't have anything that far behind that I know of which needed immediate payment. What am I going to tell the partners? Tam, I just can't do it anymore."

"Do what?" I asked.

"I just can't continue to raise money anymore. I'm totally worn out. I won't make promises to the partners that I can't keep. And I can't continue to raise millions of dollars for Dortch to do with as he pleases. Tam, I don't know what to do anymore."

"Jim, you're just tired. Once we get back home, you'll feel better. But you have to talk to Dortch. You cannot allow him to do things like this time and time again. You are the president, not Dortch! When are you going to get that fact through your head?" But I saw something go out of Jim that day that never returned. I don't know if it was confidence, enthusiasm, or that old "we have to do whatever it takes" spirit. Something happened, and he just was never the same. A few weeks after that, we lost PTL. I think he just couldn't face the fight anymore.

Part Four

The
Falwell
of PTL

Knocking at Death's Door

The last year PTL was still going strong, Jerry Falwell entered the picture. His children had been coming to Heritage USA, and we welcomed them with open arms, especially Jerry's son. He was freely allowed to roam our offices and other sensitive areas that the general public did not see. After all, he was Jerry Falwell's son. We extended him the courtesy because his family was also in the ministry, and besides, we had nothing to hide from anyone.

Neither Jim nor I knew Falwell closely. The only times we had ever met him were at the White House and political functions. In general, we assumed that Jerry, as leader of the Moral Majority and a close confidant of President Reagan, was one of us, and we were flattered when he made a move toward friendship and closer ties with us.

I remember well our first real conversation.

"I am a real fan of the *PTL* program and all the great work you've been doing," Falwell said. "This is important work, the type of work America truly needs, and I just want to let you know that I'm one hundred percent behind you." Falwell could really lay it on thick.

"It's really kind of you to be so supportive, Jerry," Jim said. "You're an inspiration to us as well."

"I know what you two are trying to accomplish. We're all trying to accomplish the same thing. That's why we've got to work together. You know in unity there is strength."

Falwell just sort of crept in, and Jim began to trust him more and more until he trusted him totally. Neither of us in our wildest dreams imagined that someone like Jerry had a dark side of jealousy and destruction.

Naturally Reverend Dortch was also beginning to buddy up to Falwell. Jim never thought anything about it, since he had no reason to fear Falwell in any way. In fact, he looked up to Falwell as a respected and nationally known leader. Time after time, Jerry did everything he possibly could to ingratiate himself with us.

We thought it would be so wonderful if our two ministries could be friends. This had never happened before, but it certainly was not impossible. Most of all we believed that creating a strong bond with Falwell would be pleasing in the eyes of God.

In 1987, PTL was gearing up to erect its greatest building ever. We needed a bigger meeting place to hold the thousands of people who came to Heritage USA every week, so Jim decided to construct a replica of England's Crystal Palace. Jim read everything he could and also had Roe Messner research the project. With a capacity for more than thirty thousand people, it would be the size of a football field and the largest structure of its kind in modern church history. The Palace was envisioned as an all-glass building rising up to the sky for the glory of God.

And it was the first building about which I ever fully agreed with Jim, which is really ironic, considering it never got built. I will never as long as I live forget the day we dedicated the land. It was in the middle of December. The winds were blustery, and no one was prepared for the weather. By the time we arrived it had been raining very hard, and the field was nothing but soft, oozing mud. But I have to admit, our staff were troupers. Hundreds of our personnel plus the mayor and other dignitaries stood out in that freezing cold to attend the ground-breaking ceremony. And it turned out to be a beautiful dedication, despite the miserable conditions.

In the midst of all this, I was called upon to sing. But by the time I took the microphone, my fingers and my face were already numb because the temperature had dropped so rapidly and I wasn't properly dressed. Anyway, following the dedication we all went home with a warm feeling in our hearts—in spite of the bone-chilling cold.

The next day Jim decided we should go to the little house we had purchased in Gatlinburg, Tennessee. It was almost Christmas, and we all needed a break. Jamie and Tammy Sue were exuberant, but I told Jim I wasn't feeling at all well. Still, I didn't want to spoil our plans, so thinking it was just a terrible sore throat, we decided to go anyway.

Feeling weak and feverish, I swallowed some aspirin and then an Ativan, a tranquilizer that originally had been prescribed to ease my fear of flying. But it seemed to quell so many of my other anxieties that I had begun to rely on it more and more, much more than I should have.

We had desperately needed someplace close where our whole family could get away; the children resented all the people who were constantly around us and loved the times that the four of us spent alone together. The trip to Gatlinburg was only an hour and a half, which made the house we'd bought quite convenient as a getaway.

At this point, just let me clarify our housing situation. Jim and I had three houses altogether. The home in Gatlinburg, our main residence on the lake in Charlotte, plus a small place out in Palm Desert, California, which we hardly ever got to use at that time.

Anyhow, our house in Gatlinburg was far up a mountain and tucked way back, a secluded cave where we didn't have to dress up and the children could be free to roam without being accompanied by guards all the time. We would go on picnics and sit for hours by the sparkling brooks hidden in the nooks and crannies of that beautiful mountain. We would hike the steep paths and listen to the birds and observe all the forest animals. It was as close to heaven as our family ever got.

When we finally arrived, I was weary to the bone and still feeling very ill. Jim immediately got the fireplace going in the living room, and we all huddled around the flames to get warm. Jim and the kids were able to get heat going through their bodies, but no matter how many layers of sweaters I put on, I just couldn't stop shivering. I took some more aspirin, sprayed my throat, and then crawled into bed.

We had only been there a couple of days when Jim received an urgent call from PTL. They needed him immediately. I don't remember exactly why, but it was important enough for him to leave me and the kids. Considering that I was not feeling well, before he left he called Vi Azvedo and asked her if she would come up and be with us. She said yes, arriving before Jim drove back to Charlotte.

I don't think anyone realized how sick I was, including me. Not being a complainer, I had begun treating my symptoms as best I could with aspirin. But aspirin wasn't doing anything. So I swallowed some cough medicine. But the cough medicine wasn't doing much of anything either. I couldn't stop coughing. My breathing became strained and shallow. Each inhalation hurt, as if I had broken ribs.

I even tried more Ativan, assuming that if my nerves could get calmed down, I would feel better. Early one afternoon Vi walked into my bedroom and asked, "Tammy, why do you have the TV on so loud?"

"Huh?"

"Why do you have the TV on so loud?"

"What? I can't hear you."

"WHY DO YOU HAVE THE TV ON SO LOUD?" Then she went over and shut it off.

"Oh, Vi. My ears are ringing so loud that I can't even hear what's on the TV." She looked very concerned and left the room. Coming back a few moments later, she took a thermometer and put it in my mouth. She waited a few minutes, then pulled it out.

"Tammy, do you know what your temperature is?"

"I don't think I want to know."

"You're a very sick girl. Your temperature is too high, Tammy. We need to get you into a cold tub of water fast and see if we can't get it down a little." The thought of getting into a tub of cold water was not a pleasant thought, but I did as I was asked. Vi filled the tub, and I got in. I stayed in that cold tub until Vi told me I could get out. Then she put me back into bed under the nice, warm covers. I could see in her eyes that she was really worried about me.

"I'll be okay, Vi," I managed to say. "Don't worry." With that, I closed my eyes.

A little while later Jamie came in and quietly sat down on my bed beside me. He kept asking me over and over again, "Mom, are you all right?"

Even though my head was spinning, I told him, "Yes, honey, I'm fine. Don't worry." But then something frightening happened. All of a sudden I began to hallucinate. I started seeing huge, Disney-type elephants falling out of the sky onto my bed.

"Watch out, Jamie!" I screamed. "They're going to hit you! They're going to crush your head in!" Well, that was enough to send my son dashing out of the room to get Vi. The next minute I saw horrible black demons coming at me with huge pitchforks. I thought I was going stark raving mad! I became hysterical, doubled up in terror. "Please, oh my God! Don't let them kill me! Please, someone save me! Hurry, they're going to kill me! Can't anyone please hear me? Oh, my God! Oh, my dear God!"

Vi called PTL and told Jim he better get to Gatlinsburg as quickly as possible. He instructed her to call Dr. Nichols, our close doctor friend in California, who subsequently dropped everything and took the first flight out. Following his examination he looked gravely concerned, saying that if I didn't get to a hospital immediately, I probably wouldn't make it.

Upon checking my lungs Dr. Nichols diagnosed severe pneumonia. Vi contacted Jim, and he ordered her to get me to the Eisenhower Hospital in Palm Springs. Without a moment's hesitation, a private airplane was chartered and I was off, accompanied by Vi, Dr. Nichols, and the children. Jim decided to send me all the way to California because he felt there was much better medical care there. In fact, I had been there before for tests when they thought I had heart problems. Not to mention that in Charlotte we were so well known that if I had been put in a hospital there, I wouldn't have had a moment's peace.

I hallucinated during the entire six-hour trip to Palm Springs. I can still remember Dr. Nichols holding me tightly as I tried time and time again to get off the plane, telling me that everything was going to be all right if I would just sit still.

Upon landing, we rented a car and drove to Eisenhower Hospital. Our entire party was met at the registration desk by another friend of ours, Dr. Marvin Brooks, who immediately checked me in to intensive care. Within minutes I was put on a respirator.

Instantly the staff started pumping me full of antibiotics, trying to draw the fluids out of my lungs. My condition was touch and go for a week, with the doctors giving me about a fifty-fifty chance of pulling through. To further complicate conditions, my blood pressure was through the roof.

The only time my pulse wasn't racing was when I was taking Ativan. So they thought in addition to the pneumonia that I had a heart problem.

Subsequently, the doctors put me through a whole series of cardiac tests. I even wore a heart monitor for a long time, but it turned out my heart was perfect. Their final diagnosis was that severe stress was causing the high blood pressure. Thanks to those dedicated medical professionals and the grace of God, my condition improved.

Following my arrival in Palm Springs, Jim had grabbed the first flight out to the Coast, leaving Reverend Dortch to run PTL in his absence. Jim stayed night and day at my bedside and was an absolute angel during my recovery. Together we'd watch the *PTL* show from my hospital bed. I could see how much he really cared for me, and that helped alleviate my distress.

During my recuperation I received hundreds of bouquets of flowers. There were so many that the hospital filled gurneys up and down the hallways with them. Every patient got bunches of flowers, thanks to the kindness of the PTL partners. I still cry when thinking about those people's love today.

I can't possibly describe the feeling of knowing that thousands of people are pulling for you, praying for your recovery. We had been looking into their faces via TV cameras for almost twenty-five years; we had been in their living rooms, bedrooms, and dens. We loved them and they loved us.

Meanwhile, back in North Carolina, Reverend Dortch appeared to be very concerned about my condition and even spoke to me once or twice on the telephone. "Tammy, I just want you to know that I've been praying for your recovery. And I can't wait to see you and Jim back here."

"Thank you, Reverend Dortch."

"I'm just trying to fill in as best I can. Do the program as best I can. But you know no one could ever take your places. Who in the world could take the place of Jim and Tammy Faye Bakker?"

But even though his voice was warm and comforting, something in his tone didn't ring true. However, I was too weak to concern myself over that. I couldn't even walk a straight line from my hospital bed to the door. All I wanted to do was go home—to our little house in Palm Desert— and try to get my life back to normal.

On the day I supposed I was being released, a lady came to my hospital room. I couldn't figure out who she was or what she was doing there. Without even introducing herself, she asked abrasively, "How long have you been taking Ativan?" My mind was still swimming.

"Uh, ever since . . . let me see. It was—"

"How many of them do you take a day?"

"Oh, I'd say no more than two or—"

"What other medications are you using?" All I wished was that she would go away and leave me in peace. But since she seemed to be part of the hospital staff, I answered her questions as politely as I could, trying not to reveal my increasing agitation.

When she finally left, Jim and David Taggart and some other staff members came into the room, informing me that I was well enough to leave the hospital. I was so excited! They helped me pack. I said my good-byes to all the wonderful nurses and devoted doctors who had helped me get well. They put me in a wheelchair, and I was taken out to the car. Finally I was going home.

I was so happy. In a few minutes I would be in our own little house, all safe and sound. I would be with Jim and Jamie and Tammy Sue. There I could get my strength back and continue getting well. But to my surprise, we drove up instead to the Betty Ford Clinic, which was located right there close to the hospital. Jim began to talk to me: "Tam, the lady who came to see you this afternoon was from the Betty Ford Clinic. She feels that because of the Ativan you've been taking so long, you need to be admitted. Here they will help you so that you don't have to take it anymore."

"Jim, what are you talking about? I don't need to go to Betty Ford! I am not a drug addict! I can stop taking Ativan! I promise you I'll never take any more of it."

"Tam, she feels like you can't do it by yourself, that you need help." I was flabbergasted! "She is afraid that someday you might overdose on it, honey, and none of us want that to happen."

"I would never do that! Please take me home. Please!" I begged him over and over. "Jim, she only talked to me a few minutes. How could she make that diagnosis in such a short time?"

By this time, tears were streaming down my face and my weakened body could hardly move. I was numb! All of a sudden I hated my husband. Why hadn't he at least asked me before he made such an important decision. Why? Why couldn't we at least have talked it over? I felt like a prisoner being taken away to jail. And I didn't know what I'd done. And I was still so sick and so weak. I begged Jim, but it was no use. His mind was made up.

Jim was supposed to protect me, and here he was conspiring with all these people. I felt betrayed, horribly betrayed, and an utter hopelessness flooded over me. I continued to implore him, but I was too weak, too exhausted, and as the door swung open, I was led inside.

In any event, the first thing I noticed was that the clinic was not a hospital. In fact, it looked more like a hotel than a clinic. The registration desk looked straight out of any Hilton or Sheraton. Following my check-in, a counselor led me to a small office. He was courteous but professional and to the point. He told me exactly why I was there and what my prognosis would be if I left.

Very politely, he told me to send all the things in my suitcase home with my husband, including my pillbox.

The only items I could keep were my makeup, my hot rollers, my pajamas and bathrobe, my underwear, and a couple of pants outfits. After all this he assigned me a room. And while I was sitting there, still in a state of shock, he left to tell Jim and the people with him that they could go home. I was devastated.

Why had I not been consulted beforehand? And why had they chosen to do this while I was still so sick? Even as I write this after all these years, I am amazed at how much anger I still feel toward Jim for this decision.

The Betty Ford Clinic is truly a no-frills building. All the rooms have two beds, two dressers, two nightstands, two lamps, and two closets. The carpet was plain, the walls a neutral beige. My first instinct upon being led into my room was to curl up and die. I didn't belong here! By the time my roommate walked in I looked like a wreck from all my crying. She was a considerably older lady and a chain-smoker.

They handed me a list of rules and chores that I was expected to do every day. They also gave me a list of classes I was to attend. It literally overwhelmed me. I was still so sick that I could hardly stand up. I was so distraught that my roommate insisted I come down to the cafeteria with her. Upon entering, I was instantly surrounded by a group of fellow women patients. They were phenomenal!

"Come on, Tammy," one woman said, "sit down and we'll get you some iced tea and a cookie. It's going to be okay. Don't cry. We all felt this way when we first got here, but it isn't a bad place." I could not eat the cookie, but I drank some of the iced tea. It felt good on my parched throat. And all the hugs just made me cry harder.

My roommate and I went back to our room, and I lay down on the bed, fully clothed, sobbing my heart out. "Somehow I have to get out of here. I don't belong here! Please, God, help me!" I begged silently. Despite the fact that my body was totally exhausted, I could not sleep. So quietly, I walked out into the hallway.

I went over to the front desk and asked, "Please, sir, may I use the phone? I need to call my husband."

"As a new patient," he said in a detached voice, "you are not allowed to use the phone." Then he went back to reading his paper. I could not believe that I could not even call home. It was then I spotted something called the Meditation Room. I walked inside and was awed by its beauty. It was really more like a lovely garden. There was no furniture, just a series of carpeted steps arranged in a semicircle. There you could meditate in an enchanting setting, filled with plants and trees of all kinds and a small pond surrounded by flowers. I began to feel more calm.

I finally went back to my room and collapsed on the mattress, begging God to get me out of this place. More excruciating minutes rolled by. It was 11:00 P.M., and I still could not sleep a wink, so I got up and went out toward the front desk again. There was a different guard sitting there, with a benevolent, sympathetic face. "Sir," I asked, "do I have to stay here?" I must have been a pathetic sight, standing before him with my eyes nearly swollen shut from sobbing so hard.

"No, Tammy," he responded, "this is not prison. You don't have to stay here against your will. Now, why don't you pretend this is a nice motel and stay just tonight? I promise you that when morning comes, you can call your husband." His smile was reassuring, and suddenly I knew everything was going to be all right. I will never forget the kindness of that precious man. He was like an angel to me. Thanks to his compassion the terrible panic I felt began to ease. I told him I would do what he said, and I walked back to my room and lay down on top of the covers, still dressed. I was up at 5:00 A.M. I went into the bathroom and put cold washcloths on my swollen face, then redid my makeup. At about 6:30 I called Jim. "Please come and get me. I want to come home."

I don't think Jim could believe what he was hearing. "Tam," he said, "you really need to give it a chance, honey. We are all so worried about you. But if you insist, I'll come and get you. I have a meeting planned for this morning, but I will be there as soon as I can get away." I started to cry again, but this time out of pure gratitude.

In the meantime I'm positive Jim called the clinic, because almost on cue a counselor showed up and tried to convince me to stay. She stated that I really did require professional help in getting off Ativan, adding that my panic attacks were symptomatic of someone whose body had become overdependent on the drug. I answered by saying that if they allowed me to go home, then I would join the outpatient clinic and do whatever was required to complete the course of treatment. She wasn't enthusiastic about the idea, but eventually she agreed.

By noon I gathered my things and Jim reluctantly checked me out of the Betty Ford Clinic. But as I was leaving, a very elegant, statuesque woman was just coming in. Placing her hand on my shoulder with great sympathy, she said, "Tammy, if you don't get help here, please try to get help somewhere else." I nodded my head weakly, only to realize a few moments later that this lady was Betty Ford herself.

I arrived home to hugs and kisses from my children as well as presents and flowers from well-wishers. I finally got undressed, got into my robe, and cuddled up in my own bed. As promised, I had Jim sign me up for the outpatient clinic. He signed up as well, something that marriage partners are encouraged to do. Later that afternoon, Jim placed a call to Reverend Dortch. "I'm going to be staying at Tammy's side."

"For how long, Jim?" Dortch asked.

"For as long as she needs me. Could be several weeks."

"That long?"

"Whatever it takes."

"Well, I'll mind the store in the meanwhile. Everybody misses the two of you. And listen, Jim, we expect you back soon."

Jim and I went through the entire six-week Betty Ford program together. Vi stayed with us to help our family through that time. She was such a comfort, and since she was so familiar with the Betty Ford approach, she made it easier for me to face each day of classes. I think that Jim benefited every bit as much as I did from the program, and even Jamie and Tammy Sue learned a lot from the times they visited. (Every so often, children were encouraged to attend with their parents.)

The Betty Ford experience turned out to be a real blessing. I learned that I didn't want Ativan or any other drug controlling my life anymore. I was sick of crying day and night. I wanted to live! I wanted to laugh! I wanted to feel! Finally I wanted to be at peace with myself. From the program I discovered that I was in control of my life and that God was in control of me and everything else. I discovered you had to face the pain head on—in the raw, if you will. And it worked.

I couldn't wait to get home to Charlotte, back to our house on the lake, back to our friends, and back to Heritage USA. Little did I know that Jim and Tammy Bakker would never return to PTL again.

The Plot Sickens

As they say, when the cat's away, the mice will play. And that's exactly what happened in Jim's absence from PTL. No one had a better understanding of our situation and how vulnerable we were than Reverend Dortch. He knew it was only a matter of time before Jim Bakker would be tarnished by accusations of marital infidelity, since there were already powerful people lurking in the shadows waiting to twist the entire Jessica Hahn affair to their own advantage.

Inside sources at *The Charlotte Observer* reported that the paper was preparing to break the story wide open. Ever since 1976, when we first moved to North Carolina, that newspaper had run hundreds of features smearing PTL. They had sustained a vicious vendetta against us for being televangelists and charismatic Christians.

Soon the cat would be out of the bag. I believe Jim knew as well as anyone else that this was coming, but he still couldn't accept it. He was exhausted. And I had just gotten out of the hospital. For anyone who knew the dire truth, it would be an ideal time to play on Jim's deepest fears and thereby extract the maximum amount of concessions.

Had I known the seriousness of the situation, I would have insisted that Jim return to PTL to fight the usurpers and subversive forces within our midst. But Jim's absence only served to further undermine his influence. When proclaiming his message of salvation, Jim was unassailable, impervious to attack from either within or without. But once he was gone, no longer appearing daily on TV stations across the country, the entire can of worms could be opened.

I kept telling Jim that we should go back to Charlotte. We had been gone for over a month, and the children wanted to go home. I felt that Jim needed to get back to the ministry. But he couldn't seem to face going back. He kept putting it off. I really think that Jim was in a state of burnout—in fact, that's what they told him at Betty Ford: that he needed a year's rest from television. Which is why he felt justified in not going back, and justified in doing TV spots from California, and totally comfortable with the idea of Richard Dortch doing the daily show. In fact, contributions actually rose by over 15 percent during the months we were in Palm Desert.

It was people's way of saying they had faith in us, praying for me to regain my health as fast as possible. The partners were always angels. The treachery came from within PTL itself, as certain opportunists saw their chance to take the ministry for themselves. All they needed was a little outside help. And they got it—in the form of Jerry Falwell. But first John Ankerberg and Jimmy Swaggart would have to be dealt with, since it appeared that they also knew about the tryst with Jessica Hahn.

That these two men despised Jim Bakker is no secret. John Ankerberg hosted a show on the PTL network called *Talk Back*, featuring highly controversial subjects concerning the state of Christianity. The circus atmosphere was more like *Family Feud* than an intelligent forum to discuss the spiritual issues of the day. Ankerberg's inflam-

matory rhetoric infuriated millions of viewers. It was designed to incite the passions of his guests, often of
different denominations, so that they would start raising
their voices and pointing fingers at one another.

Jimmy Swaggart also came after us, which was ironic
because his show had appeared on the PTL network for
many years. Not exactly a stranger to infidelity, Swaggart
had been caught red-handed with a high-price call girl
down in Louisiana, which he tearfully confessed to a massive TV audience during a special broadcast.

His constant attacks on PTL mushroomed into a full-
fledged assault. There was no letup in Swaggart's vicious
statements. He labeled PTL "a cancer eating away at the
heart of the church." Loyal readers of Swaggart's magazine
The Evangelist were treated to condemnations of Jim and
me for more than fifteen months.

But that's not the reason Jimmy was eventually taken
off the air. We were forced to act because for months Swaggart had been saying awful things about the Catholic
church. It raised a furor everywhere the PTL satellite network was broadcast, more than fifty countries. The Catho-
lics had always been our friends and partners, and we
could not let him continue to do this. After Swaggart's
show was canceled, he became enraged and called Jim.

"I'll get even for this. You can't push me off the air!"

"You pushed yourself, Jimmy. You went too far—much
too far."

"You are denying me access to my people. You are denying me my right to communicate."

"I'm denying you the right to spread hate. 'Cause that's
all you're doing, Jimmy. You're spreading hate, and I won't
have you spreading it from the pulpit of PTL!"

"You're making a big mistake pulling the plug on me,
Jim," Swaggart asserted. "A real big mistake."

"Jimmy, you're putting this all on me, when you've only
got yourself to blame."

"This is not going to end here, Jim. You know that—you know what I mean! No matter what it takes, this is not going to end here!"

After that incident, Jim was genuinely concerned about Swaggart "coming to get him."

In my opinion, Jimmy was trying to bring PTL down out of sheer envy. Swaggart had been "the biggest" until Jim came along. And preachers seem to have a real problem with that. So when he somehow found out about Jim's affair with Jessica Hahn, he jumped at a chance because he now had a weapon.

Religious politics, just like the more secular kind, make for strange bedfellows, and you probably couldn't get a stranger combination than Ankerberg and Swaggart. I don't know who they hated more: Jim Bakker or each other. I think it was a toss-up. But I suppose the deciding factor was that Jim had what both of them wanted. I believe each of them would have loved his own satellite network, to be the person in charge of one of the nation's greatest media enterprises. Small wonder they would have cut off their right arms to be in Jim's position, to have the prestige and worldwide power he wielded. Therefore even though they were polar opposites on the theological front, they decided to join forces.

But why was PTL host to all these strange intrigues? In my experience television has a peculiar effect on people. That little red light comes on, you look straight into the lens, and a unique metamorphosis takes place, sometimes good, sometimes bad. As people become enveloped by their own stardom, personal qualities are amplified. For instance, I believe the camera brought out the best in Jim.

But for others the fame becomes a drug, an addiction that has to be constantly fed and can never be satisfied. Is that what happened to Dortch? Was the kind, gentle man we originally employed somehow transformed by the seductive power of fame? We can only speculate.

By his own admission on *The Larry King Show* of February 1, 1988, we know that Dortch arranged a furtive meeting with Jerry Falwell. He was approached at a ball game down in Florida by two men. One turned out to be Mark DeMoss, son of the wealthy DeMoss insurance family and a Falwell operative. The other man was Jerry Nims, another member of Falwell's inner circle. In any event, the particulars were set up. The meeting was to be held down at the Tampa airport at eleven o'clock in the evening.

Dortch was to wait for them on the secluded part of the airfield reserved for corporate jets. But the plane was extremely late, arriving well after midnight. Making no apologies for his tardiness, Falwell quickly exited, and the four men adjourned to a private conference room upstairs. They dispensed with the usual pleasantries, and then Nims got right down to brass tacks.

He told Dortch that John Ankerberg and Jimmy Swaggart were fully aware of the entire Jessica Hahn scandal and that they wanted to enlist Falwell as their powerful ally in order to intimidate Jim Bakker into submission. But there was only one small fly in the ointment. Jerry Falwell did not trust Jimmy Swaggart; in fact he despised him.

To this day, Dortch insists that whatever his subsequent actions, they were taken only to save the ministry and Jim Bakker. He claims that he never said anything to Jerry Falwell about the Jessica Hahn affair until it was brought up at this meeting. His defense is that he took Falwell at face value, believing him a fellow man of God unselfishly offering his services in time of distress in order to thwart Swaggart and prevent a great injustice to PTL.

However, unless there is some tape recording floating around that we don't know about, there is no accurate way of telling exactly what was said in that famous meeting— what was promised, what was offered, what was planned, and whose plan it was.

Is it possible that Dortch was playing both ends against the middle? Believing that no matter who brought Jim Bakker down, he would be the winner? Or was this meeting merely the culmination of earlier discussions with Falwell in order to topple Jim Bakker, a strategy session to dot the *i*'s and cross the *t*'s? On the other hand, it's possible Dortch was convinced he was acting in the best interests of PTL, as he perceived them to be. It's hard to say. All we can do is look at the far-reaching consequences of that meeting, then draw our own conclusions.

To solidify the arrangement, Falwell's people suggested that Dortch employ an attorney named Norman Roy Grutman as counsel for PTL. Grutman was a heavyweight who had defended *Penthouse* magazine in a major lawsuit, and won. The plaintiff was none other than Jerry Falwell himself. Apparently Falwell believed that if you can't beat your enemies, let them join you. I have every reason to believe that Grutman—at the time he was hired as PTL's attorney—was also Falwell's attorney, which presented a clear conflict of interest, to say the least.

If you accept Dortch's version of the story, he was duped into believing that Grutman was fully independent of Falwell's influence and therefore could be trusted with confidential information. But if you don't have faith in Dortch's recollection, then you might assume that Grutman was expertly used as another nail in Jim Bakker's coffin.

Jerry Falwell had cleverly seized upon this time, one of the lowest points in our lives, to do his dirty work. I don't know how long he had been planning it. I have been told that he had been working out the details for well over a year. A short time after his powwow with Falwell, Dortch placed an emergency call to Jim to apprise him of the grim facts. "Jim, everything is coming to a head. Soon it will all boil over. Swaggart and Ankerberg are right on our tail. *The Charlotte Observer* is about to run the Hahn story. A decision has to be made."

Out in Palm Desert, Jim was absolutely panicked. "What can we do? If the Hahn story comes out, I'm sunk, through. You know that."

"It's going to come out, Jim. There's nothing we can do about that. It's how it's going to come out that's the question."

"What do you mean?"

"I think we can do a lot of damage control if we go with Falwell. He wants to help us. You know how much he's always liked you and Tammy. He's a friend—a powerful friend with powerful friends—and I know we can trust him."

"I'm not sure. There's got to be another way."

"Look, Jim, let me lay it on the line. You have no choice. No choice whatsoever. Your neck is way out there, and this whole thing could break any minute now."

"Maybe there's something we haven't thought of."

"Face reality, Jim. This is it. Time's up. There's only one man in the whole world who can possibly save you, and that man is Jerry Falwell."

Jim did everything he could to get a grip on himself. Finally he was able to put his thoughts together. Dortch was right. There was no turning back. It was now or never. "What does Jerry want to do?"

"I don't think we should discuss that on the phone," Dortch quickly responded. "Here's what we'll do. Tomorrow I'll fly on Falwell's jet with him out to where you are."

"So we're going to meet in Palm Desert?"

"Exactly. But don't worry. Everything is going to be all right. I think Falwell has a terrific plan that's going to fix everything," Dortch proclaimed, finishing on an upbeat note.

While the situation was definitely critical, Jim felt comforted. Dortch's soothing voice had brought a sense of peace, some hope into his heart. Jim had confidence in Dortch's ability to defuse this emergency. Their previous clashes were petty compared to a crisis of this magnitude. Jim was absolutely convinced that Dortch would rise to the occasion, using his considerable skills to save PTL. In other words, whatever it was, Daddy Dortch would make it all right. He would never let anything hurt Jim. He would have the answer to Jimmy Swaggart's threats, and the answer was Jerry Falwell—yes, Jerry Falwell would be Jim's savior!

Jim Breaks the Bad News

here was no avoiding it now. Jim knew that in twenty-four hours Jerry Falwell would be arriving and I would find out everything. For as long as I live, I will never forget the moment I found out about Jessica Hahn. Vi Azvedo was at our house. Jim said that he and Vi needed to talk to me, and he asked me to go with them into the bedroom. I don't know why, but as I went with them I shuddered with utter dread. "Why can't we talk out here, you guys?"

"Tam, we can't talk in front of the kids," Jim answered. In our bedroom was a cozy little sitting room that I loved. It was my special spot. We ended up in there on the plush white couch and matching chair. The next words I heard were to change my life forever. Vi started the conversation. "Tammy Faye, Jim has something he needs to tell you."

I immediately became defensive. With both of them there, I felt like a trapped animal. "Well, Vi, if he has something to say to me, why can't he say it by himself? Jim's a big boy. Why does he need you here?" Vi had been a part of the marriage-workshop team that had counseled us many times, and she knew our problems well. "Well, Jim, what do you want to tell me? Just say it."

I already sensed that he was incredibly uncomfortable, but nothing in the world could have prepared me for what came next. "Tam, I need to tell you about something that happened seven years ago. I have never told you because everyone told me not to. I wanted to tell you many times."

"Jim, just tell me!" I begged. My heart was pounding. I was literally shaking with fear. What could he possibly tell me that I didn't already know?

"Tam, seven years ago I met a girl. I had sex with her one time, and I have never seen her since that day. The reason I am telling you this now is that she is blackmailing me, which is why Jerry Falwell is coming in tomorrow. Jimmy Swaggart has found out and is threatening to go to the news media with it. Falwell says that he wants to help me. Reverend Dortch is flying in with him on his private plane. We'll meet with him tonight and with Falwell tomorrow. I'm sorry, Tam. Please forgive me."

With that he came over to me and tried to kiss me and put his arms around me. But I was frozen with grief, anger, and a sense of betrayal I had never felt in my entire life. "Don't you ever touch me again!" I screamed at the top of my lungs. I wanted to escape, to run away, but there was no place to go. Tears were streaming down my face.

"Why, Jim, why?" I sobbed in pure agony.

"I don't know, Tam. I'm so terribly sorry, so sorry."

By this time Vi had discreetly left the room and we were alone. I went from feeling sorry for Jim one moment to wanting to kill him the next. Dortch knew, Falwell knew, Swaggart knew, Ankerberg knew, Vi knew, Dr. Gross knew, even *The Charlotte Observer* knew. Everybody knew except me!

I felt like a fool. How could so many know, and I had never once even suspected? "Jim," I screamed in agony, "how could you have been so stupid? What if she'd gotten pregnant? What if you'd caught some disease? Did you use any protection?"

"I wasn't thinking," Jim said, almost to himself.

"You sure weren't. You weren't thinking about the kids, about me, or about your ministry. You weren't thinking about anybody but yourself. Jim, how could you have done a thing like that! One thing you didn't need more of was sex! You know I never denied you anything you wanted. Never! What did she look like?" I screamed in his face. "Was she beautiful, Jim? Was that the reason? You couldn't resist her beauty? What was it, Jim? Tell me, what was it?"

"Tam, I don't even remember what she looked like. I don't think I ever really saw her face. I was so nervous. I don't think we even spoke ten words. Tam, you've got to believe me."

"That makes me feel better."

"It meant nothing. Absolutely nothing! You satisfy me more than that Jessica Hahn ever could. Being with her made me realize how wonderful you were."

I looked at him. I didn't know whether to laugh or scream my head off. I felt as though I were falling and falling and there was no one to catch me. "How could you, Jim, how could you?" I kept repeating, but by then he wasn't answering. He just withdrew and became quiet, deathly still. Finally all I could say was, "Jim, please leave. Just get out of my sight." He shuffled out of the room, leaving me weeping. I don't think there were two more wretched human beings on the face of the planet that day.

I never denied Jim anything, not ever. I never denied him what he needed. I never said that I wasn't in the mood. I was always a good wife, both inside the bedroom and out. Now I sat in that room feeling like less than nothing! I blamed myself over and over. I must not have been enough for him. I wasn't pretty enough, talented enough, a good-enough mother, a good-enough lover. I was a total failure as a woman. I just wanted to die.

On and on, these thoughts were spinning through my head. My emotions were a jumble. I wanted to wring Jim Bakker's neck. This was as low as we had ever sunk. This was the bottom of the pit. I felt I was being crushed by the weight of the world, as if all the life was being squeezed out of me.

To this day, people ask me why I didn't file for divorce right then. Believe me, I thought about it. Trouble was, I hated the word *divorce*. My mother and father had gotten divorced—over another woman. I had always vowed that I would never get a divorce.

My religious beliefs told me that God hates divorce, and that a man and woman are supposed to live together "till death do us part." I felt the reason God hates divorce is because He loves the family, and divorce forever destroys at least one part of the family. One parent is always missing, and that is truly sad. At Christmas and Thanksgiving, it would be so hard on our children if we got divorced.

I don't know if it was these thoughts, but then something happened inside me. My maternal instinct somehow came out and took control. I dragged myself off the couch and walked out into the living room. Jim was curled up in a tight little ball on the couch. I could see that he too was in pure agony. I put my arms around him.

"It's going to be all right, honey. Somehow we will get through this, get through this together. We have to." Jim buried his face in my bosom. "We just have to." A few minutes passed, and we heard a knock on the door. It was Reverend Dortch. I was never so glad to see anyone in my whole life. Now everything was going to be fine. It had to be.

The Trap Is Sprung

In order to succeed with his ambitious scheme to acquire PTL, the PTL mailing list, and the PTL satellite network, as well as become the undisputed leader of the Christian world, Falwell needed friends in high places. Well, it just so happened that Jerry's plans coincided with campaign strategies being formulated within the White House. For as George Bush made plans to run for the Oval Office in 1988, there was great concern over Pat Robertson's entry into the race.

The Bush people were apprehensive that Robertson could siphon off enough conservative votes to throw the election to Dukakis and the Democrats, and perhaps even more terrified that Jim Bakker would throw the full weight of the PTL network behind him. As the outspoken head of the Moral Majority, Jerry Falwell was a powerful and influential force, a frequent guest of the Reagan White House, a close confidant of George Bush, and a familiar face on Capitol Hill.

Early in their campaigns, candidates George Bush and Pat Robertson got in touch with Jim in hope of gaining his support, fully realizing that the far-flung PTL communications empire and its millions of loyal viewers could be a critical factor in their success. Even though Jim always honored Pat, crediting him as the man who allowed him to learn television, Robertson had barely if ever spoken our names since we left his ministry. I recall long after we left his organization that Pat had a Founder's Day and both Jim and I were invited to it.

I do not know why Pat even invited us. He did not even acknowledge that Jim was there. The celebration was held in a huge white tent filled with tables all decorated in white and gold. At the front of that huge tent was the head table, reserved for the people who had had a part in building the CBN television network. There were people sitting at that table that I know were not part of building that network.

And here was Jim, the man who worked so hard for Pat, the man who almost singlehandedly had built the network so many years before, the man who started *The 700 Club*—here was Jim Bakker sitting at a table in the back of the tent. Pat never mentioned his name once. I ached for Jim that day. Jim never said much to me about it, but I knew that inside he must be hurting bad.

As we left the tent, Pat and his wife, Dede, were standing in a receiving line. Pat shook Jim's hand and thanked him for coming. Pat could be so cold. Of course, this was long before he decided to run for the presidency. But that moment said a lot to me about the type of man Pat was.

But when Robertson realized that the PTL network could be of enormous help to him, he swallowed his pride and came down to Heritage USA. In fact we still have footage of him there, enthusiastically talking about his run for the presidency and treating Jim like his best friend again. But from the moment of his arrival, I sensed that Pat couldn't believe what had been achieved.

"You know, Jim, who would have thought that you could have gone on to build your own television ministry."

"Uh, thank you, Pat," Jim said tentatively, not really knowing which way to take the remark.

"No, Jim, trust me. I mean that in a good way," Pat said, attempting to clear up any confusion. However, I think what particularly irked him was the fact that Jim wasn't even a college graduate. Robertson was into education, so finding someone who could accomplish all this without higher schooling just rubbed him the wrong way. "Just look how you've grown."

"We're getting there."

"Look, Jim, I know we've had our ups and downs. But I've always believed in you. I believed in you from the very first. I had a powerful belief in what you could do, didn't I?"

"I've always said that," replied Jim, thinking back to the days when Robertson was running CBN on a shoestring budget. "I've always said that without you I wouldn't be where I am today."

"I appreciate your words, Jim. I truly do," said Robertson, turning up the wattage in his smile. "With all my heart."

"It's good to be speaking to you again, Pat."

"Too long—it's been much too long, Jim. Much too much water under the bridge. But we're going to fix all that. We won't let that happen again, will we?"

"Of course we won't."

Not to be outdone, George Bush contacted Jim and waxed effusive about the great admiration he had for PTL, Heritage USA, and everything else Jim had accomplished. "Barbara and I are great fans of yours, Jim. Just great fans of the show."

"Thank you, Mr. Vice President. Those are very kind words."

"You and Tammy are terrific. PTL is certainly a huge undertaking."

"A lot of work."

"You said it. Anything that's worthwhile takes a lot of

work. That's why it took real leadership to get all this off the ground."

"Thank you."

"Jim, you know how much the president and Nancy admire what you've done. How you've stayed the course for decency."

"I've always felt the president was on my side."

"He certainly is, Jim, certainly is. We're both on your side. That's why it's important to keep that ball rolling. To make sure that what Ronald Reagan started doesn't get swept under the rug."

"That's true."

"We're all going to have to stick together in this thing. We can't divide up into little groups, no matter how well intentioned those groups might be. Because that's what the Democrats want us to do. They would like to see us divided—you know, divide and conquer. Now, listen to me, Jim. We have to keep the conservative vote under one roof."

"I see what you mean."

And so the conversation continued, until Bush had to leave.

But no political group would enjoy the support of PTL, because Jim's firm policy in all such matters was to stay totally neutral, although privately we were Republicans.

Nevertheless, and this is strictly my opinion, the Bush people knew of Jim's previous affiliation with Robertson and the similarity of their religious stances, so they may have assumed Jim's silence was merely a prelude to an announcement of support—but unfortunately not for them.

Jim Bakker was a wild card, a bomb that could explode in their faces at any moment, and they just weren't willing to take the risk. This is where I believe Jerry Falwell saw his chance. Falwell would show the government how to get Jim Bakker, and as compensation he would get all of

PTL—no questions asked. It is hard for me to believe that without outright complicity from the highest levels Jerry Falwell could have gone to the extremes he did without incurring the wrath of somebody in government.

Looking back, I realize how incredibly naïve Jim was. He just didn't realize that you had to make friends in high places, that one hand washes the other. Richard Dortch constantly urged Jim to pursue friendships with rich and powerful individuals.

"Jim," he would say. "You always need to have people in your corner who are heavy hitters, people who know how to get things done with one phone call. That's the way of the world, Jim, the law of the jungle. You've got to start making some friends high up in politics, in industry, in the financial and business world, and in the media. Because you never know when you might need them. Now, don't get me wrong. You and Tammy have really nice friends now, but they're not influential. They're not going to be able to help you out of any jams."

It was a blind spot Jim had. He didn't really feel comfortable around movers and shakers, those who wielded real authority, maybe because he didn't feel good enough about himself.

Looking back, I've often speculated about what would have happened if Jim Bakker had indeed supported George Bush for the presidency. What if he had ingratiated himself, say, as Jerry Falwell often did, with the most authoritative men and women behind the scenes? Tell me, would the subsequent prosecution ever have taken place? Would Jim have remained a free man? Would he still be heading up PTL? Or wouldn't it have made a difference? Your guess is as good as mine.

To return to the day that changed my life: While there had been serious problems with Dortch, we believed this present crisis far transcended anything that had happened between us previously, and it was therefore in our mutual interest to solve it together. So upon his arrival at our home in California, there were hugs and kisses; then the three of us sat down on the couch. "We're so glad you're finally here," I said.

"First of all, Jim and Tammy," Dortch announced cheerfully, "don't worry, everything is going to be fine. I just left Falwell and his men at the hotel." Of course, the very fact that Reverend Dortch had flown in with Falwell on his private jet should have raised a red flag, but somehow it didn't.

"Are you sure that we can trust Falwell?" Jim asked Dortch. "Is he a man of his word?"

"I have complete confidence in him," Dortch responded. "I wouldn't be here if I didn't."

Jim mulled this over. "I don't understand. Why would he want to help a charismatic ministry when he himself is Baptist?"

"Because if they can tarnish you, they can tarnish him, and all the other religious leaders in the country. Jim, let's face it. In unity there is strength. Falwell realizes that."

But Jim was still wavering. "How did he find out about the Jessica Hahn problem?" he asked.

Dortch leaned back a little and took a deep breath. "Just as I told you on the phone," he replied, shifting his weight. "Swaggart spilled the beans."

"But who told Swaggart?"

"Beats me. Could have been anybody. Maybe Fletcher. Even Profeta. Roper. Weitsman—or Hahn herself." I noticed at this point that Dortch left himself off the list. "But that's not really the issue now. The issue is how do we best handle the situation and make absolutely sure that PTL is preserved."

As Jim continued questioning him, I observed Dortch getting more and more uncomfortable. And I grew more and more suspicious. But Dortch's honey-tongued voice gave all the right answers, and I could see that Jim was believing everything he said.

"The idea can't miss. It's practically a sure thing."

"Okay, how will it work?" Jim inquired anxiously.

"Well, this is the plan Falwell and I have worked out," Dortch replied, taking time to emphasize every word. "Falwell will take over the ministry for you for three or four weeks."

Instantly Jim became alarmed. "What do you mean, take over?" But Dortch quickly settled him down.

"Well, at least that's what it will look like."

"I'm not sure I'm following."

"The bottom line is that nothing will change as far as the public is concerned. I will be in charge as usual—doing the TV show as usual."

"I'm still not—"

"It's real simple, Jim. You'll videotape an apology about the Jessica Hahn thing, and we'll play it on PTL and tell the partners that you've decided to take a leave of absence. Falwell will go on the air and explain that he's temporarily taking charge in order to help you and encourage you. Then in four weeks you can come back to Charlotte and everything will be fine. All the partners will see that you're genuinely remorseful."

"So you're saying four weeks and that's it?"

"At the most, at the very most." Then Dortch started really pounding away. "Look, Jim, you've got to do this. You *need* to do this! And then we'll let you come back in four weeks. Four weeks is nothing. In four weeks we'll put you right back where you belong."

I listened in ever-increasing horror until finally I had to say something. "Are you sure there isn't some other way of doing this? I have to tell you, this doesn't seem right to me."

"Tammy, there is no other way," Dortch pronounced,

abruptly standing up to leave. "Just trust me." Those were the last three words Dortch ever spoke directly to me. "Now it's getting late and I need to get back to the hotel. Falwell wants to meet at nine o'clock tomorrow morning. We'll see you then." Jim looked relieved; I was panic-stricken. Something was terribly wrong, but I just couldn't put my finger on it.

Jim and I tossed it back and forth half the night. "Listen, could Swaggart have found out from Dortch?" I asked Jim, not actually expecting an answer. "I know they've been friends for years."

"I don't think so. Even Dortch wouldn't betray the confidence of a hurting man."

"Are you a hundred percent sure?"

"I'm not a hundred percent sure of anything," came the reply.

"Could it be that Dortch told Falwell too, so that when Swaggart called him, Jerry already knew and was playing it cool?"

"Look, Tam, I'm getting a migraine from trying to figure this all out. It doesn't matter who told what to who or when."

"Somebody is being disloyal to you, Jim, and you better find out who before it's too late."

"Can't we just wait till tomorrow? Let's just see what happens. I'm sure it will all be resolved when we get to the hotel."

"That's just the point, Jim. Why are we going to the hotel? Why are we meeting them on their turf? Why don't they come over to our place? Why is everyone being so secretive?" But Jim just withdrew. As we finally got into bed around 3:00 A.M., I whispered softly to him, "There's something wrong here, Jim. Be careful. Be very careful."

After a couple of restless hours' sleep, Jim and I drove to the Palm Springs Hotel at around eight-thirty in the morning and went up to Dortch's room. After chatting for a few minutes, the three of us went down to the lobby. There we met Jerry Falwell and his operatives. Falwell embraced us with open arms. I can still picture the scene: Falwell in his immaculately tailored, conservative gray business suit surrounded by four or five of his associates, also wearing gray suits.

The only person wearing something flashy was Grutman, whose sports jacket was just a little too tight around the middle. For the meeting a large suite had been reserved, and after everybody made their introductions, we all adjourned upstairs. Falwell suggested the three of us go into the bedroom in order to ensure privacy.

In the bedroom Falwell shut the door and put his huge arms around me and Jim. Tears came to his eyes as he spoke. "Jim and Tammy, you know how much I have always loved your ministry. My children love it too. My son was just at Heritage USA, and he had a wonderful time. In fact he couldn't quit talking about how much fun he had on the water slide and just what an amazing place it was. He said it was the best vacation he had ever had."

Then Jerry projected a look of deep concern; his voice became lower. "Now, Jim and Tammy, I've been getting calls from Jimmy Swaggart recently, and he knows all about the Jessica Hahn situation. He was asking me for my help in having you removed as the head of PTL. Swaggart thinks that you are no longer worthy of running such a large ministry, and he feels you should be forced to give PTL up."

Once again his arm went around Jim's shoulder, a comforting arm, the same arm of forgiveness that a father might offer a son who just broke a neighbor's window. Jerry was very convincing; even I was taken in for a moment.

"I think Jimmy Swaggart is wrong," Falwell continued. "We all make mistakes, and he should know that better than anybody. In any event, I wouldn't want anyone going through my dirty laundry. We are just human, and sometimes we fail. But God forgives us, therefore we must forgive ourselves too."

Falwell drew my husband even closer to him. "Jim, someone tried to destroy another minister friend of mine a few years ago; but I went in and helped him. They tried to disgrace him, but the man renounced his sins and his ministry was saved. I want to do the same thing for you and Tammy," he declared, flashing us his most benevolent smile. "After all, we are all brothers and sisters in the Lord, and it's time we all start working together as one instead of being divided."

Bingo! I could see that really struck a responsive chord in Jim. Jerry was tossing out the bait, and Jim was buying it, hook, line, and sinker. It had always been a goal of Jim's to see all denominations working in accord. Falwell sure knew what he was doing. "Now, Jim, I've talked this over with Dortch on the plane on the way here, and I feel like we've come up with a workable solution."

Then he proceeded to outline the same scenario Dortch had offered. He would take over the ministry for three or four weeks to give the partners a chance to hear Jim's apology for the Jessica Hahn problem.

"But I won't be staying in Charlotte," Jerry added. "I've got my own ministry to tend to." Falwell concluded by saying that he would videotape a message to the partners that he was standing behind Jim, supporting him 100 percent; also he would urge the people to forgive Jim. He would encourage them to stand with Jim in every way to continue the great work that PTL was doing.

Then he put his arms around us again and prayed for us both. Tears welled in his eyes again. We left that bedroom and went back out into the suite to meet Grutman and the other men Falwell had just happened to bring along. My mind started going wild again. Why would he bring a lawyer if all he wanted was to help Jim out with some moral support?

Suddenly I felt claustrophobic, a little nauseated. All I wanted was to get out of there. Telling Jim I'd meet him back at the house, I left—but not without warning him to be careful.

Upon arriving home, I immediately went out and sat at a little table by the pool. Everything was happening so fast. How much more could I take? I had only learned about Jessica Hahn the day before, and here she had become the focal point of the most important decision Jim would ever make in his life—in our lives. It was too much to bear.

The sun was getting hot as I sat there thinking, hurting inside and scared, so I went to the kitchen and got a pitcher of lemonade. Just as I sat down again I heard a car drive up. It was Jim and Grutman. Jim looked miserable as they came out and sat down next to me at the table. My heart ached for him.

"Tam, we need to talk to you," Jim began. "I told them I wouldn't make any decisions until I talked to you first. They're all waiting for me back at the hotel." I couldn't figure out for the life of me why he had Falwell's lawyer with him.

"Honey, here's the plan Falwell and Grutman have worked out." And as he spoke, I couldn't believe my ears! They wanted Jim to resign from the board of directors with a letter, *which they would write for him.* Grutman told Jim that in reality he would still be running the ministry through Dortch. When the four weeks were up, the board of directors would reinstate him—and he would automatically take back the TV show.

"Think of it like you would a play," Grutman said. "And, Jim, you are the lead character. It's only a play, and you are just playacting. People will recognize how remorseful you are by the fact that you've given up your ministry because you are no longer worthy of running it."

Those were his precise words. I couldn't believe he was comparing this tragedy to a play and playacting. "Wait a minute!" I interrupted. "Does it mention anywhere in this agreement about Jim returning? Is that part written down?" Grutman was glaring at me. Sweat dampened his brow, as if he was scared to death that I was going to mess up their plan.

"Now, Tammy, you know putting that in writing would only appear to invalidate the sincerity of Jim's noble gesture," said Grutman smoothly. "I believe it's better to keep that part of the arrangement on a handshake basis." That's when I knew the whole scheme stunk. We had already been destroyed by people who insisted on working on a handshake basis.

I looked at Jim in desperation. "Jim, please don't do this!" I begged. "Please don't give up your place on the board of directors. You will never get it back if you do. It will rob you of your power! That is what they want, Jim. Please don't do it!" I was practically down on my knees at this point, pleading with him, but Jim just sat there like a zombie, as if he were paralyzed. "This is not just your ministry, this is something I've worked hard for too. Don't give it away. Don't give PTL away. Don't give away your birthright!"

Finally Jim said, "Tam, I have to get back."

"If you feel you need a few weeks off while this all blows over, fine! Just don't resign from the board. Tell the partners what's happening. Talk to them. They'll understand. They really will understand. I don't care what Dortch is telling you—something isn't right here. Please don't sign anything! Please, Jim! Just listen to me this once!" Well, if looks could kill, Grutman would have had me dead on the spot.

"Tam, I have to get back," Jim repeated.

"Jim, please . . ."

"They're waiting for me."

As they left, I could see that Jim was petrified by fear and anguish. I don't know what he thought or believed at that moment. All I know is that nothing I said had taken hold in his mind.

I think everyone felt betrayed by what Jim allowed to happen that day. Why didn't he stop and think about what this was going to do to his family? Why didn't he stop and think what it was going to do to the faithful partners of PTL? Why didn't he stop and think about the effect it was going to have on the thousands of people who worked at PTL?

I believe he was so scared of screaming headlines in *The Charlotte Observer*—JIM BAKKER RAPES CHURCH SECRETARY—that he couldn't think straight. Time and time again, Falwell, Dortch, and Grutman had told him those headlines would be running all over the United States if Jim didn't do what they said. They stampeded him into making a foolhardy decision. It's a mystery to me. Jim is such an intelligent man. I will never know why he couldn't see through their ploy. And why he couldn't see that Dortch, by going along with the plan, was serving as the catalyst for the destruction of Jim Bakker.

Without first asking the people who loved PTL, I believe Jim had no right to sign it away. Before saying another word to Falwell, he should have gotten on a plane and flown back to Charlotte. He should have gone to the board of directors and told them what was happening. He should have talked to Roe Messner and the other men he trusted. And he should have gone on TV and talked to the partners about the situation.

Had he performed this one act of courage, I know that everything would have turned out differently. Jim should have stood up and said out loud, "I made a mistake seven years ago, a terrible mistake that has haunted me every single day of my life. Do you want me to give it up, do you want me to leave PTL—or will you forgive me?"

And the people would have forgiven him. They would have rallied by the millions. In every state, in every town across America, they would have condemned the black-mail by Jessica Hahn. If only Jim would have gone on the offensive, summoning the courage within himself, instead of caving in. If only Jim had . . . if only . . .

If there is one thing I've learned, it's never do anything important quickly, and never do anything out of fear. Jim acted without thinking. He didn't speak to the people who really cared about him and the ministry. Therefore, as they agreed, the next day Grutman wrote out Jim's letter of res-ignation from the board of directors, and Jim numbly signed it. With a single stroke of that pen, I knew it was all over.

Jerry Falwell had found the key to Jim's soul and shrewdly turned it, unlocking the golden doors to PTL.

All Hell
Breaks Loose

J IM BAKKER RESIGNS FROM PTL, JERRY FALWELL AS-
SUMES LEADERSHIP, blared the huge black-and-white
headline of *The Charlotte Observer* on March 20,
1987, a date that will forever make me cringe, the day my
worst fears came true. Jessica Hahn became a household
name, and overnight we became the vortex of a national
storm, with news coverage equaling that given to the O. J.
Simpson trial years later.

We were still out in Palm Desert when everything blew
up, still shell-shocked by the rapid-fire barrage. About a
week after we lost PTL, Roe Messner got an interesting surprise. It was a direct call from Jerry Falwell. "Roe, I was
wondering if you could fly to Lynchburg and meet with me.
I have something I would like you to do for Jim and
Tammy."

"Sure, Jerry," Roe responded, somewhat taken aback.
"I'll be more than pleased to do anything I can." On the
very next day Roe flew to Lynchburg and was picked up at
the airport by one of Falwell's men. He was driven to the
Hilton Inn.

"Hello, Roe, thank you for coming," Falwell said warmly. "Brother, I have a message I would like you to personally deliver to Jim and Tammy in California. I have made out a list of things here that I would like you to give them. It shows some of the extras they've been getting at PTL. I know that they're having a hard time of it, and I'd like to help them out until they can get back on their feet again." Roe was moved by Falwell's act of kindness.

"Sure, Jerry, I'll be happy to fly out and personally deliver your message to Jim and Tammy." With that Falwell handed Roe a piece of paper. And this is what was written down on it: "I want to provide Jim and Tammy with a $300,000 salary this year, plus pay for a year's worth of health insurance and telephone expenses. I want them to be able to keep their maid, a secretary, and a guard for a year."

"Well, Jerry, that sure is kind of you. I know that they will appreciate your thoughtfulness. They are hurting so bad."

"Now, Roe, there is one condition," Falwell added. "I want you to have them copy this statement on their personal stationery exactly as I have written it and then send it back with you."

"Well, thank you, Jerry. I will, and I'm sure your kindness will help ease some of the terrible pressure they're under. God bless you, brother." Roe was shortly off to the airport with the list Falwell had given him, and the next day there was a knock on our door.

"Roe, what are you doing here? It's so good to see you again." Jim welcomed him in, and after a few minutes of general conversation Roe got down to the reason for his visit.

"Jim, I've come at the request of Falwell," Roe said with a gleam in his eye. "I have some good news that he's asked me to bring you." Both of us instantly brightened. Maybe

Jerry was already planning to have Jim return and video-tape his apology, just as we had agreed. But instead Roe took out Falwell's note and gave it to us.

"Wait a minute," I interrupted. "This doesn't sound like we'll be back anytime soon. It doesn't sound like the four weeks we talked about."

Jim mulled over my concerns. "Look, Tam, I think this reflects Jerry's compassion for us. Just in case things take a little longer than planned. In my opinion, it actually makes everything look more legitimate. It gives me faith that Jerry is honoring his commitment to us."

"Could this be only to make Jerry look good?" I asked. "Some kind of public relations ploy?"

"Even if it is," Jim responded. "I think we're too desperate not to accept."

"Well, that's certainly the truth!" At least we were all in agreement on that. Jim looked over the statement one more time.

"Roe, are you sure of all this?"

"Yes, Jim, I just came from Lynchburg, where I met with Jerry personally, and he wrote these things down in his own handwriting. All he wants you to do is copy it as he wrote it on your own letterhead in your own handwriting. Then he wants me to deliver it back to him."

"Tam, go find a piece of stationery," Jim said. I found a piece of my stationery, which had a little picture of me on it.

"Will this do, Roe?" I asked.

"It's just what he asked for. It will be fine." I took the list and copied Falwell's words. We signed our names at the bottom.

"Roe," Jim said. "I want you to write something down on Tammy's stationery for me."

"Sure, Jim, what do you want me to write?"

"Write that Tammy and I are not making any demands on PTL at all." So Roe wrote that down at the bottom.

"Please tell Jerry we both say thank you. And, Roe, thanks for coming all this way."

"I was more than glad to do it, Jim. I'm praying for you." With that Roe left to go back to the airport. What happened next was beyond belief.

Practically the next day Falwell marched into the TV studio. Looking indignantly right into the television camera, he announced, "I just received this letter from Jim and Tammy making the following demands." He then read out the list: $300,000 salary, health insurance, phone, maid, secretary, and security guard!

This doesn't look like someone who is repentant but like a greedy person, Jerry proclaimed. His outrage intensified, and he started calling this, notoriously, the "wish list." Falwell sure knew how to hit a man while he's down, when he can't defend himself. But the "wish list" was merely used as the first bullet fired against Jim Bakker in a veritable holy war of words.

It was now apparent that Falwell was determined to make Jim look so repugnant that he could never return to PTL. He said Jim was a homosexual. He said Jim had stolen money. He said we had Swiss bank accounts. Jerry Falwell even made a big deal out of our old houseboat. Falwell took everything that was precious to us and our family and trashed it before the world. All the trumped-up lies came straight from Falwell's mouth. He knew the Christian world, so he knew what buttons you push to destroy someone. He also knew human nature. He knew the key words that incite and infuriate and enrage—he was no dumb man! Words like "sex," "stealing," "greedy," "homosexual," "wealthy"—he used these words as his keys to Jim's destruction.

He had just used Roe to make it look like Jim was greedily demanding everything on that list. He was standing in front of the CNN cameras, a minister of the gospel, looking into the faces of the people and telling terrible, destructive lies that would end up wrecking not only our family but an entire ministry. A true born-again Christian could never do that to his brother in Christ. It was at that moment that I wondered if Jerry Falwell had ever really had a real born-again experience. A true born-again experience changes a wicked heart and replaces wickedness with love. There was certainly no evidence that change had happened within Jerry Falwell's heart.

Roe was in shock. He could not believe what he was hearing. He called Jim on the phone so shaken he could hardly talk. "Jim," he managed to say, "I am so sorry that I was part of what Jerry Falwell did to you and Tammy. I only wanted to help you. I never dreamed he could be using me as part of a scheme to destroy you. Please forgive me, Jim."

The networks were like sharks at a feeding frenzy. They went crazy with the story. ABC, NBC, and CBS dispatched immense trucks with direct satellite uplinks to Heritage USA and parked them right outside the gate. The story was going live around the world. The BBC picked it up; Parisians drooled over the sordid details; even in Taiwan the press was having a field day. Swarming over Heritage USA were more than two hundred reporters, interviewing anyone in sight, and when there was no one in sight, they interviewed one another. They roamed the grounds as if they owned the place. Their appetites were insatiable.

The most powerful and prestigious news organizations sent in their top correspondents, many even having the audacity to take up residence at our hotel. You couldn't miss them. Seasoned staff representing *The New York Times*, *The Washington Post*, the *Los Angeles Times*, *Newsweek*, *Time*, *USA Today*, *U.S. News & World Report*, and dozens of others feasted at our restaurants, exchanging rumors and gossip that instantly got transmitted as facts.

Within only one week our pictures were blasted all over the covers of *Time*, *U.S. News & World Report*, and *News-*

week. The broadcast of the *PTL* program went on every day as planned, but under tremendous stress. Hundreds of reporters climbed over one another to get into the studio, snapping shots of whatever and whomever they could, sticking microphones in the partners' faces as if they were criminals.

The shock and confusion hit PTL like a sudden death in the family. The vast majority of the staff and partners couldn't believe their eyes and ears. Jim's sudden departure was unfathomable. It had to be a bad dream. Even more incredible was the fact that complete control had been seized by Jerry Falwell, a man who didn't even share the same faith that we did, a complete outsider.

The whole situation was outlandish, a farce beyond belief. Employees walked around in a daze, too stunned to accept what was going on. Over and over they asked one another questions. "Oh God, how could this be happening to our beloved PTL?" "Who could possibly do this to us?" "Where are Jim and Tammy? Why don't they come back and explain to us what's happening?" But there were no answers.

Far beyond the idyllic gates of Heritage USA, the entire Christian community seemed to be reeling from the charges and countercharges. Our management team was equally in the dark, without a clue as to what to do. No one knew if they would even have a job tomorrow. In spite of that, to demonstrate their support for us, thousands of yellow ribbons were tied around acres of trees at Heritage USA; but Dortch made the staff take them down. Dortch was in all his glory. He was now in charge of PTL—Falwell's right-hand man!

Meanwhile our home was under siege by the media. Under their constant surveillance we were virtually held hostage. They'd stand up on top of their trucks and try to get a clear shot into our home with their cameras, so we had to hang sheets over the windows, since we didn't have curtains. Helicopters passed back and forth, sounding as though they were going to land on the roof. I knew then exactly how poor souls dying of thirst felt out on the prairie, watching the vultures circling overhead, waiting to pick their dying carcasses clean.

There wasn't any way to get groceries without being followed. There wasn't any way to do anything without being stalked by members of the press. I remember Jamie wanted to go out and play basketball in the little courtyard, and they would keep the cameras on him playing till it would make him so nervous he'd have to come back inside.

We were like exhibits at a zoo. I felt so sorry for our children. They couldn't comprehend what was happening to them and to their mom and dad. We were painfully honest with them, and yet they looked up at us with eyes that still did not understand. Outside our house the road was three and four deep with reporters, TV trucks, and cameras. Lights like you'd see in a baseball stadium were erected for when it got dark. They had satellite dishes sticking up in the air. Rows of Porta-Johns were moved in to accommodate the hundreds of reporters.

In order for our family to escape the house without detection, we would have to lie down on the floors of cars; and then friends would cover us with blankets. For if the media ever found out we were in a car, they would follow us day and night with their vans and cameras.

Every so often we would appear at our front door and instantly be barraged with one question after another. "Hey, Jim, Jerry Falwell says that you're a homosexual. Is that true?"

"Absolutely not. I am not a—"

"Then why would Jerry Falwell say that?"

"You'll have to ask him."

"So you're calling Jerry Falwell a liar? Why would he lie?"

"All I can say is that I'm not—"

"In other words, you categorically deny that you're a homosexual."

"I'm denying it because it's not true."

I have to admit Jerry Falwell was smart. He knew that the partners would probably forgive Jim for an indiscretion with a woman. There were certainly other preachers—like Jimmy Swaggart—who had fallen from grace and come back. But Falwell knew that many people could never forgive Jim if he were homosexual.

"Is Jessica Hahn the only woman you've had an affair with? Weren't there others?"

To which my reply would be "If there were others, they would be coming out of the woodwork. They'd be all over the TV, wouldn't they?"

"Jim, what about little old ladies eating cat food because they sent their money to PTL?" On and on it went. The same questions all the time. Jerry Falwell said this, Jerry Falwell said that, and then we had to defend ourselves. I couldn't even watch TV. No matter what the station, every few minutes there would be a flashing "update" on what the media was heralding as "the Holy War" between Jim Bakker and Jerry Falwell.

Even then, if Jim would have taken Falwell to court, challenged him in public, I'm convinced our partners would have stood by him. In the first month after the story broke, thousands and thousands of letters and phone calls were received at PTL, begging us to come back, telling us that all had been forgiven. But Jim just didn't have what it takes to go back.

My children suffered the most through the ordeal. They were not allowed back on the grounds of PTL, which they loved so much; they were not allowed back in the school they'd been attending there; they lost their friends, even their home in Charlotte and most of what was inside. Since the ministry leased our car, that had been taken as well.

We were forced to come back from Palm Desert to claim our furniture and whatever other personal items we still had. I will never forget that day as long as I live. The terror of it still haunts me. They came in like you see Nazis do in the movies. They walked through the rooms of our house like we were not even there—through the bedrooms, into my closets, even into the bathrooms. I don't know what they were looking for. We certainly didn't have anything of much value.

We had no paintings or great works of art. It was just an old house filled with what was left of our family and our memories. I remember we had taken the kids and left town for a few weeks to get away from the press. But all the time we were away, Falwell's men were trying to get into our house and empty it before we could get back. In our absence, Jim's sister, Donna, had been staying at our place. I can still recall her frantically calling us as they were trying to break in—even with her there. It was such a horrible time. I have tried so hard to forget, but still, so many years later, I sometimes have nightmares about what they did to our family.

People who remained loyal to us helped us pack. I will never forget those unselfish men and women as they got all the boxes ready. Having twenty-five years of living crated up was painful. I can still see Jamie and Tammy Sue trying to help by being strong. Jim was almost catatonic. I was sobbing so hard that I could hardly stand. I begged the movers sent by Falwell, "Please let us keep our bed! Please just let us keep our bed!" I didn't want to see them auction it off. I didn't want the news media to come in and take pictures and make fun of the bed we had slept in.

We packed boxes of dishes, knickknacks, books, toys, and pictures, then Falwell's men would deliberately unpack them to make sure we weren't stealing anything that belonged to PTL. I don't know how they decided what belonged to PTL and what didn't. It was our home, and we didn't have anything that I knew of that belonged to the ministry. It was just our stuff. The memories that families are made of—personal mementos, things that are treasures only to us. To see them handle our belongings and rummage through those boxes that our friends were working so hard to pack made me physically sick. I wanted to vomit!

I was so worried for Jamie and Tammy Sue. How would it affect them to see people who once worked for Jim and me doing this to us? Jamie was only a little boy, ten years old. He ran outside and climbed up in the tree house his daddy had built for him a couple of years before. While he was out there he saw about twelve men carrying the doghouse up the hill. What a pitiful sight, those hefty men and four little dogs looking at them taking away their house too.

We ended up leaving most of our furniture. We were just too weak to fight for it, and at that point I didn't care about furniture or anything else except my precious children, who were suffering so awfully. By the time we were supposed to leave, the whole place was empty. I don't know why, but I stayed in the house all by myself that night. For some reason I slept on the floor in the closet of our bedroom with Tuppins, my little five-pound Yorkie.

Everything I loved was gone, every*one* I loved was gone, and it was just me and Tuppins and that big old house. All night long I didn't sleep. I just lay there in the dark remembering the wonderful times we'd had there. I could still picture Tammy Sue deciding that Jamie Charles had slept in her room long enough and it was time to kick him out. So we decided to build him his own room. Jamie was so thrilled. "Just make sure it doesn't look like a girl's room, Mom!" was his only command.

I recalled when we built Jim an office in the basement. He wanted to try and spend a little more time at home; but Jim didn't use the office as much as anticipated. It was just too hard getting away from PTL once he got there. Too many people needing to talk with him about too many things, always one thing after another.

Then there was our dining room. I remember making it just like a little restaurant with five small tables instead of just one big one. I put tiny white lights in the ficus trees that filled the room. They were live, not silk, and I loved that! I loved anything that was alive. It was such a charming room, with a distinct warmth and personality all its own. Our dining room was always filled with loved and trusted friends.

At almost every gathering were the Dortches, as well as Doug and Laura Lee Oldham. I thought of Blair and Judy Bycura and their two children, who were about the age of our two kids. There wasn't a day that went by without us getting together at some time. Judy and I spent hundreds of hours together in those years while the guys were off doing their things. Her husband was a podiatrist. Judy looked just like Sandy Duncan, the actress.

Our kids had played together constantly. Darin, Ryan, Tammy Sue, and Jamie—what a team they were! I was so glad that Judy and I had each other as neighbors. I could share anything with Judy and know it would go no further.

Now the house was quiet and still. Here and there I could hear a familiar creak. There was no laughter, no sound of little feet running up the stairs, no dogs barking joyfully as I came through the door, no phones ringing, no warmth, no love, just an emptiness that overwhelmed my heart. But the memories continued to pour through me. It was like my mind was on fast forward, all the images coming and going in a blur.

Stepping out of the closet, I walked through that house for the last time, saying good-bye to what would never be again. In each room I stopped a moment, paused and reflected. But I couldn't linger much longer. It was already morning. Time to look forward, not back. There were far more urgent matters at hand. So I fought back the sobs and asked myself, "Where are we going to go? What are we going to do?" I don't think we ever formally said good-bye to Blair and Judy. It just hurt too bad.

With just a few suitcases in the trunk, we drove up the hill and tried not to look back. Today our family home is just a black hole in the ground. It burned down a couple of years after we left it. Soon afterward someone placed a single red rose where the front door had once been. I think it was one of the staff members who still loved us. That gesture, that simple act of remembrance, meant so much to me.

I felt that God allowed that house to burn down. It was a closure for our family. All that was left was burned wood and the cement under the garage where we had all put our names while it was still wet—Jim, Tammy, Tammy Sue, Jamie, Blair, Judy, Darin, and Ryan. Beside the names it read: "We are going to eat fish tonight at the fish camp!" Simple words that mean nothing to you but everything to me.

The Blitzkrieg Continues

*J*erry Falwell's steamroller flattened our lives and everything else in sight, but nobody had the courage to stop his plunder of PTL. Falwell ordered his workers to dig a huge pit and then buried thousands of my recordings, and books we had written, and Bibles with our pictures on them. They dumped all the inventory at midnight, thinking no one would see them, but their actions were secretly filmed by a camera crew as they covered the landfill with cement.

The pillage continued unabated. From the Heritage Grand Hotel, witnesses saw truckloads of furniture being hauled away, presumably to Lynchburg. It was beautiful, expensive furniture, bought and paid for by the partners of PTL. Falwell forced all the employees into signing loyalty statements and warned them they could no longer correspond with us—or even say our names—or they would be fired. My secretary was among the first to leave. Claiming that he was just reducing costs, Falwell let hundreds of staff members go, only to bring in replacements from Lynchburg for every single one he fired.

One of the first people Falwell let go was my mom. She

needed her job, and she pleaded with him to no avail. Losing her position broke my mom's heart. Something went out of her after that. She was never quite the same. After she had raised eight children, that job had given her a new lease on life, and a new self-confidence and independence. With those two words—"you're fired"—Jerry Falwell destroyed Mom's dream and her security. She would never have hurt him in any way.

But that was Jerry's standard way of operating. In a decision billed as an economy move, Falwell transferred all mail operations over to his brother in Lynchburg. Heavy sacks brimming with mail would arrive every day, and Falwell's people would just *take the money out* and throw the letters away. Personal letters addressed to us were trashed, despite Falwell's pledge that they would be forwarded. Even checks with our names on them were pilfered.

But this was just the beginning of Falwell's heavy-handed tactics. One day Pinkerton armed guards showed up with no warning like invading storm troopers. They surrounded the administration building in a massive show of sheer force. In complete bewilderment, staff members peered out their windows as megaphone-wielding guards in the atrium below blared out that the whole place was now fully secured; no one dared leave the premises without first being searched. And they meant business!

Anyone entering or leaving the building was harassed. Handbags were opened and examined. Contents of briefcases were rifled. Packages were unwrapped. Even Roe Messner wasn't allowed entrance. Jerry had clenched his iron fist. This was no longer a democracy, it was a dictatorship. Apparently Falwell felt nothing but contempt for the people working at PTL. They weren't his followers, they owed no loyalty to him, so therefore they were his enemies, a hostile force to be demoralized.

One of the most valuable items Falwell was able to wrest

from PTL was our mailing list, a veritable gold mine worth millions of dollars. By invading our computer records, Jerry was able to obtain the names and addresses of every person who ever sent in a contribution. This gave him a powerful weapon against us, plus a tool for raising millions of dollars.

Shortly after his takeover the partners were fairly besieged by mail from Falwell, asking them to donate as much as they could. These good people couldn't figure out what was happening, since they had had nothing to do with him beforehand. With the mailing list Falwell held the heart and soul of PTL in the palm of his hand, and he had every intention of putting the squeeze on.

But perhaps the most sought-after possession of PTL— the satellite network, the space-age communications link to virtually hundreds of stations around the world— Falwell was never able to get his hands on. It eventually fell into the hands of Ted Turner, who was busy building his own media empire. That international link would have made Falwell the premier force in televangelism, with enough media clout to dominate the airwaves. Luckily, no matter how he schemed, begged, and borrowed, he just couldn't pull it off. I guess the good Lord decided to draw the line somewhere.

Acting as official "spokesperson" for PTL during this time was the lawyer Norman Roy Grutman. Finally, after being paid hundreds of thousands of dollars as PTL's attorney, he saw his chance to have his moment in the sun, and he wasn't particularly intent on letting it go. But although Grutman's behavior was predictable, Doug Oldham's was not.

One of the saddest things that happened, and which hurt us the most, was when Doug and Laura Lee walked out on us and went back to Jerry Falwell. I was in shock. Doug was Jim's best friend in the ministry. These were people to whom we had bared our souls. Our children saw the Oldhams as a surrogate aunt and uncle, and here they were going back to work for the man who had wrecked our lives.

Remember that before he came to PTL, Doug had worked for many years as a gospel singer on Falwell's television show, *The Old Time Gospel Hour.* But when Doug became ill and was no longer able to work, Falwell kicked him out—at least that was the story Doug told Jim.

Through the years I have heard rumors that while Doug was with PTL he was secretly feeding Jerry Falwell information. Many have accused him of being a spy planted within the ministry. We knew from time to time that Doug called Falwell, but we thought nothing of it, knowing they were former coworkers.

Doug knew whenever Jim and I were having problems, so if he did inform Falwell, then Jerry had at least one reliable source to confirm our situation. What Doug did or said is between him and God. All that I know, as of this writing, is that he and his wife are still working for Jerry Falwell and live in Lynchburg.

As I said before, the senior staff and employees were ridden with anxiety when Falwell arrived—and with good reason. Within a few days of seizing power Jerry showed up with a group of bodyguards, each one solidly built with a perpetual scowl. They were an intimidating presence, and the people at PTL quickly labeled them "Jerry's Goon Squad."

In the first few weeks of his reign, Falwell double-crossed Reverend Dortch. Since Dortch had served his purpose, Jerry didn't need him anymore, and consequently he was fired at the very first board meeting. After his entire plan backfired, I heard Dortch was completely distraught. Staff members had to virtually hold him up as he left the administration building. I think Dortch learned a powerful lesson that day. When you go swimming with the sharks, you better have the sharpest teeth. Obviously, Dortch was no match for the fangs of Falwell.

Through all these upheavals, Uncle Henry continued to be seen on the *PTL* program. He lived on the Heritage grounds in a beautiful home he had bought with some inheritance money. But Uncle Henry was in ill health, and I think it was very important to him that he keep his job at PTL. So when Falwell came, he decided to play it smart and just keep his mouth shut. Uncle Henry confided to us that he never believed a word of what Falwell was saying. In fact, privately he defended Jim; unfortunately, he never did so on the air.

Meanwhile, Falwell's media strategy was simple: The more charges against Jim Bakker, the more the press would eat it up. One of the most shocking allegations Jerry made was that $80 million was missing from PTL's account. Cleverly, Falwell called this "the Black Hole," and the media instantly picked up on it. *USA Today* immediately headlined Falwell's preposterous assertions. Every wire service and TV network ran the story, and within hours "the Black Hole" and the "vanished" $80 million became the latest fuel for the PTL fire.

Of course, just a couple of days later, "corrections" appeared in small print, buried in the back pages of newspapers across the country. It turned out there was no such thing as "the Black Hole." It never existed. It was so outrageously bogus that neither the IRS nor the federal prosecutors ever made it an issue. Lies were disseminated all the time; but when they were found to be lies, just one sentence was printed, and just once, to "correct the mistake."

Few people saw or heard those retractions.

But Falwell had a history of telling incredible lies. On one occasion he claimed to have been wined and dined by President Jimmy Carter at a lavish White House reception in his honor. But Carter quickly set the record straight by saying that Jerry had never been entertained at the White House during his administration, nor had he even been invited. In typical Falwell fashion, when confronted with his false statements, he merely laughed them off.

Recently a lady came up to me who had seen me on *A Current Affair.* With tears filling her eyes, she said, "You were not guilty of what they said about you, were you? I'm sorry for believing them." Then she turned and walked away. I couldn't even speak. At last someone else could see what had happened. And if she realized that she had been had by the press, then there were others out there who felt the same way.

Of all the hundreds of media invitations we received, Jim and I finally elected to do *Nightline.* We felt it would be the best forum to tell our side of the story. The program had a prestigious reputation, and while we knew Ted Koppel was a hard-nosed interviewer, we also knew that he had a reputation for fairness and would keep the questions out of the gutter.

The *Nightline* interview was one of the bright spots in our media nightmare. Ted Koppel treated us professionally and courteously, a true journalist. I believe they even extended the length of the show by about fifteen to twenty minutes, and the show was the highest-rated in *Nightline* history. Ted Koppel let us say what we wanted to say, and we felt it was a very successful interview.

Nonetheless, there was little solace anyplace, not one word of defense, even from our brethren, the other ministers we had so faithfully supported. Where were all the pastors and religious leaders Jim had shared his TV program with for all those years? Why did they refuse to lift a finger in Jim's defense? There were literally hundreds of them whom Jim had helped by giving them thousands of hours of free airtime and contributing huge amounts to their churches when they were in need. I could count on the fingers of two hands the number of preachers who even told us they were sorry for what happened.

The ones we called and asked for help (and believe me, these were all the biggest names at the time) either wouldn't take our calls or were out of their offices or away on trips or any other excuse you can think of. None of them wanted to be associated with us now that we had no more TV time to give them—or big checks to write out in their names. In fact, many of them even helped further destroy us from their pulpits and in private.

The things people told me they heard from ministers we thought were our friends made me never want to trust another human being as long as I live. I couldn't believe that when the chips were down, these men did not in any way practice what they were preaching.

But I have my own theory as to why these preachers acted as they did. Especially those who were on the air with their own shows. If they could destroy Jim Bakker to the point where he could never again appear on television, then the millions of PTL partners would have to turn somewhere else with their donations. And that is exactly what happened.

The king of the mountain had been knocked off his throne. That's the reason they all deserted us in droves, shunning Jim and making him look bad. The only one who stood up for Jim was Billy Graham. He was the single televangelist who remained silent during that time. Billy Graham, godly man that he is, said nothing. What a wonderful thing it would have been if others had only followed his example. But everybody wanted to get in on the act. Greed and jealousy overwhelmed love and forgiveness.

And lest anyone believe I'm overstating the case against Jerry Falwell or misrepresenting his true intentions, I'm going to reprint here excerpts from a transcript of a sermon given by Dr. Bob Gray, a Baptist pastor and a very close friend of Falwell's, before his congregation on March

15, 1987. It was taped with his full knowledge and consent:

> While I was in Germany for the month of March doing missionary work, the news broke on the immorality of the sponsor and MC of the PTL television club. . . . And of course the thing that perhaps shocked you and shocked me the most was that Dr. Jerry Falwell, who's a very dear personal friend . . . took over this ministry and became the chairman of its board. When I learned that he had taken over, I was frankly shocked. I could not comprehend what was going on.
>
> . . . And so I got one of the letters that he sent out to everybody on his mailing list asking for money to save *The PTL Club.* Several of you had told me that you had seen a televised news conference where he was answering questions from the press. . . . You said that on that news conference he said that there would be no change in the format of *The PTL Club,* which meant that the charismatic influence and program would go right on. Well, that shocked me also.
>
> . . . So I flew to Lynchburg on Thursday. Dr. Falwell gave me an appointment and I met with him and I'll give you the essence of our conversation. . . . I said, "I'm not trying to tell you how to conduct your ministry, but as your friend, I think you've made the biggest mistake you've ever made in your life and your ministry by identifying favorably with the PTL format. . . . Unless you've changed since the last time we talked in your doctrine, I know that you certainly have not changed to embrace the charismatic position."
>
> And he said, "You're absolutely right. I haven't changed one iota. I've always been against it and I still am. Let me explain to you what my motive is and where I'm going. When I received word that this was about to happen, I was determined that if at all possible, I would try to get the PTL network for *The Old Time Gospel Hour,* and this is the only way that I felt like I could do it."
>
> And I said, "Well, I personally don't agree with your methods and I don't agree with your philosophy, but that's be-

tween you and the Lord. But I do feel that it was wrong for you to identify with this movement."

"Well," he said. ". . . I don't care what happens to the country club down at Charlotte and all the jamboree stuff that goes on there. I'm only interested in the PTL cable network. It's the largest Christian cable network in the nation and I'd like to get that . . ."

And I said, "Well, I feel that you have placed your friends in an indefensible position and I'm one of them. I am one hundred percent opposed to PTL and when I got your letter asking for money to save it, my first reaction was why not go ahead and bury it and everybody would be a lot better off? I've never felt that God was in it from the beginning. . . . I think it's been the biggest religious charade that's ever been telecast . . ."

And then he went on to say this. "I think you'd also like to know that this coming Tuesday I'm having a press conference and at that time we plan to expose Jim Bakker not only for immorality with a woman, but homosexual immorality— and not only him, but Dortch and all of those in a leadership position on PTL. I plan to fire sixteen hundred workers on Tuesday and probably it'll be in bankruptcy before too long and the sooner the better. All I want out of it is the cable network for the Lord."

And I said, ". . . but again, I do not agree with what you had to do to get it, because millions of people across this nation are confused and wonder what in the world is going on and why would you suddenly identify with a movement that you've always been in opposition to . . ."

He also said that he thinks the sooner the organization goes bankrupt, the better off it will be because the assets will then be auctioned and disposed and the network will then be free for purchase and they hope to purchase it and go on from there . . .

I want to close by saying this. I love Dr. Falwell. He's still my dear friend. . . . But until this issue is clear, I hope you'll not send money. I mean that. Until this issue is clear, I believe you'll answer to God if you put a dime in PTL or any other charismatic ministry. . . . That's a stand I've always taken. But I felt that you needed to know. . . . So I wanted you to know the full scope of what's happening there. Don't be shocked by what happens in the next few days. It's going to get worse. It's not going to get better.

Quite obviously, Dr. Gray was no fan of our ministry. Yet despite this he had the strength and conviction to speak out against lies and injustice. I shall always admire the man's integrity, the courage it required to reveal Jerry Falwell's true motives for wanting control of PTL.

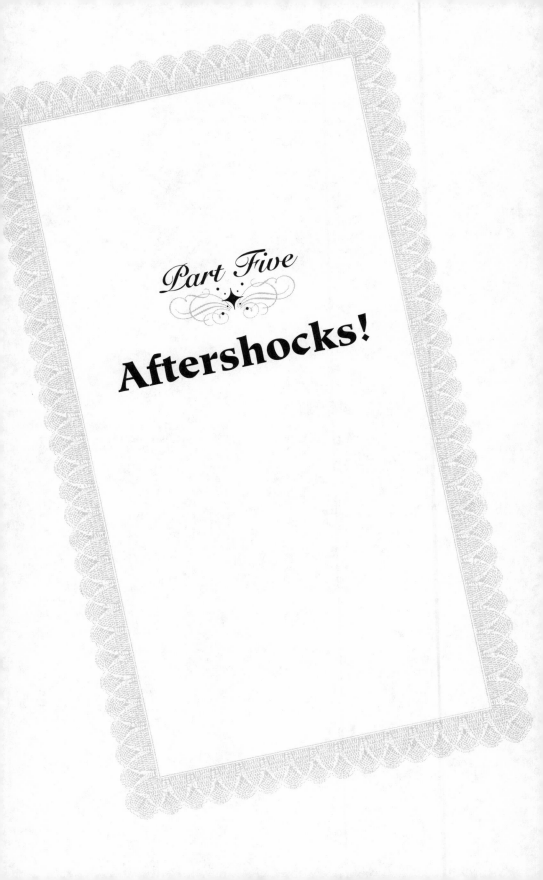

Part Five

Aftershocks!

Lost in the Desert

After losing our home in Charlotte, Jim and I truly felt like nomads. We were like people without a country. We were either loved or hated by every person we met, treated with either disdain or profound sympathy. There was no in-between. We never knew whether the person approaching us was for or against us. Would they shake our hands or curse our faces?

We couldn't go anywhere in the country, what with Jerry Falwell accusing us hour after hour on CNN of being thieves and ruining Christian television for everyone. Reporters were still hot on our trail, bombarding us with questions whenever they could. "Tammy! Tammy! Is it true that you had an air-conditioned doghouse!?"

"For the millionth time, we don't have an air-conditioned doghouse!" During the winter our dogs were kept in the garage so they could stay warm. But the odor was nauseating, and our constant spraying with water was ruining the wooden floor and walls. So Jim simply built a doghouse. He found an old heating/air-conditioning unit no one was using and placed it inside the doghouse as a source of heat. That doghouse was never air-conditioned, only heated.

"Tammy, we hear you've got gold faucets. How can you possibly justify having gold faucets?"

"I don't have to, because we don't."

"Are you saying you don't have gold faucets in your bathroom?"

"They're made of chrome, just like your faucets. All we had were gold-colored swans instead of silver-colored knobs. They cost only pennies more per unit, and I liked the gold color better than the silver color. That's all there is to it!" Yet the news media declared we had fourteen-karat gold fixtures. The fiction became a fact. So many lies became "facts" in people's minds as a result of Falwell's untruthfulness, concocted to make Jim look bad in the eyes of the public.

When we lost PTL, Jim and I ended up with virtually nothing. In actuality, we'd lived just like everyone else. Our charge accounts were maxed out to the limit, we had house payments and other bills to be paid, and we didn't even have a savings account. Yes, we had a wonderful income, but like most people we spent what we made. Losing PTL, we had to sell the house in Gatlinburg and the house in Palm Desert. We had to sell the two cars that we owned. There were no Swiss bank accounts—as Falwell stood before the cameras and declared there were. There were no huge savings accounts of any kind. We did not have expensive collections of art treasures—the government came and checked on things like that when Jim was indicted. They would have confiscated anything valuable we had. There was nothing to confiscate!

To this day, people still believe the Falwell lies propagated by the press. I guess that's human nature. The Communists have a theory: They say that if you say something loud enough and long enough, people will believe it. And they're right!

I don't try to defend myself anymore against those people. The older I get, the less it makes any difference to me what other people think. All I can do is to tell the truth and allow people to believe what they want to believe.

We didn't know where to go, what to say, what to do. People were not only cruel to us, but they were cruel to our children. That I did not understand. I guess that people just weren't thinking. The media had stirred everyone up into such a frenzy that people probably would have kicked our dog had she been walking with us. The popular thing to do was to hate Jim and Tammy. Even little children who I know were not capable of understanding our situation parroted what their parents were saying. It was horrible even to try to go anywhere. I didn't care what people said about me or Jim, but I did not want my children to be hurt by crude, cruel remarks. The media took lies and made them the truth, and they took the truth and turned it into lies—lies that people believed.

My heart felt like a piece of liver that had been beaten until it was nothing but a bloody pulp. I felt like it was hanging outside my chest. I constantly found myself walking around with my arms folded over my heart, as if I were attempting to shield it from more blows. Where were all the thousands and thousands of people we loved so much? I felt totally alone, forsaken by both God and man. "God, please let me die. Please let our whole family die!" How could people possibly believe the hideous lies being told by Falwell and his cohorts in the press? We had stood in front of those people every day for over twenty years and bared our very souls. They had been with us through the good times and the bad times.

They had seen me though two tough pregnancies and through marriage problems; we had hidden nothing from them. They had watched our children grow up and shared every area of our lives. How could they accept the falsehoods Jerry Falwell was telling about us? I just didn't understand. I believe everything would have turned around if we could have gotten to our PTL partners and let them know what really happened. But from the day he took over, Falwell would not let us anywhere near Heritage USA. It was as if we had just disappeared off the face of the earth. The people we loved so much didn't understand what was happening, and we had no way of telling them.

So I don't blame them. I just feel sad. We were hurting too bad to know there were actually thousands of our partners fighting for us, but their hands were tied. Thousands and thousands of letters were written on our behalf to Falwell, but they were simply thrown unanswered into a Dumpster and burned. No personal mail was ever sent to us, so no wonder people thought we didn't care!

Despite the ceaseless attacks, we knew that we had to get Jamie back in school and get some semblance of normality back into his little life. So we found another tiny two-bedroom house in Palm Desert, California, and started over again. We had lost everything except a couple of storage rooms full of mementos, furniture, and knick-knacks. We didn't even own a car.

Reverend Mike Murdock, a frequent guest on *PTL* and a dear friend, found out that we didn't have a car and promptly sent us one. God bless you, Mike! It was like God dropped it right out of Heaven. We registered Jamie in a wonderful Christian school, and for a little while we tried to live a somewhat normal life, although it was constantly shrouded in sadness.

Eventually one day Tammy Sue couldn't take it anymore. She told us that she was going out to dinner with friends. We didn't think anything of this, as she did this often. When it started getting late, we got worried. We called the friends she was supposed to be with, and they told us to go outside and look on our car windshield, that Tammy had left a note for us. Her message said that she was leaving for Dallas to stay with friends.

Tammy Sue disliked being famous. She always used to say, "Mom, I just want to be a normal person. I want to live a normal life. I just wish we were a regular family." Consequently I do not blame Tammy Sue for what she did. She was hurting so bad, unable to face living in a fishbowl anymore. Tammy Sue was running away to try and find "home."

And she made that wish come true. Soon after leaving she eloped with Doug Chapman, one of the bellboys at the Heritage Grand. Initially we had discouraged their relationship, since she was only seventeen and he was about six years older, but eventually we accepted him warmly into our family. The two of them moved into a darling mobile home on a piece of land that Doug's grandmother owned in North Carolina.

Without Tammy Sue the house felt colder, emptier. We had lost one of our family. But this was just one of the many blows we would have to endure. Not long after our daughter left, *Playboy* magazine came out with nude photos of Jessica Hahn plus an interview with her. I don't know how many thousands of dollars she got for doing that spread, but it showed me what kind of a girl she was. And it showed other people too. I mean, she didn't even have boobs. She was just this skinny little nothing girl. In one way I was relieved because she was not even pretty. She was not who I thought Jim would ever be turned on to.

Still, I was so embarrassed for Jim. But even more embarrassed for myself. In the article, Hahn said horrible things about me. She alleged that Jim revealed to her I had never satisfied him. Jim cried like a baby and swore over and over on a Bible that he never said any of those things, that he never once mentioned me or anything about our relationship.

Often Jim woke up sick to his stomach, his ulcers burning like fire. It was almost more than our minds could handle at times. We survived through the sheer will to live and by reading the Bible. Thank God we had Jamie to take care of and his well-being to worry about. We had to go on for him. Luckily we had friends who stuck with us. We had known Don and Emma Howard for a long time, and they loved us and believed in us. They were a source of great strength and inspiration to us and worked hard to help us cope with the tragedy. They forced us to socialize.

We were frantic, as we had no health insurance. What if one of us should get sick? We had a friend who was a doctor and who had been on television with us many times. Dr. Marvin Brooks and his wife, Sally, told us that if we had any medical problems, they would help us. I cannot tell you the dreadful weight that was lifted off our minds by their kindness. I wish there was a way to personally mention every person who helped us through those traumatic times.

After a while people began to find our address in Palm Desert. The word spread like wildfire, and within a few weeks we were receiving huge boxes full of mail, heartfelt correspondence begging for Jim and me to come back. "We forgive you, we forgive you," they wrote by the thousands. We had to bring people in just to read all the letters, actually setting up a mini-mailroom. The response we were getting from our partners imploring us to come back was overwhelming.

Some of my women friends worked day and night in 118 degree heat to get that correspondence answered. Fran Moore and Sally Wall will never forget one particular day that they had answered boxes of mail. They got the huge boxes ready and took them to the post office, only to find out that they had not zip-coded them properly. In the stifling heat, their clothes soaked with perspiration, they had to stand there and sort zip codes for an hour. They told me afterward that the only way they were even able to complete the task was by laughing so hard that they were done before they knew it. They still talk about it to this day.

We lived day to day. I will never know how we bought

groceries and made house payments except that when we were at the end of our rope, someone would always send us a check. Every day we spent hour after hour answering mail. At times we had to wait to mail our letters, as we could not afford the postage.

Fortunately I had my constant companion, my dog Tuppins. I would just sit there telling her everything. And Tuppins was there to jump up on me and lick my tears. They call a dog man's best friend, and Tuppins was mine, a little bit of life cuddling up to me and kissing my face. She was something I could reach out and hold on to, something cozy and soft and warm and furry—someone who loved me no matter what.

Meanwhile Jim became so wrapped up in his own grief that it was almost impossible for me to be around him. He stayed all curled up in a fetal position on the couch, underneath the blankets, listening to "praise tapes," recordings of classic gospel songs. He wouldn't utter a word, just listen to them hour after hour. I would say anything I could to motivate him: "Jim, you've got to get up and fight for yourself. Fight for the partners. Tell the people what really happened. They will believe you. Don't just lay there and let Falwell and the news media trample on you. Stop the pity party, Jim. You have as much power to command the news media as Falwell. Get out there and give them the truth. Please, Jim."

But soon I just couldn't handle it anymore. I felt he never listened to me, that there was no hope for our marriage. We were caught in a net of hurt and suffering from which I could see no way out. I could no longer carry Jim's pain. I could no longer carry his heavy burden of guilt over Jessica Hahn or his regrets over losing PTL.

We were hurting each other more by staying together. My sorrow was feeding off his sorrow, my pain off his pain. It was just more than my mind could possibly bear. I felt that if I didn't leave Jim, I was going to die.

People ask me why I didn't take Jamie and leave at that time. But I could not leave Jim when he was suffering so. He needed somebody so bad. And I was so afraid that he was going to go through with the threats he was making.

"Tam," he'd say, "I'm thinking about committing suicide. I just can't live like this anymore. I cannot live with people thinking that I would do the horrible things Falwell has accused me of. And I can't live with the fact that people are actually believing him."

"Jim, you can't do that! You know that suicide is wrong. Besides, it's the selfish way out. What about poor little Jamie, what about Tammy Sue, what about the thousands and thousands of people who still love you and believe in you? What about me, Jim?"

But it continued to get worse and worse. Every day I was petrified to leave him, for fear that when I got back home I would find him dead somewhere. I felt as if I were losing my mind. Finally, after days of these threats, I finally screamed in desperation, "Jim, please quit threatening me. If you're going to commit suicide, just go ahead and do it! Get it over with! I can't take it anymore!" Tears were streaming down my face.

Suddenly we heard a knock at the door.

I didn't want to see anyone. I decided not to answer, but the knocking continued. I was screaming, "Please go away! Whoever you are, whatever you want, please just go away!"

"Mom, someone's at the door," Jamie called out from his room. "Can't you hear them?"

"Yes, Jamie, I hear," I responded wearily. But still I didn't move. Jim didn't either. It was as if we were paralyzed. Eventually Jamie went to the door and opened it. In walked our friends pastor Ty Beason and his wife, Jeanette. They had driven nearly a hundred miles.

"We were praying, and God told us that you needed us," said Ty. "We want you to pack a few things and come stay at our house for a while. We want to love you and take care of you until you both feel better."

"Jim can go with you," I answered, "but I'm not going anywhere." Then I did something I normally would never do. I went into my bedroom and shut the door. I could hear Ty and Jeanette talking to Jim and Jamie.

"Jim, we know God spoke to us, and we are not going to leave this house without you and Tammy."

Through the door I could hear Jim talking to them. "We don't want to go anywhere. Thank you so much for coming, but we'll be all right." Then there was a knock on my bedroom door; it was Jeanette.

"It's open," I said.

Jeanette marched into the room and started toward my closet. "Tammy, if you don't put some things together yourself, then I am going to do it for you. We are not leaving here without you and Jim!" And I knew that she meant business. With tears streaming down my face, protesting all the way, I got out my suitcase for the trip that I did not want to take. Jim and I wearily walked out to their car.

We were in such an agonized state of mind that we didn't even know where we were going. We didn't know what we were doing. We couldn't talk. We couldn't think. There was nothing we could do. Jim and I could not communicate. We were on totally different wavelengths. Two people in a state of shock, complete basket cases.

But the Beasons stood right there with us. They were determined to get us back on our feet. Over the next several weeks they counseled us, prayed with us, loved us, and cared for us, and by the time we left their home, I felt like Jim had gotten himself more level, past the flirtation with suicide.

After Jim and I returned home, we both concentrated on poor little Jamie. We were trying to make life as normal as possible for him, which wasn't easy. Here's this little ten-year-old boy all bewildered, his world turned upside down. I couldn't even send him to school anymore, because kids made fun of him. To make sure he got an education, we wound up trying to home-school him.

One evening some of my girlfriends came over determined to get me out of the house for a couple of hours. "Tam, we want you to dress up and let us take you to Sonny Bono's restaurant for dinner." I needed desperately to get away from Jim's grief for just a little while, so even though I felt guilty for leaving him, I told the girls that I would go. I got dressed up for the first time since doing the *PTL* program. I told Jim we'd be right back, and we left to go eat.

Sonny Bono's restaurant was so pretty and romantic. It was dark, the tables lit by candles. Live music was wafting through the place, and for just a little while I forgot my suffering. No one would recognize me here because of the darkness, which meant I was safe to enjoy the evening. We sat down and ordered our meals, and just as mine arrived I heard Jim's name mentioned. It was at the table right next to us; they obviously didn't know that I was there.

I didn't want to listen, but I couldn't help but overhear what they were saying. And it was not nice. I thought, what am I going to do? Any minute now they're going to see me sitting there, and it will be terribly embarrassing for everyone. So I made a decision. I turned around and tapped one of the men on the shoulder.

"Sir, my name is Tammy Faye Bakker, and I just heard you talking about my husband and me." But before I could go on, horror of all horrors, I started sobbing. But fighting back more tears I told the man, "Don't believe everything you hear. There are two sides to every story. At least give us a fighting chance."

Well, I have never seen a table of people so flustered in my life. They were obviously very nice men and women. They weren't naturally mean. They were considerate, upper-class couples. Almost instantly, one of them apologized profusely by saying, "We're sorry, Tammy. All we know is what the newspapers and the television have been telling us. We're very sorry. Please forgive us for behaving like this." Then they instantly got up from the table, leaving their dessert behind. I felt bad about that. I wasn't trying to humiliate them.

As the days passed, Jim was trying his best to live normally. But how do you live normally when you are used to doing programs every day and running a huge corporation with hundreds of people around you, then all of a sudden there you are living in this tiny two-bedroom house doing nothing, your reputation destroyed? It was an impossible situation for him to deal with.

About six months passed, and Jim was beginning to feel almost normal again. I could see him coming back to life. "Tam," he said to me one day, "I want to go back to Charlotte and do some television again." Dale Hill, our former director of television at PTL, had called and told Jim that the old gang was ready and willing to start over again. Dale felt that there were enough partners wanting us back on television, and that we really had a chance. He and Jim had worked together since the Pat Robertson days, and Jim valued Dale's opinions and advice.

However, as bad as I wanted Jim back on TV, I felt that the worst place in the world we could go was Charlotte. "Jim," I said, "I believe it's a good idea to start over again, but why go back to Charlotte? We're settled here in California. Why don't we just find a studio here?"

I knew if we went back to Charlotte and they thought we were trying to get PTL back, all hell would break loose. But once again, regardless of what I said, we packed up our things and moved back to North Carolina. Which, as I predicted, turned out to be the biggest mistake we ever made—and we had made some beauties!

The Scavengers' Feast

After our departure, events at PTL continued to unfold at a dizzying pace. Positions of power and influence revolved like musical chairs. Trustees and board members came and went. Money that was raised disappeared. Friends turned into enemies. Order became chaos as everybody tried to slice off their piece of the pie. Now, while I wasn't directly involved with any of this, I know people who were. These reliable sources told me everything that went on. All the fraud and chicanery could fill up a book. So even though the situation was crazy, I'll try to make sense of it for you.

It is my belief that from day one Falwell intended to wipe out PTL's cash flow. This way he could throw PTL into bankruptcy and try to buy it back for pennies on the dollar, coming in the back door and getting control. Consequently PTL would have been transformed from a charismatic to a Baptist ministry. Naturally it was a complicated legal scheme, but Jerry thought he could pull it off. With friends high up in the Reagan White House, he had every reason to think they wouldn't be overly concerned with his financial maneuvering.

And he was right.

Jerry Falwell raped the ministry over and over again. From the day he took it over it began to crumble into ruins. Millions of dollars destined for PTL programs mysteriously went unaccounted for and remain so to this day.

On his very first day at PTL, Falwell invited Roe Messner to fly back to Lynchburg with him on his private jet. He said he wanted Roe to be on the *PTL* show the next day when he made a direct appeal to the PTL partners to continue sending in their support. So Roe went to Lynchburg to be with Falwell on TV the next day.

Falwell told the TV audience that PTL owed Roe millions of dollars on construction projects, plus it was also way behind in paying the television stations for airtime. Falwell declared that if the money didn't come in, PTL would soon go bankrupt and that all the building would stop, including the much anticipated Heritage Towers, which Roe was in the process of completing. Heritage Towers would provide 513 more rooms for the partners. Jerry virtually begged Roe to keep working and promised to give him a large payment on his past-due invoices. Roe had more than three hundred people employed on various projects at PTL.

In May of 1987 the pressure increased dramatically, with Falwell issuing an urgent message to the TV audience. Immediately he needed to raise $8 million for Roe Messner or PTL would go under. Jerry labeled his sacred crusade the "May Emergency to May Victory" and duped everybody, including Roe Messner—PTL's biggest creditor, who was owed over fifteen million dollars.

His voice trembling with emotion, his eyes watery, Jerry gave an impassioned performance, richly deserving of an Oscar. Falwell even sent out letters to the partners begging them for money. I don't know exactly how much money came in as a result of his pleas, but reliable sources place it at over $16 million. Nevertheless, I do know for a fact that Roe never received a dime of this money (though he eventually did get $600,000 as part of the later bankruptcy settlement). He wound up having to lay off all his employees.

In the meanwhile Falwell got rid of all the animals in the petting zoo Jim had so lovingly planned for the children; he gave away the beautiful thoroughbred horses that the partners had donated to the ministry; he sold the charming carousel that the children and older folks alike had loved so much; he auctioned off the little trains that went through the park filled with moms and dads and kids; he sold the buses and the trams; he closed the home for unwed mothers; and he turned Kevin's House, the home for crippled children, into a bed and breakfast.

Then on June 12, 1987, in an effort to gain complete control for himself, Jerry Falwell plunged the ministry into bankruptcy. Soon afterward he filed his bankruptcy reorganization plan, which would have granted him virtual ownership of PTL. This was a deliberate act of deceit, as PTL was in no way ever bankrupt. But with Falwell at the helm, bills suddenly went into arrears and became way overdue.

At the bankruptcy hearing this was all confirmed. One creditor after another testified that they had always been paid until Jerry Falwell came in. Falwell's plans to totally control the remaining assets of PTL went sour. The judge in charge of the bankruptcy proceedings allowed the PTL creditors to collectively file a competing plan. On the day that ruling came down, Jerry Falwell knew he was beaten.

Because each creditor would now get the chance to vote in the reorganization, with every dollar they were owed equaling one vote. Since the largest creditor by far was Roe Messner, he could easily swing the outcome. Falwell knew that Messner wouldn't support him, not in a million years. So Jerry just resigned in October of 1987. But he had already accomplished what he set out to do—which was to grab as much as he could, destroying Jim Bakker and the entire PTL television ministry in the process.

And Jerry Falwell calls himself a man of God! And has a college that trains young minds!

So Close
but So Far Away

When we returned to Charlotte, some good friends of ours, Dexter and Birdie Yeager, notified us that we could move into a big log cabin they owned. And that if we began doing TV again, we could rent the office building that was also on their property. But it was simply horrendous being so near Heritage USA and not being a part of it anymore. It seemed impossible! My heart would break every time we had to drive past the place.

Still living in a subdivision on the grounds was my mom, as well as Jim's mom and dad. But it was a battle just to go visit them. The guards—some of them the same ones who had loved us and taken care of our family—now watched us as if we were criminals. It was beyond belief! So terribly, terribly sad.

To get the ball rolling, Jim called together some members of our old team. They were mostly people who had either quit or been fired by Falwell. After a few months we were back on television once more with church services every Sunday. Jim's hope was that he could build the dream again.

At least we were busy doing something. In all honesty, I

felt the circumstances were more discouraging than bene-
ficial to us. Jim held on as best he could, bravely filling his
days and nights with the only thing he knew—television.
Despite my initial reservations I feel that in those few
months we did some of the best shows we've ever done. TV
guests flew in at their own expense to show their continued support of Jim and me.

Our house was always filled with PTL partners who refused to give up on us and who were elated that we were
back. Jim's days were once again filled with doing television and pastoring a growing church. But since Falwell
had confiscated our partner list, we had no way of solicit-
ing contributions through the mail. Hence we could not
afford good television time, and we were forced to broadcast on low-power stations, which reached hardly anybody.

And then insult was added to injury.

Jim received word that we could no longer do TV from
the Yeager estate. It was not zoned for commercial production or church services. We tried to fight the order but to
no avail. So once more we had to pack up and leave our
home. Yet despite this bad news, a miracle occurred;
Tammy Sue presented us with our first grandchild, a
beautiful baby boy named James. It was truly the only
bright spot in our lives since we lost PTL. How we thanked
God for that precious baby. He gave us the first hope we
had in a long time—the feeling that no matter what, life
goes on.

From then on, our situation started to improve. A sympathetic Florida minister who heard that we were going to
have to close down our TV production facilities offered us
his place to continue. Before I knew it our TV crew and
several volunteers were headed down to Florida along with
us. We arrived to find one of the most breathtaking spots I
had ever seen.

Located on the water was a beautiful two-story home. It

was very large, with a huge living room, a large dining room, a very large restaurant-type kitchen, many bedrooms, and many baths. Also located on the property were a couple of small cottages. The house and cottages were virtually hidden by the huge trees surrounding them. Our entire crew moved in, and although we were crowded beyond belief we enjoyed one another's company and did more great television programs.

Again, people flew in from all over the country at their own expense to be with us. I don't know how, but somehow the partners found us again and came to view the TV shows we were doing. But after a couple of months of septic tanks overflowing and everything else that goes along with overcrowded conditions, we knew we were going to have to look for larger facilities.

That's how we ended up in Orlando. We rented an abandoned shopping center and began preparing it for TV. Our whole staff painted and fixed and cleaned, and before long we had it looking very nice. It was plenty big enough. We had enough room for a large TV studio, TV control rooms, and offices. We even had a couple of stores open up while we were there. The shopping center already had a bar. It was the only thing that had survived, until we got there.

But a local preacher decided that he didn't want us around and took it upon himself to make his feelings known. One day during our broadcast we heard some commotion, and when we went outside to investigate we saw him and some members of his congregation unloading a casket. They dragged it in front of the TV studio with a sign hanging from it: BURY JIM AND TAMMY!

Jamie Charles was so scared. What a cruel thing to do when they knew we had a little boy who would see it. I cannot figure out what was going on in the mind of that cruel pastor, who claimed to be a man of God. I thought at the time, "No wonder people don't want to be Christians, when they see so-called Christians being so mean to one another." I also began to wonder, "How many Jerry Falwells are out there?" I don't blame people for not wanting that kind of religion. I think it upset all of us more than we would admit.

The pastor's tirade didn't stop there. He handed out posters condemning us, he took out anti-Bakker ads in the newspaper, he lambasted us on TV and radio. I guess he was trying to pull a Falwell, but he didn't have what it takes to generate any real support. Soon the media ignored him.

Another time we heard that a local radio station was bringing Jessica Hahn to town and that she was going to appear scantily clad at the bar located in our shopping center. What's more, she dared Jim Bakker to show up and talk to her!

Well, thank God we got wind of that before it happened. Canceling our TV shows, we left town with Jamie for a week. Later we heard that Hahn was lying almost naked on a waterbed challenging Jim to come and see her. It was all thought up by a local deejay and broadcast live on the radio. I guess they were all disappointed when no one showed up to watch the circus they had prepared for us.

My nerves were frayed in those days. Nevertheless, I wanted to support Jim in any way I could. I felt so sorry for him. But it was like living in a dream. My body was always there, but I had shut off my mind. I did television, I cohosted with Jim like always, I sang, I went to church, I ran our home—but I was numb.

It was then that Jim made a catastrophic move—the move that I believe set the forces of the criminal-justice system against him, intent on removing him from the picture once and for all. Jim attempted to buy back PTL and Heritage USA. This was not a matter of money. Jim was getting thousands and thousands of letters imploring him to head the ministry once more. Jim wanted to go back and make everything right with the partners, to vindicate his name and undo what Falwell had done. All along I had strongly encouraged him to do exactly this and claim what was rightfully his. But I felt he had waited too long, that it was too late by this time. However, Jim went ahead with the plan anyway.

Some of the PTL partners with a lot of money contacted Jim and urged him to make a bid on the Heritage USA property. Before he knew it, checks were coming in from all over the country toward the purchase of PTL. With promises from some of the large donors for much more, should his bid be considered, Jim contacted a man named Red Benton, who was the trustee of the property at that time. Jim said that he would have the money together within days.

Benton said that if he were to accept Jim's bid, then he must have $3 million within forty-eight hours. These forty-eight hours just happened to be over a weekend, when it is virtually impossible to transfer funds. Of course Benton knew that, so even though the funds were arriving at lightning speed, Benton held fast to his position. He was never going to allow Jim to buy anything. The $3 million was raised but had to be returned to the donors.

It wasn't long afterward that Jerry Falwell began calling for an investigation; maybe even the government put him up to it. Again, the presidential election was shortly coming up, and if Jim ever regained his prominence, you can be sure he wouldn't have been too grateful to Falwell or his friends in the Reagan or Bush administrations.

I believe this is the reason the government started in on him. And again I feel that Jerry Falwell was the man who spearheaded this attack. He said that if people wrote and insisted there be an investigation against us, then the government would have to conduct one. I believe that Jerry was panic-stricken at the thought of Jim somehow regaining Heritage USA. If that had happened, then Jerry's lies would have been uncovered, and he could have possibly ended up in prison. And I feel that Jerry Falwell is the one who should have gone to prison, not Jim Bakker.

Was there a plot hatched by Falwell and the Justice Department? You be the judge. Edwin Meese, then attorney general of the United States, was asked by Jerry Falwell to give the commencement address at Liberty University in Lynchburg, which Falwell had founded and where he now served as chancellor. Also in attendance was Mrs. Meese. After the ceremony Falwell invited the Meeses to spend time with him and his wife. A few weeks later it was proclaimed that a grand jury was being convened to investigate Jim. I don't think this was any coincidence.

Even so, I wasn't paying any attention to Falwell by this point. I figured the worst that could happen had already happened. And then Jim walked in one day with the news. "Tam," he said, his voice dry and hoarse, "they've notified me I'm being investigated."

"Who's investigating what?"

"The Justice Department. They are going to get a grand jury together and they are going to try and indict me, Tam."

I was not too concerned, and I told him I didn't think he need be worried. "Jim, the PTL records have nothing to hide. Everything was in order when we left."

"That's just the point. The records were in order *when we left*. But Falwell and his men have been in there since then. They could do anything they wanted to the records. And they probably have, in order to validate their lies."

I could see what he meant, and I too began to panic.

"Jim, I just wish that you'd tried to get PTL back sooner or just left it alone. By the time you did try, it was just too late. You must have known that trying to buy back PTL would scare Falwell to death. Him and everyone who was working with him."

"Tam, I did what I felt I had to do."

"Jim, if they do get a grand jury together and if you *are* indicted, what will we do with the shopping center and our television program?"

"We'll just have to shut it down, honey."

I could see once more our world coming to an end. I've lately compared the treatment given Jim Bakker with that afforded O. J. Simpson. Jim was accused of taking too big a salary and overbooking a hotel. O.J. was accused of the brutal murder of two people, including the mother of his two small children. But never once was O.J. paraded around in shackles and handcuffs. Since the day he arrived in prison he was granted great respect and given preferential treatment over all the other inmates. He was allowed visitors every day, unlimited phone calls, special food, the list goes on. But Jim Bakker was paraded around in shackles and handcuffs like a circus animal; he was allowed only one phone call a day and visitors only once a week, and even they had to give their entire life history before being allowed to see him. One defendant was a famous sports hero, the other a famous television minister. One jury was sequestered for nine months; the other jury was allowed to live freely and do what they pleased, to be prejudiced day and night by TV reporters and newspaper columnists. And we call this American justice!

Not to mention that the O.J. trial was presided over by Lance Ito, who bent over backward to give the defense every benefit of the doubt and remain impartial. No such luck at Jim's trial. Judge Potter, who conducted the proceedings, was inflammatory, arrogant, and openly contemptuous of Jim Bakker in court, at one point calling him "a sawed-off little runt" right in front of the jury. If you don't believe me, look at the videotape.

O.J. had millions of dollars to hire the very best defense

lawyers in America. We had no money. In fact, as of this writing, Jim still owes lawyers money for that trial. The lawyers he had to use were certainly no match for the government prosecution. In my estimation, Jim never had a chance.

To begin with, I'm not a legal expert. All I can offer is my view on these events as they unfolded. During the course of the investigation, I pleaded with Jim to talk to the grand jury himself. "Defend who we were and what we did. Tell them we aren't thieves. You're the best speaker I've ever heard. Go tell these men and women the truth. They will understand. Storm in there if you have to!"

But he refused, listening instead to what his lawyers advised. "Tam, the grand jury is being led around by the nose by the prosecutors. I wouldn't stand a chance in there. The government could arraign Mickey Mouse if they wanted to."

Then the decision came down. About six months after the Justice Department started its probe, Jim was indicted on the fact of "overselling" the Heritage Grand Hotel and for using the airwaves, the phone lines, and letters to do it. They indicted him on twenty-four counts.

Charged along with him was Reverend Dortch. After the reverend had been cut loose from PTL, he was set adrift without Falwell's protection. By adding Dortch to the list, the prosecutors could bring into play the conspiracy statutes. For anytime two or more people allegedly enter into an illegal arrangement, you can label it a conspiracy. The idea of conspiracy allows greater punishment and more prison time if convicted. And that's exactly what the government did. Of course the federal prosecutors also knew that by indicting Dortch they could bring even more heat against Jim. To them Dortch was just the little fish. They wanted the big fry. I remember when we got the word.

"Well, Tam, they have indicted me. *The United States versus Jim Bakker.* Can you believe that? The whole United States against one person, Jim Bakker."

I started to sob. I was horrified! "Jim, what can we do, what can we do?"

"I don't know, Tam, I don't think we can do anything. Once a grand jury is assembled, I don't think you have any recourse. All we can do is pray, be prepared for anything, and tell the truth. But I feel sure that once we are actually in the courtroom in front of the jury, they'll be able to see the truth of what really happened."

I felt that way too.

Jim and I were both convinced that he was fully capable of answering any questions under cross-examination and believed he could gather enough evidence to prove his innocence. "Tam," he said, his mood upbeat, "this whole thing could just be a blessing in disguise. Get everything out in the open. I welcome my day in court."

Then we heard that something unbelievable had happened. We were stunned! Richard Dortch submitted to a plea bargain. When I was informed by our lawyers what a plea bargain is, I felt that it was all over for us. In a plea bargain, you make a deal with the prosecutors. You agree that if they'll save your neck, you'll do anything you have to do, say anything you have to say, to convict another person. That way you'll receive a lighter sentence, or, in some cases, no sentence at all.

I feel that government plea bargaining should not be

constitutionally allowed. I feel it is criminal! It encourages people to lie about other people—and get away with it—in order to save their own necks. I feel that many people have been punished for crimes they weren't guilty of as a result of being forced, with fear tactics, to plea-bargain. I don't understand how the government can get away with this! I always thought our Constitution was built on truth, not lies. How could we, as a nation, fall so low?

It is my understanding that Dortch said that he would lie and say that he and Jim were co-conspirators. By doing that he became a key government witness against Jim. Now they could charge Jim with fraud and they would have him. In other words, Dortch sold Jim down the river to save his own neck. I will always believe that if Dortch had stood behind Jim and stuck to the truth, they could have won the case.

Yes, terrible mistakes were made at PTL: mistakes of judgment, mistakes of ego, and mismanagement of large sums of money—but these mistakes were not criminal. If the leadership of PTL had not become intimidated by the government, they might have brought out volumes of proof—which still exist—that there were no criminal acts committed at PTL.

Let me try to explain the government's accusations. When Jim was running PTL, even though contributions were coming in at record amounts, he still needed additional funds to erect the Heritage Grand Hotel, which was slated to be our largest and most impressive hotel, equivalent to the most luxurious Sheraton or Holiday Inn resort. To accommodate the ever mushrooming number of visitors, the Heritage Grand Hotel would have offered partners first-class amenities second to none.

In order to finance the ambitious project, Jim created an innovative plan, which seemed quite feasible at the time. It was a basic vacation-resort time-share concept, the very model upon which many such similar programs are built today. His idea was simple. He started a special lifetime-partnership club. Everyone who donated $1,000 to help the ministry got a special gift: Once a year they could stay four days and three nights at the hotel. But the government accused Jim of "overselling" these partnerships. In other words, if everyone decided to come at the same time, there wouldn't be enough rooms for all of them. In my opinion, this was exaggerated.

The times people visited were to be managed just as in any other time-share facility. In a condo in Maui, for example, you wouldn't schedule fifty-two members the same week. That's common sense, and Jim was aware of that. The Heritage Grand Hotel had 504 rooms. The Heritage Towers had 513 rooms. Plus there were other motels on the property, with hundreds more rooms available. With that much visitor capacity, Jim was positive he had enough rooms to accommodate everybody.

When we were there, no one had ever been turned away from the existing hotels at Heritage USA. They might have had to accept alternate dates, as everyone could not come for Christmas, but we did have more than enough openings for them to visit another time of the year. And to most of the partners this was perfectly acceptable. The partners were told time and time again that if they wanted a special time, such as Christmas, they must make their reservations months in advance. So all partners were aware of this. They would arrange their vacations accordingly. We never dreamed it was a problem.

Curiously enough, Jerry Falwell was never indicted, despite the fact that he continued to sell lifetime memberships after Jim was gone. The government was trying to put Jim in prison for one thing and one thing only: overselling lifetime memberships. Falwell was then guilty of the same crime. Why wasn't Falwell indicted and given a prison sentence too? Wasn't he as guilty as Jim was? I can only speculate on how he escaped being charged as well.

We were forced to close down the television show in Orlando. Jim had just received word from his lawyers in Charlotte that he was going to have to spend the next few weeks preparing for his trial. We were living in a beautiful little house then, and we were both frantic, trying to figure out how we were going to make the rent payments without any income coming in.

The night before Jim had to leave we went for a walk with our dog Tuppins. The sunset was so beautiful as we walked through our neighborhood. We spoke of many things, to keep our mood light and upbeat.

Then Jim said something strange to me: "Tam, it just can't end this way."

At first I couldn't figure out what he was talking about. When it finally dawned on me, I said, "Why are you talking like this? What do you mean, 'It can't end this way'?"

But he never answered me.

Jim must have had some kind of premonition that night. Anyway, it was getting dark and we went back into the house, fixed ourselves and Jamie something to eat, and then went to bed. We just lay there, talking about the day it would all be over and we could go back to living a normal life.

Jim felt that he could win, but on the other hand he was nervous about the lawyers he had hired. He knew that they had never fought a case with such national scrutiny. He also knew that we had no money, and he was worried about how we were going to pay them. The government had millions at their disposal, and prosecutors who were experts at winning cases such as this. Jim was also worried about leaving me and Jamie for so many weeks. But I assured him that he needn't be concerned about us. We would be just fine. I told Jim that he needed to put his every waking moment into getting the needed material and documents together to fight his case.

The next morning came all too soon. I helped Jim pack. He would need clothes to last him several weeks. We worked in silence, not trusting ourselves to even talk to each other. Tears were running down both our faces. It wasn't long before we heard a car horn blow. We both nearly jumped out of our skins. It was Shirley Fulbright, Jim's longtime secretary. She had come all the way from Charlotte to drive Jim back there. She informed him that his dear friend Herb Moore, who had worked with Jim for years, had rented an apartment for him so that he would have a place to stay and work on the case.

I will never forget the moment Jim and Shirley drove out of our driveway, leaving Jamie and me with tears streaming down our faces, waving good-bye. I never dreamed that this would be the last time we would ever be together as a family. And thank God I did not know the heartache that was ahead. I don't know if my heart could have taken it. I'm so glad that God in his mercy prevents us from knowing what the future holds.

Jamie and I did not see Jim much those next few weeks. Jamie had just started at a new school, so we could not take any trips. Plus we had just enough money to pay the next month's rent, and I had no idea what we were going to live on when that was gone. Jim called every night. He told me that he and Herb Moore and the lawyers were making great progress, gathering all the boxes of paperwork, videotapes, and financial records they needed to prove their case. They were busy lining up people to testify in Jim's defense. They were working day and night.

The time finally arrived for the trial to start. Jim's nerves were worn to a frazzle. His ulcers were acting up again, he was having terrible bouts of depression, and he was feeling tired all the time. Jim spoke to a doctor friend of ours, who felt that Jim needed to take something to calm his nerves. He also felt that Jim was in need of an antidepressant. So

Jim had these prescriptions filled and began taking the medications. But as the trial began, Jim began to experience horrible side effects.

One day when court was supposed to start, Jim's lawyers told the judge, Robert Potter, that Jim was sick and needed a couple of days off to get well. Potter went ballistic and ordered his deputies to go get Jim; he didn't care if Jim was sick. When the deputies got to the lawyer's office where Jim was, they found Jim curled up in the fetal position under the couch, shaking like a leaf. They pulled him out and jerked him to his feet. Then they handcuffed him.

They walked him out of that office like they were leading an animal, and paraded him in front of the news media. That footage has been played around the nation hundreds of times: Jim in handcuffs and shackles, so sick he could hardly walk, tears streaming down his face. And people laughed and poked fun at one of our nation's leading ministers of the gospel—not knowing, not caring, that he was so ill and confused from the medication that he didn't even know where he was, or why they were doing this to him. I have this question for readers of this book: What if Jim had been one of your sons or your dad? How would you have felt then?

Jim was brought before Judge Potter, who ordered that Jim be put away in a prison for the mentally ill. He then ordered that the trial resume in a week. The deputies took Jim away.

The lawyers called and told me what had happened, that the doctor had put Jim on a combination of drugs. I became absolutely furious! I called the doctor and screamed until my throat hurt me. Tears drenched my blouse. "Why did you give him that stuff? You know that Jim's system cannot take those kinds of pills! Then to mix two kinds together, how could you?"

The doctor listened as long as he could stand to and then told me he was going to hang up and call back later, when I had calmed down. I walked through the house crying out to the God I so loved. "God, how could you let them do this to Jim? He does not deserve to be treated this way." But I felt that God was a million miles away and wasn't even hearing my cries. Where was God? Why didn't He do something for Jim? For the first time my faith began to waver, and a cold fear came over my very soul. If the government could do this to Jim, what else were they capable of doing?

Jim was not even allowed to call me until the second day he was incarcerated in that dreadful place. He told me horror stories about the way they were treating him. "They never turn off the lights—day or night. A guard sits outside my cell constantly, talking and yelling and rattling his keys. They feed me through a hole in the door, and there's no pillow for the cot I'm sleeping on. Tam, the toilet next to me is always full of excrement. Every time the prisoner next door to me flushes, it comes up on my side. The first day they didn't even give me bathroom tissue." I listened in pure horror. "Tam, the nurses come and take blood samples twenty-four hours a day. They test me for hours at a time. I'm terrified that they're trying to drive me crazy—or that they're trying to kill me! Then they could say I died from something else."

I don't know how Jim withstood all that. When the week was up, they took him directly from the prison to the courthouse floor. Then Judge Potter had the prison doctors testify about the results of all the tests Jim had taken. I was appalled as I sat there and listened to all those doctors or psychiatrists or whatever they were reveal Jim's most private self to the world. But I was so grateful that in spite of those inhuman circumstances, God gave Jim presence of mind, and he tested above-average to the genius level of intelligence. I wanted to stand up and cheer!

I cannot recount each and every moment of the trial. I have tried to shut it out of my mind. Having to sit there and listen to them accuse your husband—and a minister

of the gospel—of everything short of murdering his mother
was more than my heart could take. I wanted to die as I
watched the government prosecutor, Debra Smith, march
back and forth in front of the judge and jury proclaiming
that the Heritage Towers had never been built. That was a
bold-faced lie! It was sitting right there on the property for
all to see and walk through.

In fact, it was just weeks away from occupancy. The carpet had already been laid on ten floors, and thirteen floors
were wallpapered. The centerpiece of the government's
case was that there weren't enough rooms for all the lifetime members. But with the opening of the Towers, there
would have been. Is it a coincidence that Jim was indicted
a short time before its completion?

Debra Smith told one lie after another and got away with
it because the judge would not allow the jury to check on
any of her stories. And our lawyers were so unprepared
that they could not repair the damage she was doing. I
don't know why they didn't jump to their feet and say that
she was lying. So I tried hard to just shut her out of my
mind.

For weeks I lived in a state of pure agony, anger, and
despair. I felt that our lawyers were enjoying the publicity
and the TV cameras more than they were researching the
pertinent facts, and that they cared very little about the
actual outcome. I can still hear Jim after a grueling day in
court asking them, "Why didn't you tell the jury that
wasn't true? Why didn't you bring out the charts?" Over
and over he would try to help his lawyers get the facts
straight, but all to no avail. I think that near the end even
Jim gave up in desperation, seeing that the cards were all
stacked against him.

The Honorable Robert Potter, Chief Judge of the United
States District Court of Western North Carolina, was
known far and wide as a hanging judge. They called him
"Maximum Bob." He was very cruel in subtle ways. Potter

called Jim a "little sawed-off runt." During the trial he would close his eyes and lean back in his chair, as if he were asleep. Several times he was seen acting like a little child who doesn't want to hear something, sticking his fingers in his ears. He would yawn and belch and wink at the jury. I saw him do those things with my own eyes.

How they could allow a man like this to be a judge in the first place is beyond me. In my opinion, and in the opinions of many others, he was biased against Jim when the case first came his way. Potter did not like television evangelists, and he made no secret of it. Therefore, the jury was not even allowed to go see Heritage USA or our "mansion of a home," as one prosecutor put it. Potter forbade the jury to see any evidence that could have kept Jim from going to prison. Again, that is my opinion.

"Tam," Jim would say to me, "Judge Potter is really out to get me. Anything that shows me in a sympathetic light he's ruling inadmissible. He will not allow the jury to know about the millions of dollars PTL has contributed to foreign mission projects and to charities, or about the thousands of hours of free airtime we have given to pastors who could not afford to buy it. I don't know what to do. I've talked to my lawyers about it, but they just act like they don't even hear me."

To further prejudice matters, proof that Jim and I donated to PTL over $8 million in royalties on records, tapes, books, and other items, such as the retailing of Suzy Moppett dolls, was never allowed to be heard by the jury. When you examine the figures, the bottom line is that Jim and I were the largest contributors to PTL. Period.

One of my good friends asked me the other day, "Tammy, do you still receive royalties from all the albums you made and the books you wrote?" I was upset by her assumption. Then I realized that if she thought that way, many others did too. And rightfully so, since this would be the way such deals are normally done. Let me explain exactly how these items were handled: Neither Jim nor I ever received one penny for any of the albums I made or the books we wrote. All the royalties from the albums and books went directly to the PTL ministry. We never even saw the royalty checks. For example: For a gift of $25 we would send our partners an album, or perhaps a book or a Bible especially designed by us. Thousands upon thousands of records, books, and Bibles were sent out over the years. My albums alone earned up to $2 million a year for the ministry.

Had we taken royalties, we would have received much more than we were ever paid by the ministry, which we felt would have been wrong, because I sang on the show every day and we constantly spoke about the books we were writing, offering them to our audience as love gifts and thank-yous for contributions. Consequently, we felt that every cent of that money belonged to PTL.

The jury that convicted Jim was not even permitted to come visit Heritage USA and see for themselves where the money went—the money that Jim was accused of spending frivolously. To me this was unfair. Small wonder they didn't have a clue what Heritage was even like, what was finished and what was not finished, what was built and what wasn't. The government prosecutors didn't want the jury to see where the millions of dollars they were accusing Jim Bakker of misusing had gone. They didn't want the jury to see for themselves the acres and acres of beautiful buildings costing millions of dollars. To this day, I don't know why our lawyers didn't insist that the jury be allowed to see Heritage USA for themselves, to see for themselves that the Heritage Towers were just three weeks away from completion, three weeks away from being able to accommodate the partners. What a terrible injustice! I remember Jim calling me after this decision was handed down.

"It's too bad, Tam. I wish so much they could have taken

a tour of our 'mansion.' They would have been so disappointed! They would have seen it was just a big old house. I guess the prosecutors don't want them to know that we lived just like regular, normal people."

This is what I believe happened. One of the factors in the verdict was simply that the jury was overwhelmed. These were good, hardworking, decent people. They owned homes and made car payments every month. But I don't think they could even comprehend what a million dollars was. *I* can't even comprehend how much a million dollars is. I think that I could live like a queen for the rest of my life if I had a million dollars. I think that is how the jury felt.

I really do not understand the jury selection process. Because in most cases, anyone who would make a good prospective juror is automatically eliminated by the prosecution. Say you are being tried for bankruptcy fraud. Forty people have been called in as prospective jurors. The judge asks, "How many of you have ever had to file for bankruptcy?" Ten people raise their hands. They are automatically eliminated. Why? Would they not be the ones best be able to understand that situation? This is what happened in Jim's case.

It is my understanding that if you had ever watched the *PTL* show, you were not allowed to be a juror. If you had ever visited Heritage USA, you were not allowed to be a juror. If you professed to be a born-again Christian, you were not allowed to be a juror. So what are you left with? People who have no understanding of the situation. Then when it comes to the actual trial, all they are allowed to hear is what the judge allows them to hear.

In Jim's case, Judge Potter disallowed important facts that could have made Jim a free man. The prosecutor said that buildings Jim promised to build had not been built yet, when in fact they were sitting right there, weeks away from being finished. I still believe and always will that if

Jim had had a judge who was not prejudiced and lawyers who were more thorough, the outcome of his case would have been much different.

As a consequence of the government going through our books, there was one startling—and I'm afraid very disheartening—revelation. We found out that they were going to investigate David Taggart, who had worked for Jim for many years. David, as I mentioned before, was Jim's right-hand man, keeping track of expenses and receipts and traveling everywhere with Jim; he had occupied an office right next door to Jim's. We loved David, and he made a great impression on everyone he met; he was intelligent, sophisticated, and had a quiet yet cultured manner. He was also more than capable of doing anything Jim asked him to do. He was a hard worker, extremely organized, and he put in long hours for PTL.

You'll also recall that David was from a very wealthy family, and that he and his brother, James, were eventually to receive an enormous inheritance from their grandmother's estate—at least that's the story David told us when he was hired. We had no reason not to believe David.

Never did David give us any reason to suspect that he was anything other than what he told us. So when we heard that he too had been indicted, we were shocked! We came to learn that his entire story had been a falsehood. Auditors found that David had been embezzling money from PTL for a long time, and that his extravagant living style had been paid for with PTL money. Jim and I nearly died when we heard the news. When Jim asked the auditors why this hadn't been looked into months before, they said that when they'd asked David for receipts or proof of money spent that he would always have an excuse why he didn't have the information ready, and that he'd say he'd get everything they needed as soon as he could. The auditors said that they had no reason to doubt David, but that he never seemed to get the stuff together. Now, that is the story as I heard it. What I cannot figure is *why* the auditors allowed David to get away with that. I thought that an audit couldn't be completed if everything wasn't in order. And why wasn't Jim or Richard Dortch told that David was not providing necessary receipts and other information?

David and his brother, James, were found guilty by a jury—I believe the charges were tax evasion, not embezzlement—and sent to jail, where they both served about five years. I didn't pay too much attention to their case, as I was so crushed about what was happening to Jim, so I'm still not clear about all the particulars. From the bottom of my heart I apologize for David Taggart's actions. It was PTL's responsibility to root out corruption, and in this case we failed. I can't offer any excuse for that.

Through the tortured weeks of the trial, the major force sustaining me was my mother. She was the only source of comfort I had. She would pray for me by the hour. She would call me and say, "Tam, it's going to be okay, honey. It's going to be okay. You just keep your faith in God. He will take care of you." Luckily, Jim's parents were very good support for him. So we had a group of people that stood with us as we were being purged of the last shred of our dignity.

As the trial approached its last days, Alan Dershowitz appeared on the scene. I don't know who called him in. All I know is that he arrived with much fanfare. I don't even know what he did. He was only there for one day. He was supposed to stay for longer than that, but he had to leave for some reason. He claims that *he* is the reason Jim's sentence was eventually reduced. I don't know. All I remember about Alan is his frequent calls to me in Orlando and the threatening letters he wrote telling me that he had to have the thousands of dollars we owed him for that one day he was there. I would get so scared whenever I got one of those letters or received one of those calls. I was desperately trying to raise money to pay him, but I was alone, pastoring a tiny church, trying to get enough money to-gether to take care of my son and pay the rent and the electric bill plus the huge telephone bills—the only way Jim and I could even talk to each other was if he called collect. I called everyone I knew to see if they could or would help pay off Dershowitz's bill. A man finally gave me $25,000; I gave this directly to Alan. Even though that did not pay the whole amount we owed him, it was enough to satisfy him for a while. I know that Alan Dershowitz had every right to attempt to collect his fee, and I'm not faulting him for that. But it was one of the straws that helped break the camel's back for me.

By this point our reputation was destroyed, our ability to work and make a living was also destroyed, and any linger-ing doubts were gone. Everybody thought we were crooks. And there was no way left to prove that we weren't. We were in a no-win situation. All we had left was God. I cried out, "God, where are You? Oh, God, where are You?" I'd pray and pray, but it felt like my prayers didn't even reach the ceiling.

The verdict came as no surprise. I had been prepared for it from the first day of the trial. Maximum Bob gave Jim forty-five years—basically a life sentence, when you con-sider that Jim was fifty years old when convicted. There was no money for an appeal.

Even so, just seconds after the sentence was pro-nounced, the lawyers were whispering to him, "Don't worry, Jim. We'll have you out in less than a month. This is just a temporary setback."

Jim was put into handcuffs and led away from the court-room off to jail. They didn't even give me the chance to put my arms around him or give him one last kiss. What was the big hurry, anyway? From the moment Jim was con-victed, I became locked in a terrible prison as well—the darkest prison you could possibly imagine.

The Punishment
Is a Crime

A good friend of mine once wrote a song that says, "There are times when you think you've hit your highest low yet, and there's just nothing left to go wrong." Every time I hear those words I think of Jim in prison. Of everything I have ever gone through, it was always my "highest low yet." Only those who have been there can possibly know the effect it has on the rest of your life, no matter how hard you try to forget, to put it in the past.

All through the trial, the long jury deliberations, right up to the last moment, my mind would not, could not, believe that something like this could happen to our family. There must be something protecting the mind during severe trauma—so that you don't go insane.

I felt that the thousands and thousands of people we'd loved so much and served for the last twenty years on television had all turned against us. They had let us down by believing the negative press that was continually bombarding them every hour on the hour. How could they believe we would steal from them?

By the time Jim was finally tried and put in prison, I was numb—numb with fear, anger, discouragement, and disbelief. I had seen my husband led around like a serial killer in shackles and handcuffs, paraded across the television sets of America. Our family had been accused of everything but murder. In fact, Jim would have received less time if he had murdered someone. I had no more faith in the judicial system, and I still don't to this day.

After the sentence was issued, they led Jim away, not even letting us know where they were taking him. I thought that was appalling.

I placed a call to Jim's lawyers. "Where have they taken him?" I screamed between sobs. "You are supposed to know. Where is he?" I was frantic.

Jamie was crying too. "What are they saying, Mom? Where is Dad?" The lawyers did not know, but they told me that Jim would call me as soon as he got where he was going and that I wasn't to worry.

"I don't know, Jamie. I don't know, honey," I said. "But they say that Daddy is okay and will call us tomorrow." Jamie and I held on to each other as we cried.

We did not find out where Jim was until two days later, when he was finally allowed a collect call from the federal prison in Rochester, Minnesota, sixteen hundred miles away from us in Orlando, Florida. Why had they put him in a prison so far from his family? I feel that it was just to be cruel. Why couldn't they have put him in a prison in Florida? How would Jamie and I ever be able to afford to go visit him? I about jumped out of my skin when the phone rang. Waiting for that call, I had not left the house in two days.

"Hello, Jim, honey. Where are you? Are you all right?" I realized I was screaming.

"I'm all right, Tam," he answered in a voice so weary I could hardly understand what he was saying.

"You don't sound fine. What are they doing to you?"

"I'm sorry I didn't get to say good-bye, Tam. They wouldn't let me. I begged them, but they shackled my hands and feet and put me in a police car. We drove all the way from Charlotte to Minnesota. I didn't bring a coat with me, and it's cold up here. I can't seem to get warm."

"Tell me what happened once you got there," I said, suddenly filled with curiosity about what prison was like. But I wish I hadn't asked, because what I heard make me sick to my stomach.

"Well, when we finally got here, it was late at night. I was so tired and so cold I wanted to die, Tam. And I had to go to the bathroom so bad I was getting sick."

"Didn't they allow you to stop and use the rest room on the trip?"

"Yes, they would stop if I asked them, but we had to use gas stations and restaurant bathrooms, and they had to go in there with me because of the shackles and handcuffs. I was too embarrassed to go unless it just got to be an emergency. When we finally got here, they took me into this big empty room. They took off my handcuffs and shackles and then told me to take all my clothes off.

"There were a lot of men standing around and I said, 'In front of all these people?'

" 'Just do as we told you,' the officer barked at me. Tam, I was so exhausted, so nervous and embarrassed, I didn't know what to do. I was shaking all over. They let me stand there naked in front of all those men who kept poking each other and making snide, crude remarks as they watched me being strip-searched.

"Tam, they felt all my private parts, went into every opening in my body, even made me stick my tongue out so they could look in my mouth. I don't know what they were looking for. I had been with them in handcuffs and leg irons for two days. It was so humiliating.

"I heard one guy say to his fellow officer, 'I was wondering what Jim Bakker had between his legs.' "

I was livid as I listened to Jim talk. "I'm going to call and complain to the prison warden," I screamed.

"Don't do that, Tam," he warned. "If you do, they'll just take it out on me."

My mind went back to Jim dressed in his beautiful suits, in front of millions of people on TV preaching the gospel, one of America's best-known ministers. Now he was being treated worse than an animal.

I sobbed as I hung up the phone. "God, where are You? Where are You? Can You hear me, do You even care?" I cried myself to sleep and woke up the next morning still crying. I could not understand.

When I think of it, I think of the little poem about Humpty Dumpty we learned as children. And just as all the king's horses and all the king's men couldn't put Humpty together again, I will never be the same again. Tammy Sue and Jamie will never be the same again; and I know that Jim will never be the same again. Prison steals something from a human being that you never get back again. It takes a part of you away.

You realize your vulnerability, that it is indeed possible to lose control of your own life, that you are powerless over certain situations, that you can be destroyed. It humiliates and degrades you beyond belief. Let me tell you what it is like for the families of prisoners when they go to see their loved one.

I remember the first Christmas Jim was in jail. The small room where we were checked in was filled to overflowing with women and children waiting to visit their husbands and daddies. The guards at the desk were never in a hurry and as usual were taking their time. Families were kept waiting outside in the twenty-below weather for sometimes half an hour because the guards wouldn't open the doors one minute early—even for the mothers with tiny, freezing babies.

Standing outside hearing those babies crying from the cold made me almost hate for the first time in my life. What had happened to simple human decency? But there is no kindness in prison, only rules, and you had better follow them to the letter.

Everyone must sign in, giving your name and address and the number of the inmate you are visiting. The guard calls you one at a time, and the first thing he does is to take your coat, any bags you may be carrying, baby blankets and whatever else, and run them through an X-ray machine. Then he asks you to walk through a metal detector.

Since it was so cold, everyone was dressed warmly with heavy coats, boots, and scarves. If you buzzed going through the machine, you had to take things off until you didn't buzz anymore. Nearly everyone had to take off their shoes or boots, all their jewelry, and their belts; the system was so touchy. Some people would wind up standing there almost naked. I will never forget one time standing there in my stocking feet begging them not to make me take off my jacket as I didn't have much on under it. I was so embarrassed.

After finally making it through the X-ray machine, you stand in a line to get your hand stamped with a mark that glows. Then you are marched about fifteen at a time into this little room, and the heavy metal doors close with a thud. In there you put your marked hand under a machine that reads it. When everyone has done that, the bolted door on the other side opens and you walk outside in the freezing cold again. You walk several feet to another building. Where once again you stand outside and wait for a lethargic guard to come along with his keys to open the door.

You file into a huge room filled with plastic chairs and short wooden tables, much lower even than your average coffee table. Two guards sit in the front of the room. You go immediately up to one of them and once again check in, signing your name and the number of the inmate you are visiting.

Over on one side of the room are vending machines filled with sandwiches, popcorn, drinks, and candy bars. This is what you will be eating all day long, providing there aren't too many people visiting and they don't run out of food. You bring rolls of quarters to purchase the food with. The inmates are not allowed to carry any money, so you must remember to bring enough for them, too. You wait and wait until at last the door by the guard opens and your loved one walks out.

You are allowed one hug and a quick kiss, but you are not permitted to touch after that. The inmate must sit facing the guards at all times. If you have to use the bathroom, you check out a key from the guard. The guard goes right into the bathroom with the inmate. I recall Jim would not use the bathroom from 8:00 A.M. until we had to leave at 3:00 P.M. because he didn't want to have to do so in front of a guard.

My heart ached for him. What a terrible, degrading, inhuman place prison is. I felt so sorry for the little children. From eight o'clock until three in the afternoon is such a long time for children to be confined. The prison would allow no toys inside. The only thing the children could play with was a big box of dirty wooden blocks and a few torn-up children's books.

When it's time to leave, the guards yell out, "Visiting hours are over! Visitors step to the back, inmates to the front!" I can hardly write about what takes place at that time. Little children hold on to their daddies crying, "I don't want to go!" Tears are streaming down everyone's faces. Some join hands and pray, others turn and literally run out the back so that husbands will not see them weeping. I was one of those. You keep waving and waving until the guards let you walk out the door, it hurts so bad!

I will never forget one time when Tammy Sue was there with her babies. Jim took off his glasses so that he could play with little James and Jonothan. And Tammy Sue, not thinking, put them in her diaper bag for him. When it came time to leave she remembered her daddy's glasses, but she was already outside the first building.

"Could you please give these to Jim Bakker," she asked the guard politely, taking the glasses out of her bag.

"Prisoners aren't allowed to receive anything."

"But these are his. I accidentally took them."

"I told you. Prisoners aren't allowed to receive anything."

"It'll just take a minute."

"Move on."

"I can't believe you won't—"

"Move on, or you'll never be allowed back in here!"

Tammy Sue started to cry, and with tears running down her cold little face put her dad's glasses back in her bag. Which meant that Jim was without his glasses until he could get another appointment with the prison eye doctor and get another pair. And that took weeks! That was unnecessary cruelty.

Jim's hypochondria made being in prison very difficult for him. Of course the officials gave him the dirtiest job in the prison. All the five years he was incarcerated, he had to clean the prison toilets. They were filthy places, with urine, excrement, spit, and vomit everywhere. And when there were fights, they would generally take place in the toilet, so add blood to the list of disgusting messes Jim would have to clean up.

Nevertheless, Jim informed me that his floor had the cleanest rest rooms in the whole prison. He double-gloved to clean the toilets, and got on his hands and knees to clean the floors with disinfectant. Jim said that in one way he was glad he had been assigned that job—because in doing it himself, he knew it was really clean.

Jim has never been afraid of hard work. I have seen him, hundreds of times, doing the same tasks that his employees were doing. He'd join them with a shovel, a hammer, a paint brush, cleaning tools; no job was too hard or too dirty for Jim to help out with. He always said that he would never ask a man to do a job he wouldn't do himself. And I saw him prove that time and time again. So if the prison officials thought they were further punishing Jim Bakker by making him do manual labor, they were very much mistaken. Jim told me that hard work is what kept him from going crazy while he was there.

Even in prison, Jim never stopped giving. He's terrific at doing ceramics, as he's so creative, and he was constantly sending me beautiful vases that he had designed. Knowing that I love fake food, he fashioned a ceramic pizza for me and a cup of hot chocolate complete with a marshmallow floating on top. Jim made me jewelry and darling little ceramic animals, even a miniature version of my dog Tuppins. Even though I loved the things he made for me, it was always so sad to see them sitting around my house and knowing the pain and suffering they represented. I could hardly look at them without crying.

Despite all the obvious hardships, Rochester was still a white-collar prison and was probably one of the best facilities Jim could have been in. The medical care was good. If the prisoners got sick, they were sent over to the Mayo Clinic, which was close by. Rochester was very clean, very neat, and very well kept. But even at its best, it was still a horrible place.

While Jim was in prison, my major concern was just trying to keep my mind together. I was also attempting to make a living for Jamie and me. Jim called collect, the only way he could call, every day; he was hurting so bad and needed to talk. We would spend an hour at a time on the phone. I was trying so hard to help him with his depression. I would have been terribly despondent in his situation too, so I totally understood. We would cry together, and once in a while I could even make him laugh a little. That is when I learned how expensive long distance can be.

Whew! Every month I was paying anywhere from $400 to $800 in phone bills.

That was a very hard time for me, trying to keep him up, because at the same time I was so lonely and hurting so bad and feeling so betrayed by everyone. I felt God had left me alone.

"Tam, I'm in a cell with four other prisoners. And everybody's got a different idea of what time to go to bed."

"Don't let them bother you, Jim. Just try to get some rest."

"You don't know what it's like! All the noise, the guards just strutting around all day and night, clanging those thick iron key rings, until you can hear those keys clanging in your head even when they're not there."

"Then put something in your ears. Honey, just try to tune them out. You know you used to be pretty good at that."

"Then they're always slamming the doors. These thick metal doors. It sounds like they're closing the doors on a tomb."

"Hang in there, Jim. You are stronger than you think. Thousands of people still love you and are praying for you. The lawyers told me they're doing everything in their power to get you out of that place."

"I can't sleep, Tam. I am so tired. And I can't eat. The food is good, but it's not good for me. It is so greasy. And with my ulcer, you know what that does to my stomach."

Jim had to be careful what he said because they monitored his phone calls. He had to be careful what he wrote in letters because they read all his outgoing mail. So we would try to have a conversation, but really it was just surface talk, talking without actually saying anything really important. It was the same when we wrote letters. Prison was a living hell for Jim, a man who only wanted to lead people to heaven.

But to his credit, even though he was suffering miserably, Jim tried to make the best of it. He had exceedingly good relationships with the other inmates. They all respected him. There were many professional men in there, including a group of corporate lawyers. One man that Jim got friendly with was a skydiver who had organized the largest skydiving events in the world. I don't know why he was there in prison.

Of course, the professional people tended to draw together for protection, because in every prison there are many dangerous people, violent men who could hurt you real bad. Tempers flare, things get out of hand. You walk a fine line in prison. Nothing serious ever happened to Jim. Of course, I believe that God protected him. For the most part, Jim got along very well and participated in many areas, such as all those community men's groups they had in prison. He would have taken on more of a leadership role except that the guards wouldn't allow it. Jim was completely forbidden from ministering inside the prison walls, but I'm sure he talked to many men privately about Jesus and God.

Roe Messner also visited Jim on several occasions. By this time Roe was having severe difficulties of his own. Because of PTL's bankruptcy, he was owed millions of dollars, which plunged him into debt. Further complicating matters was a bad marriage. But Roe never dwelled on his own dismal situation. Instead he tried to be supportive and cheer Jim up as best he could, and he listened to Jim's ideas about the future.

I was glad to hear that Jim was talking about the future again. It gave him something to get excited about. It gave his mind something to fix on besides prison. He and Roe would talk for hours about the possibility of building again. Once again Jim was drawing buildings on napkins, and once again Roe was telling Jim what he thought the cost would be. I don't know if Jim really thought he could ever again build anything the size of Heritage USA, but I think talking about it to someone like Roe, who understood, at least gave him a sense of self-worth again.

During one of Roe's visits, Jim was really excited. He had heard from one of the other inmates that there was a beautiful place—much like Heritage USA but smaller—that was for sale in French Lick, Indiana. It was a famous hotel, built in the 1920s, and it was said to be in great condition. The place would be a perfect spot to start over, as it was already a well-known tourist attraction.

Jim asked Roe if he would fly to French Lick and check it out, and Roe did. He came back with a good report and with the news that the owners had decided to auction off the hotel instead of putting it on the real estate market. The bidding would start at $1 million. Roe felt that he could find private investors who were sympathetic to Jim's dream of building another ministry, and he did. They told Roe that they were willing to invest up to $3 million.

Jim informed me that he wanted me to move the ministry I was building in Orlando and work at getting back on television again. I was excited but overwhelmed at the thought of doing it all by myself. "Jim, you're asking too much of me," I said. "The TV stations are never going to sell time to a woman, especially to Tammy Bakker. And even though I have a mailing list of thousands of people, I've never raised money before, Jim. I wouldn't have the first clue of where to start."

"I'll teach you, Tam—everything you need to know."

I still was not convinced, but at least I was willing to try. Jim begged me to at least go see the property for myself, which I did. It was beautiful, but it would be a huge responsibility for a lady with a ruined reputation and a husband in prison. I was nearly sick with fear that the sale might actually happen. And it almost did!

Roe went to the bidding. He and one other man were the only bidders. Roe bid up to the $3,000,000 he had, and the other man bid $3,050,000. In one way I was relieved that we did not get the property, in another way I was sad. It would have been such a morale booster for Jim. But it was not to be. Jim gave up after that, I think. I never again heard him talk about rebuilding.

After Jim had been in prison a couple of years, it was time for his lawyers to try to get his sentence reduced. So Jim had to be flown from Rochester back to Charlotte. When he arrived he was put in the county jail to await his court appearance.

It was the same jail we had visited so many times before, ministered in, where we had taken the band and singers to entertain during Christmas, where we had brought hundreds of wrapped holiday gifts each year to hand out to the inmates. In fact, the warden himself had visited PTL many times and had even been on television with us, along with his deputies.

But all that seemed like a million years ago. Now I was visiting Jim there, and it was suddenly the dirtiest place I had ever seen. It made me sick to walk through that place. I remember thinking, They could at least paint the walls and make an attempt to keep things clean.

The guards led me to a small unkempt room. I sat there on a rusty chair waiting for Jim to come from his cell. I was horrified when I saw him. He had on a filthy, wrinkled bright orange jumpsuit. He was haggard, and his hair was long and shaggy. He looked sick and feeble. He wouldn't even let me touch him. Tears started running down my face as the agony in my heart overflowed.

"Jim, what have they done to you?"

He just shrugged weakly. "Tam, this place is terrible. The food smells bad, the cells are filthy. I can't eat, I can't sleep, and I have to be in court tomorrow."

I had bought Jim a suit to change into the next morning.

But he told me the next day they had made him dress in the hall and that they would not even allow him to have a mirror so that he could shave and comb his hair. After putting on his suit, they locked him in shackles and hand-cuffs and took him to the court. My stomach is sick as I write this, even after so many years have passed. Nothing was worse than seeing my husband treated like a dog. I take that back. You would be locked up for treating a dog like they treated him!

Out of the hundreds of preachers Jim had helped finan-cially, given free airtime to, I think maybe five or six of them actually visited him while he was in prison. They didn't even bother to write him. Where were these men of God when Jim needed them so desperately?

Even more devastating was the way in which Pat Robert-son conducted himself. When Jim was put away, Robert-son basically said that he deserved it—that Jim deserved to serve every last day of his sentence. I thought this was an extremely cruel and cold-blooded thing to say. It wasn't enough that Jim was buried; Robertson had to shovel more dirt on his grave. It's incredible! Only a short time before, when Pat had been running for the presidency, he had been praising Jim left and right.

Nonetheless, I will forever be grateful to a minister named Phil Shaw. When he heard they were sending Jim to Rochester, he applied to be Jim's pastor, since he minis-tered a local church in the area. Phil and his wife, Faith, visited Jim every week he was in prison.

When our family flew in to visit Jim, Phil would be there at the airport in below-zero weather to pick us up and take us to the local hotel. Beyond that, that precious man and his church paid our hotel bill many times. They cared for me, Tammy Sue, and Jamie as if we were their family. They brought us to their home, and Faith fixed wonderful meals for us. They loved our family and comforted us in our time of greatest need.

Another one of the few bright moments was when Billy Graham, who proved himself to be a real man of faith, twice visited Jim in prison and was very comforting to him. He was very kind and thanked Jim for giving hundreds of thousands of dollars to Billy's son, Franklin, for his ministry. Billy Graham was just what you would expect him to be, completely neutral, unconcerned about public opinion. Unlike many lesser preachers, he refused to score points by taking cheap shots at Jim or me. He made it a point not to talk to the press or anybody about us. But he did call us at our home and speak to us at length. Billy Graham was very supportive through the most difficult years of my life, and I'll always treasure him dearly for that.

Reverend Mike Murdock and Reverend Robert Gass also made several trips to see Jim in prison. Mike wrote most of the music that I sang on *PTL*, and Robert was a frequent guest on the program. These men did not forget us, and I will always respect the fact that they were not afraid to practice what they preached. That took guts!

On November 4, 1991, Judge Thurmond Bishop handed down a decision. This is part of what he said:

> It was not contemplated that lifetime partners would be entitled to a specific hotel room, condominium, or unit on the premises . . . nor were partners promised availability of rooms or any other benefits for the use of their partnerships. Moreover, no trust relationship is alleged to have been created. . . . In essence, the rights and responsibilities of the individual lifetime partners and the debtor were both fully operative and were being delivered and provided prior to the filing of the bankruptcy petition.
>
> These payments, solicited as gifts, and made by the plaintiffs to the debtor, do not fall under the definition of deposit. Additionally, it is important to note that at the time of payment by the lifetime partners, no deposit arrangement could have been contemplated by the parties.

In other words, the ruling of Judge Bishop clearly stated that the lifetime partnerships were really gifts to the ministry. They weren't deposits, say, of the sort you'd make on a condominium as a down payment. They were contributions. And as such they would entitle partners to four days and three nights at the Heritage Grand Hotel, no more, no less. Partners didn't have to take out a mortgage or a loan. For their gift they received our gift, a guaranteed free vacation for the rest of their lives. This decision by itself should have immediately overturned Jim's conviction. Right then and there he should have walked out of a prison a free man, but they kept him in no matter how much we appealed. The courts and the Bush administration didn't even pretend they were listening.

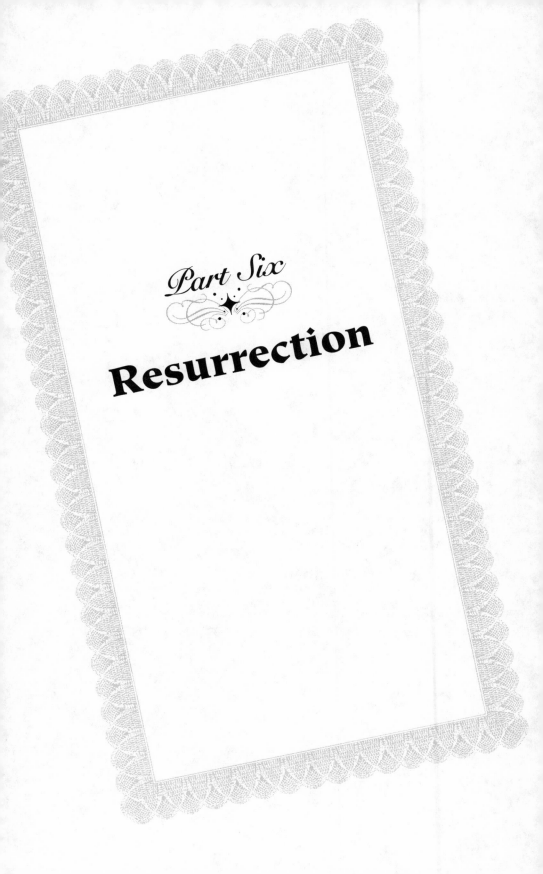

Part Six

Resurrection

Tammy Faye

Ministries

ife in Orlando was very hard on me. I was alone for the first time in my life. My husband was in prison. I had a young son to raise by myself. I was forced to make the living for our family. I had gone right from working at Woolworth's to getting married to television, so I had no experience in the modern working world.

My name, my reputation, everything that I held dear had been destroyed by the news media. I was a national laughingstock. Everything about me was being ridiculed. I could not watch television without my eyelashes, my makeup, and even my tears being made fun of. I was the butt of comedians' crude jokes and snide remarks. My heart ached constantly. My pillow would be wet with tears every night. But during the day, for the sake of Jamie, I put on a happy face. I had lost all my self-confidence, I was scared to death. The only thing that held me together was that I knew I was not the first woman who was suddenly alone with no money and a child to take care of. If even one of them had made it, then I could too.

I had a house payment that had to be made, a fast-growing child who constantly needed new clothes and shoes, doctor bills, dentist bills, phone bills, electric bills. It seemed there was no end to the expenses of just living. I was terrified! I knew I had to do something, but what? Who in their right mind would ever hire Tammy Faye Bakker? They too would become a laughingstock.

All I knew how to do was television. And no one in television would give me a job. They wouldn't touch me with a ten-foot pole, or even a hundred-foot pole! I was desperate. I wanted to run away, to hide, but I had Jamie there. I had to live for him. If I fell apart, he would have no one. At just thirteen years old he needed his mom.

The first few days after Jim went off to prison, I was inconsolable. I would drive Jamie to school and come home, put on my old pink bathrobe, and cry until I could cry no more. "God, please help me, I don't know what to do." My cries would ring out through that empty house. I felt forsaken by God. The phone would ring, and I was afraid to answer it. When I did, it would be Jim, suffering dreadfully, or it would be the school. "Mrs. Bakker, you need to come and get Jamie; he's having a problem."

Every day he would go to school, and every day I would get a call from one of his teachers asking me to pick Jamie up. His stomach was always upset. He was continually getting into fights with kids who teased him mercilessly about his dad being locked up. Jamie was having a dreadful time. I didn't know how to help him.

In truth I just wanted to die. For the first time in my life I understood the thoughts going through the mind of a person who is thinking about suicide. I knew I had to get a hold on myself and my emotions if I was going to survive. I needed a quiet place where I could go and talk to God. Once again, I found comfort inside my closet. It was there that I poured out my misery to the God I had served for so many years. Almighty God—who I had always proclaimed could help you through any situation.

I was filled with so much anger. Anger at preachers whom we had helped and who now acted as if we had died, anger at Jerry Falwell, anger at Jim for not standing up, for forcing me to be in this position. I was living in horrid grief, grief over losing a husband and so many people we thought were our friends, grief over losing the only job I knew how to do, grief for my children, grief for the PTL partners who were suffering too.

In that closet I cried out to God for deliverance, for peace, and for restoration of my joy. And He did not fail me. In my darkest moment, at the very bottom of my despair, He allowed me once again to feel His presence. He flooded my poor body with warmth, peace, joy, and faith for the future that had seemed so bleak and hopeless. My life was so filled with darkness, and He dispelled that darkness with the light of His love. He gave me the will to live again, not just to exist.

There is a great difference between just existing and living. And suddenly I wanted to live again. When I left that closet, the sky looked brighter, the flowers more radiant, the very air I breathed more refreshing. For the first time in a long time I decided that I was going to make it. That nothing was too hard if I had God on my side. I decided to start practicing what I had preached all these years.

To start with, I knew that I had to work on my anger. It was only destroying me. It didn't hurt the people I was angry at, but it was eating me alive. They say that anger does more damage to the vessel in which it is stored than it does to the object on which it is poured. I believe that. I remembered hearing once that in some ancient cultures, if you murdered someone, the person you killed would be strapped to your back. Can you imagine carrying a corpse around on your back? You couldn't eat, you couldn't sleep, the stench alone would be nauseating. Other people wouldn't come anywhere near you. That decaying corpse would eventually kill you. That is what anger and hate do to you. It's like carrying around a decaying dead body on your back all the time.

When anger and hate are all you can think about, they color everything you do, everything you say. And if you don't rid yourself of them, they will eventually kill you, emotionally if not physically. It's not worth the price! You need to drop all that negativity and move on. And that is what I made a decision to do in my life.

I often think about the words *bitter* and *better.* The only difference in those two words is one letter, the letter "i." I decided in that closet of suffering that I was not going to allow the hurts in my life to make me bitter, but I was going to use them to make me better. I have found that everything in life is about attitude. It is not the circumstances that destroy you; it is your attitude *toward* the circumstances that destroys you. I knew that I desperately needed an attitude adjustment. I asked God to help me make that adjustment, and He did. You are not a victim unless you allow yourself to be. I decided I was no longer going to be a victim but that I was going to be a victor. And that decision changed my life.

I began feeling better—about myself, about my situation, about life in general. Over the years on TV I had often sung, "You can make it." But I was learning that it's much easier to sing about it than it was to live it. Nevertheless, I was determined to live it.

I started right where I was—inside my closet. I had a huge TV wardrobe that I wouldn't be wearing anymore. So one of the first things I did was to box up all the stylish remnants of my former life. I took my blouses off the rack, my skirts, my shoes and belts, purses and jackets, and just started packing them away. I piled up the boxes one on top of another. You could hardly even get through. There were stacks and stacks of them all over the bedroom.

Then I decided to take these clothes down to a resale shop I had seen in Orlando. I filled the trunk of my car several times in the next few weeks with television clothes. And to my surprise, they sold like wildfire. The lady who ran the shop kept asking me if I had any more things I could bring in, and I did. I made $2,000 the first month from my initial trunkload of clothes. The next month I made even more. I couldn't believe it. Selling my clothes is what saved me and Jamie financially.

But I knew this was just a temporary solution. Therefore I decided to do the only thing I knew how to do, and something Jim had asked me to do right after he was imprisoned: start a church for the partners who still loved us and our ministry. I was scared to death of the prospect, but with Jim's consistent encouragement and the help of many friends, I got the nerve to begin.

We conducted our first services in hotels, in homes, wherever we could. But hardly anyone was coming because it was difficult to find us. So we distributed maps, pasted flyers inside rest rooms, and put up signs along the road, anything to let people know where the Tammy Faye Ministries were.

As word got out, our congregation started growing rapidly and I realized that I had to find a permanent home pretty soon. We located a building that fitted our needs perfectly. It had sufficient office space, a large room in which to hold services, and a suitable hall for expansion. Volunteers got together, and we cleaned and painted and laid new carpet. But just when we were getting our heads above water, in came the zoning commission—and closed us down, claiming it was because there was a paint factory next door that could blow up.

I had to go to court, but since there was hardly any money for lawyers, I didn't think I stood a chance—until a small miracle took place. When the American Civil Liberties Union heard of our plight, they went in and fought for us—filing motions left and right—and sure enough, we won. I will always be grateful to the ACLU for going to bat for me. After weeks of fighting city hall, we finally got our church back. What a relief!

It wasn't long until our new little church was making ends meet. We were able to pay the rent and all the other expenses connected with running a ministry. We were able to put nine employees on salary, and we were even able to purchase a beautiful baby grand piano for the church. Mike Murdock and Robert Gass had been kind enough to share their mailing lists with me so that once again I was able to contact the PTL partners and let them know where we were and what we were doing.

Our mailing list continued to grow. In fact, it got so big that we could not afford to write back to the thousands of people who began to write us. PTL partners were giving our address to one another. It was a real miracle, and I will always be grateful to those precious people who helped me survive while Jim was away.

Then, to my surprise, the media started showing up. I could not figure out why they would still be interested in me. After all, I had not been on TV in three years. But they were still talking about my makeup, my eyelashes, and my tears. And they were still calling me a controversial woman. That always makes me laugh. I cannot for the life of me figure out why they think I am controversial.

But the new publicity also started bringing in former PTL partners from all over the country. Some Sundays we would have people from as many as twenty states in our congregation. I would always have a show of hands and ask people where they were from. It meant so much to me that people still cared enough to find me.

For two years I worked hard pastoring that church. I spent all day Saturday preparing the message I would preach to the people on Sunday. I spent every day of the week answering mail and working in the office with our staff. But trying to be perfect, giving everything I had and even more, made my life very hard. It got to where I would rather take a beating than go to church on Sunday and face those people who were expecting something from me. In short, I was burned out.

I felt I couldn't preach one more sermon or sing one more song, that I was not really doing anyone any good, including myself. These same people could go to another church and be ministered to just as easily as they could at my church. I wrestled with the idea of closing New Covenant Ministries.

There wasn't even a spare moment to take a vacation, which further compounded my exhaustion. I visited Jim in prison every time I could get enough money together to buy airline tickets for Jamie and me. We continued to speak every day on the phone, but as time passed, his dreadful suffering began to take a heavy toll on me.

Naturally, I would always try to encourage him without getting discouraged myself. But try as I might, I just could not help him. He was hurting too bad. He felt that I couldn't possibly understand how horrible it was to be in prison. On each visit to prison, less and less was said between us. We just sat and ate popcorn or whatever other junk they had in the machine. Even though we hardly spoke a word, our mutual misery was deafening.

Divorcing Away My Life

I was busy making chili in my kitchen when the phone rang. My first thought was, "It must be Jim, he hasn't called yet today." Indeed it was Jim, and as usual he sounded serious and discouraged. I was getting ready to give him my standard "You can make it" speech when he interrupted me.

"Tam, I know that you don't love me anymore."

I was shocked. My mouth just fell open. We had barely been able to communicate since the day he went to prison, we were both hurting so bad. And I think the guilt Jim felt over what had happened to our family as a result of the decisions he made was nearly killing him. I did not want to injure him any further by talking about all my frustration toward him. The horrors of prison were more than enough; he didn't need me venting my feelings. I just couldn't inflict any more pain on him.

Therefore I lived with my hurt and anger tucked safely inside me. Naturally I was always kind whenever I went to visit Jim, but inside I could feel nothing but hopelessness, as if I didn't even know him anymore. I was numb to any feeling. He would come out of the prison holding cell into the visitors' area, and all I wanted to do was to cry. When I kissed him I felt nothing, just profound sadness. We would sit down and not even look at each other.

I would see other couples trying to cuddle without being caught. Walking hand in hand in the courtyard and doing things that would get the wife kicked out if they were caught by the guard. I envied them, wishing so much that there was still something left in my heart for the man I was visiting—the man who had been my husband for nearly thirty years. But that something in my heart had died a slow, painful death.

I don't know just how it died—from neglect, from words spoken that could be forgiven but never forgotten. I don't know if it was Jessica Hahn that killed my heart, or maybe the fact that Jim allowed such a dreadful thing to happen to our family. Death is always so sad, and all I could feel was just this terrible sadness, so deep I could not bring myself to talk about it, or even think about it.

It was destroying not only my spirit but my health as well. I had such high blood pressure they were going to put me on pills. I had trouble with my heart beating fast—fibrillating, the doctors called it. I was anemic and I had asthma. I felt bad all the time.

Ironically, I have always been the type of person who wants to make everything all right for everyone. My favorite words have always been, "Oh, don't worry, everything's going to be all right." But somehow I knew that it was not ever again going to be all right between Jim and me, that there was no way to fix it. I was not willing to go through any more marriage seminars. We had been through that ordeal twice before, and it was so hard on me. Besides, things always went back to the way they were. I don't blame that all on Jim. We both tried, but he had a huge ministry to run, and maybe I was just too needy. I don't know.

Now, as I stirred the chili that was bubbling away on the

stove, Jim said, "Tam, when you come and see me here at the prison, you look sadder every time I see you. You have nothing to say to me anymore. I don't know how much longer I'm going to have to be in here, Tam, so I am going to do you a favor. I am going to call our lawyer, Jim Toms, and tell him to start divorce proceedings. I want you to get on with your life, Tam. I really do."

At first I couldn't breathe. My heart filled with panic. My first thought was to say, "I love you, Jim. Don't file for divorce. It's going to be all right, you'll see." But for the first time in thirty years I couldn't bring myself to utter those words. As if I were paralyzed, I just sat there and listened to him.

"I know that you're living without sex, and I know how difficult that must be for you. I know how difficult it is for me."

"Yes, Jim," I responded, suddenly choking on the words.

"Who knows if I'll ever get out of here. The way things stand now, I'll probably die in prison. Look, Tam, the thought of you waiting for me all through the next years, all by yourself and alone at night, really crushes my heart. It's the straw that's breaking the camel's back. I can't let them put you in prison just because I am." I tried to find something to say, something consoling, but nothing came to my lips. "Tam, I've hurt you so terribly much that I just want to set you free. It's the one nice thing left that I can do for you."

Numbly, I heard my voice saying, "Jim, do what you have to do." A long silence came between us, and I knew right then and there that there was nothing left to say, except for "Good-bye, Jim. May God protect you. May He always protect you." There was another long silence, a darkness that seemed to fall over everything in the world. Then finally, without saying another word, we both hung up.

I turned off the stove and went into my bedroom and locked the door. I cried until I could cry no more. Divorce! I had never even allowed that word into my vocabulary. Marriage was supposed to be forever. What would my children think? I couldn't hurt them even more than they were already hurting. Especially Jamie. What would it do to his life if his parents got a divorce? I called my mom and poured my heart out to her.

Jim didn't call again for several days, and when at last he did he told me, "Tam, the divorce papers have been filed, and you'll receive a copy of them in a few days. Believe me, Tam. This is all for the best." I was dumbfounded. He was really serious. Later that day I got a call from our lawyer confirming what Jim had said. In fact, Jim had already signed the papers, Mr. Toms told me. My heart was beating so hard in my chest I thought I was having a heart attack.

A few more days went by. I didn't breathe a word to anyone, but it was the only thing on my mind day and night. I couldn't eat, couldn't sleep. People began to notice that I was losing weight. "Is everything all right, Tammy?"

"Oh, yes, I'm fine," I would answer. But they knew different, looking at my constantly tearstained face. I decided I had to talk to someone, and I didn't want to worry my mom any further. But who does Tammy Bakker talk to? Who could I trust to keep quiet? Jamie also needed some counseling desperately. Then someone told me of an experienced Christian psychologist in California. Her specialty was looking beyond the obvious and beyond what you said, discerning what your real hurts were and what you really wanted and needed in your life.

I decided to make an appointment with her for Jamie and me. In a few days we were on our way to California. Jamie talked with her first. I have never seen a young man cry so hard in my whole life. He still didn't know about our impending divorce. Jamie was inconsolable as he voiced his feelings about his dad in prison and his disappointments in Christians, particularly the preachers.

When Jamie left the room, it was my turn. I couldn't control myself any longer. My whole body shook with sobs and pent-up emotion as I poured out my heart to that doctor.

"Please help me, please help me! I have to have some sound advice from someone who is impartial."

By the time we had finished, she said, "Tammy, I have spoken to a lot of women in my many years of counseling, but I have never seen anyone as filled with pain as you are. You will never be happy until you do what you know you need to do. You have put off the inevitable for years, and you must make a decision. Everything is not going to be all right, and you know that. You need to stop pretending. Stop being Jim's mother and face reality. You really need to sign those divorce papers as soon as possible and get on with your life."

As I walked out of her office, I realized that I didn't have to carry Jim's heavy burdens anymore. I didn't have to be his caretaker. I didn't have to make everything all right for him anymore. I don't remember how I got on the airplane, when it left the ground, or when it landed. But all of a sudden I was back in Orlando again and the phone was ringing.

"Hello . . . oh, hi, Jim."

"Where have you been? I've been calling the house."

"Jamie and I were in California. We just got home. Listen, we went to see a Christian psychologist. Jamie and I both had a session with her. In fact, we had several sessions with her in the week we were there." Then Jim hit me again with surprising news.

"Tam, I have been praying, and I feel it was wrong of me to file for divorce. So I have asked Mr. Toms to just stop the proceedings." I was completely taken aback. Then I uttered the hardest words I have ever spoken in my life.

"Jim, I'm going to call him and tell him to continue the proceedings. I think we should get that divorce." I couldn't believe those words had come out of my mouth, but as I spoke them, I felt like a million pounds fell off my tired shoulders. Jim was flabbergasted.

"Well, if that's what you want, but you are going to have to say that you divorced me, not that I divorced you. I don't want the divorce, Tam."

"I'll take the blame then," I said. I hung up the phone and called Mr. Toms immediately. He was very kind to me and promised that he would move forward, that he would do anything he could to help either one of us.

But what was I going to do? Where was I going to go? How was I going to tell my children? What would the PTL partners say? How was I going to make a living? What would Jim do without me there for him? My mind was spinning.

A couple of weeks later I received a call from Mr. Toms. "Tammy, I know two judges who have loved you and Jim for years. They want to help you. They're trying a case down in Tallahassee. If you will meet them March thirteenth, they'll grant your divorce in between cases."

So I got up at 4:00 A.M. on March 13 because we had to leave by five to get to the court on time. It was cold outside, and it was a long drive. Shirley Fulbright, Jim's former secretary, who lived with me and Jamie, usually talked a hundred miles an hour, but both of us were quiet and reflective as we watched the palm trees and billboards pass by. I will never forget walking into that building. A great sadness overwhelmed me. This was not supposed to happen. It was supposed to go, "And they lived happily ever after."

I can hardly remember what came next, it happened so

fast. The judges were there waiting for me, as was Mr. Toms. Within about ten minutes it was all over and I was being asked to sign the final papers. With a sweep of my pen I simply became Tammy Faye. No more Jim. No more Bakker. I walked out of that room with conflicting feelings—sadness, relief, but most of all, loneliness. A loneliness such as I had never felt in my entire life.

I was silent all the way home. My voice wouldn't work. I entered the house, and it was not my house anymore. It seemed like I had divorced everything and everybody. I didn't know where I belonged. I went to the typewriter and began to type the last letter I would ever write to our ministry partners. I wanted to tell them before it was released in the news media. I wanted them to hear the truth from me and not from some tabloid account of what had happened between Jim and me. It worked! My letter arrived in their homes just in time. I was so grateful for that.

People often put me down for leaving Jim while he was still in prison. But I feel that leaving at the time I did was the kindest thing I could do for Jim. How cruel it would have been for me to have waited until he walked through those prison doors, happy and filled with great dreams and plans for Jim and Tammy. How cold it would have been for me to kill him with the words "Jim, I'm not going home with you. I want a divorce." How cruel it would have been for me to resist his hugs and kisses and his need to be loved. I could not do that to Jim. The way I did it, he had time to get used to being alone, time to adjust to the fact that when he got out of prison I would not be there. I know that was hard for him, too, but I feel that it was less painful than waiting until he got out.

Everyone who worked in my ministry was angry at me, and they felt I had made the wrong decision. So when it came time for me to pack the household belongings, only two people wanted to help me. I will always be grateful to Doc and Mary Ann Phillips. They worked night and day to help me pack all my things and enough furniture to outfit an apartment. I left more than half of our possessions for Jim. I wanted him to have enough to put together a home for himself when he got out. I left him the special things I knew he loved and would hate to part with.

I will never forget walking into Jim's closet for the last time. The day before, I had been to a store where they had a sale on garment bags. I bought as many as I could afford, and went home and hung all of Jim's clothes in them. He had such beautiful suits, and I didn't want anything to happen to them. With tears streaming down my face, I put them one at a time in the garment bags and then transferred them to a huge box. I marked the box JIM'S TELEVISION CLOTHES. It was the end of an era in my life, and the last thing I could do for Jim. I sat down on the floor and wept for what might have been.

Thereupon I found myself on the way to Palm Springs. It was a small town with a small-town atmosphere. Don and Emma Howard, our dear friends, still lived out there. Years earlier the Howards had just walked up to us in a restaurant and introduced themselves. They asked us if we wanted to go out and eat sometime, and before you know it, we all became the best of friends. Emma was a successful real estate agent, and to this day she remains my closest confidante. The Howards stood by us after we lost PTL.

Using her connections, Emma had found me a little place to live that I could afford. I loved Palm Springs. The sun always shone there. Maybe it would help heal my emotional wounds.

Jamie Trips and Gets Up

I begged Jamie to come with me to Palm Springs, but he was sixteen years old, and I had to allow him to make his own decision. "Well, there's not a whole lot I can do if you refuse to come," I said wearily. "I can't make you." Jamie felt that if he came to live with me he would be taking sides against his dad. I understood. The divorce was devastating for our son. He was absolutely furious with me. He couldn't believe that we were really breaking up. It shattered the last remnants of his security. Nothing could ever go back to the way it had been.

I remember the way I felt when my mom and dad were yelling at each other. I know I somehow blamed myself. How many times—I can't even count—did I hide under my bed, scared to death that my parents would separate?

So I knew something of what Jamie was going through, but he was experiencing something far worse than I could have imagined. After Jim's imprisonment, Jamie fell to pieces. Jamie could handle life as long as his dad was with him. But when they took his dad off to jail, I think something snapped inside. With the loss of Heritage USA and now this, it was like the whole world had turned against him.

Jamie desperately needed a male figure to confide in; but because he never wanted to worry his dad even the slightest, Jamie always told Jim that everything was fine, everything was just fine at school and in his life. The pressure on him became enormous.

All I could do was love him, feed him, clothe him, keep his room clean for him, and pray for him. Jamie didn't know how to deal with his pain and his fury. Therefore he turned to alcohol and drugs. Every time Jamie came back from a visit to prison he would have a terrible time for weeks. He would cry and cry. "Mom, I don't want to be like this, I don't mean to make you feel sad, but I just hurt so bad inside." Jamie blamed everything on Jerry Falwell. "Mom, I'm going to take a gun and kill that man!"

But I would tell him over and over, "Honey, you let God take care of Jerry Falwell. You have to forgive him, Jamie." But that was hard for a boy his age to understand. My heart ached for my precious son.

Jamie was smoking several cigarettes a day. I will never forget him telling me, "Mom, I feel like my cigarette is my friend. It gives me courage."

I would tell him, "I know, honey, but it is a friend that will turn on you and destroy you." However, I never harassed Jamie about his smoking. I felt that he needed something to comfort him. And at that time he did not understand that his comfort could come from God. Jamie also started to drink during this time. It started with beer. That seemed innocent enough. But the beer soon turned to hard alcohol, and before he knew it Jamie had a serious drinking problem.

"Mom, it numbs my mind. It makes me happy even if it is just for a little while." Every night when he was getting ready to leave the house for an evening with his friends, we would talk. "I'll be fine, Mom. I won't drink tonight, I promise." But I knew that he was unable to keep that promise, even though I know he tried desperately.

"I'll be home by midnight," he would tell me as he waved good-bye. "If I'm going to be late, I'll call you." Jamie was always very thoughtful and he didn't want me to worry, so I knew that he made a special effort to phone. I spent night after night after night praying that God would keep Jamie safe. I can still hear him knocking on my bedroom door. "I'm home, Mom," he would say. I could finally close my eyes.

Then I found out that Jamie was having a problem that I knew nothing about. He was experimenting with drugs. All his gang was doing it, and he got caught up in the peer pressure. I didn't know how to tell if a child was using drugs. I saw people on TV talking about it, but I never thought that could happen to my son. I never noticed anything different about Jamie, except that he slept a lot during the day. I thought that was normal for a teenage boy.

I don't remember how I discovered that Jamie was having a problem. I think he told me. He talked about putting a little piece of paper on his tongue, and how it would cause you to sit for hours hallucinating. Then something happened during one of those times that really scared Jamie: He could not stop hallucinating. It would not go away. Then he started to have flashbacks even when he wasn't using. He started getting panic attacks. He lived in constant fear of these flashbacks.

He said to me, "I'm so scared. I would commit suicide if I wasn't afraid of going to hell. Mom, I'm afraid that hell would be flashbacks that never go away. I need help, Mom, I need help so bad. I want to get my life straightened out. I don't want to smoke anymore, I don't want to drink anymore, and, Mom, I don't want to ever touch any kind of drug again."

And I knew that he meant it. But he knew he could not do it by himself.

Then a miracle happened. A PTL partner heard about the problems Jamie was having. He was a professional therapist, and his heart went out to our family. The phone rang one day, and the voice at the other end said, "Tammy, this is Dr. Jackson. I want to help your son, Jamie. I have a hospital where we treat patients with alcohol and drug addictions, but my wife, Lila, and I would like to take Jamie into our home, free of charge, and keep him there until he is able to handle life again." I started to weep with gratitude.

And true to his word, he and Lila went beyond the scope of ordinary medicine and actually took Jamie into their home. This wonderful, caring healer let Jamie live with him for weeks. He gave him medication to stop the flashbacks once and for all. The medication purified his body; the Lord cleansed his soul. From that day forward, Jamie never again went back to alcohol or drugs. He quit smoking altogether, totally beat the habit cold turkey. I shall be grateful to Dr. Jackson and his wife for the rest of my life.

When I moved to Palm Springs, Jamie decided to live with Shirley, Jim's secretary. As far as I was concerned, Shirley was family. She also had a son, about Jamie's age, who was off in school. Anyway, the two of them wound up living together in a spectacular place. One of the partners had graciously donated it to Jim for as long as he needed. It was a high-rise apartment right on the beach in St. Petersburg, Florida. Jamie and Shirley lived there. God bless Shirley. She became Jamie's second mother, and I will always love her for that. When Jim was released from prison, Jamie went to live with his father.

However, it was also during this time that a despicable article came out in one of the rag magazines. The headlines screamed: TAMMY FAYE DESERTS SON! The article said that I had left Jamie to wander from house to house like a bum with no place to go. I almost died! I still cannot believe that those magazines can get by printing such atrocious lies. And worse yet, making people believe them. Yes, such were the headlines haunting me as I tried to make a new life for myself in Palm Springs.

Roe Enters the Picture

After my divorce, I was racked with guilt. I felt like I could never get married again. What man would ever want me, given the horrible publicity associated with my name? But moreover, I didn't think I could ever trust a man again. Therefore I planned to live by myself and give my time to my kids and be a grandma and—well, that's what it would be. Love and romance seemed as far away as Mars. Then something truly extraordinary occurred.

Roe Messner walked into my life. Now, that was not unusual, as Roe had been so kind to me and Jamie while Jim was in prison. He had visited us and taken me and Jamie and Shirley out to dinner many times. His wife, Ruth Ann, had even come with him on one occasion when he came to the house in Orlando. So seeing Roe again was no big deal. I liked Roe. What I liked about him was his consistency. He never changed. He was always calm, always in charge, and I never once heard him raise his voice to anyone. He was an athletic man, and you could not help but notice that he kept himself in great shape. He always looked like a man you would see in a magazine, well dressed and very handsome. But all we ever were was friends.

When we were at PTL, I remember, I hated to see Roe coming because it meant that Jim was building another building. I don't think I ever really even spoke to Roe in all the years he was at PTL, except to say hello when he occasionally appeared on the TV show to be interviewed by Jim. We never did anything socially with Roe. In my mind, he was simply "the man who built Heritage USA."

One day I read in a magazine that Roe was Jim's best friend and that Jim, before he went to prison, said, "Roe, please take care of my family." I couldn't believe what I was reading. I asked Jim if he had said that, and he said no, he had never said anything like that. I still cannot believe how the news media can constantly get by fabricating lies and printing them as truth.

You would have thought that Roe would be awfully upset with Jim for what happened, but all I ever heard Roe do was defend Jim. He never once put Jim down for what happened to PTL or Heritage USA. Roe stood in Jim's defense in front of the grand jury, the news media, and everyone he talked with. I remember being truly impressed with Roe for that. To me he was a man of honor and principle.

I began to know Roe a little better during the trial, as he was a part of everything that was happening in the courtroom. Roe was very kind to me and Jim and the children at that time. I remember him writing out a check for $25,000 to Jim's defense fund. That touched me deeply. Roe also visited Jim in prison, something very few of our so-called friends did.

Shortly after my divorce came through, my phone rang and I was surprised to hear a familiar voice at the other end. "Hello, Tammy, this is Roe Messner. Would you mind if I came to see you?"

"Sure, Roe," I replied, not really thinking too much about it. "I would like that." Of course I never dreamed that one call would change my life forever. At the time Roe was building a church over in Jacksonville, and he flew to Orlando see me.

When he got to the house, he asked Shirley and me if he could take us out to dinner.

After we ate, and Roe was getting ready to go back to Jacksonville, he shook my hand and said good-bye and gave Shirley a hug. He didn't even hug me! I think he was playing it cool.

He never once gave me any hint that he was interested in me. Of course I thought that Roe was a happily married man, so I would have been shocked if he'd acted any differently. I never dreamed that for fifteen years Roe had lived in an unhappy marriage.

I was grateful when Roe asked me if I needed any help moving to California. Up until that time, I'd had no idea how I was going to get my furniture there. Roe said that he had an extra truck and would get a friend of his to load it and drive it to Palm Springs for me.

Roe came to visit me in Palm Springs. It was then he told me that he was getting a divorce, that he and his wife had been living separate lives for years. I was stunned!

Roe and I began to date, and he was extremely polite. I loved that about him. But one night after taking me to dinner, he just grabbed me and kissed me. I nearly had a heart attack. Roe could not possibly be interested in me, I'd thought. What man would take a chance and get involved with Tammy Bakker? The publicity would be more than most men could take. I talked to Roe about that, but from the moment we first kissed, magic happened—and it was too late!

We realized that what was happening between us was very special, something that only happens to most people once in a lifetime (and that's if they're lucky!). I don't think a man and a woman should ever marry if that magic isn't there. Because magic between two people is not something you can make happen. It's either there or it isn't. And it was there for Roe and me. I could not believe that something so wonderful could happen to me.

There was something else that meant a lot to me: I knew that I could trust Roe. At PTL, it was well known that he was an honest, true, good man. Roe never went back on his word. He was the good earth!

Another thing I loved about Roe was his gentle, quiet nature. He was not a driven man. And he believed in stopping to smell the roses every day.

About the time we started getting serious, Roe thought it would be the right thing to go see Jim and tell him face-to-face what was going on. On the way he picked up Jamie, and the two of them flew to Rochester. Roe said to him, "I want to tell Jim that I want to start dating your mother." But Jamie went absolutely ballistic.

"I don't want you to tell Dad that! There's no way you're going to tell him anything!"

"Jamie, I think it's—"

"I don't care what you think! I'm not going to let you do that to him!"

"Jamie, I wish you'd—" But Roe could see that Jamie was really hot under the collar. But it wasn't him in particular Jamie objected to. Jamie would have been furious with any man who was going out with his mother.

"No way! Do you hear me? No way!"

Finally Roe said, "Okay, Jamie, I'll respect your wishes if you don't want me to." Although they wound up staying for two or three days, Jamie wouldn't let Roe go over to the prison see Jim. So Roe just wound up camping out at the hotel, and Jamie himself told his dad about Roe and me.

One day Roe sat down and talked to me about what had happened in his marriage. He cried as he told me. My heart ached as he spoke, tears running down his face. I have only seen him cry one other time, and that was when his mom died.

I have agonized about whether or not to share what Roe told me with you. I don't think it's nice to talk about ex-husbands or ex-wives. But Roe and I have been misjudged so much since our marriage that I feel people need to know what really happened, and why we felt free before God to remarry. I have been called a home wrecker, and Roe has been called a wife stealer. I have talked to many of our friends about writing this story, and every one of them has said that I should take this opportunity to squelch the rumors once and for all—with the truth.

I would still refuse to write about this except that Roe himself has asked me to do so. I would never write this without his permission. So whether you think it's right or proper or not, at least you are hearing the truth from us and not from some rag magazine. I am not in any way trying to put down Ruth Ann Messner or to hurt her in any way.

Ruth Ann had originally filed for divorce back in January 1975. Roe said they had been getting ready to go out to a New Year's Eve party when she handed him the papers. "Roe," she said, "I want a divorce."

Roe said it was as if someone had knocked him over the head with a two-by-four. He couldn't believe what he was hearing. "Ruth Ann, what in the world have I done? What is wrong? I don't want a divorce. Let's try to work this out—for the children's sake, if for nothing else." With that, Roe told Ruth Ann that he would move out for six months and give it some time. "But before I leave," he added, "we have to tell the children first."

Roe called the kids (he and Ruth Ann had four children; the oldest was sixteen, the youngest six) to come upstairs. He told them that he and their mother wanted to talk to them. "Kids," he said, "Mom wants a divorce, and Dad will be moving out tomorrow." That was the saddest moment of his life. Roe didn't want the family broken apart.

"I won't be far away," Roe said. "And you can come and

see me anytime you want to. You stay here and take care of Mom."

The next day, he moved into a one-bedroom apartment.

Roe and Ruth Ann did get back together, but their life was misery. They were living under the same roof, but that was all. Roe worked hard, and over time he became a multimillionaire. Ruth Ann decided that she wanted something to do. She loved journalism, so Roe bought her *The Wichitan* magazine and *KS* magazine. Ruth Ann became a very powerful woman in Kansas.

Because of the fall of PTL, Roe had to file both personal and corporate bankruptcy. He lost $31 million. Ruth Ann also signed the bankruptcy papers. At that time, Roe also filed for divorce. He felt he could no longer live with someone who didn't love him. His heart was breaking. He told me that if Ruth Ann would have told him just one time that she loved him, he would not have filed for divorce.

When Roe asked Ruth Ann for a divorce, she hired herself a lawyer named Sheila Floodman. Between the two of them they took everything Roe had. Roe was left with a bedroom suite and a few other pieces of used furniture, and they had the very best of everything. Ruth Ann had a sale and sold many of the things Roe had asked for.

Ruth Ann and Sheila Floodman did some terrible things to Roe during the two years it took to finalize the divorce. One of the cruelest was that they went to Kansas U.S. attorney Randy Rathbun and told him that Roe had lied on the bankruptcy papers, and that if Ruth Ann were granted immunity she would tell whatever the government wanted to hear.

The next thing we knew, Roe got a call from Randy Rathbun, asking him if he would come and appear before a grand jury to answer questions concerning his bankruptcy. Roe didn't even bother to contact an attorney, as he said he had nothing to hide.

Roe was not worried as he boarded the airplane to fly to

Wichita. Kissing me good-bye, he said, "Tammy, don't worry, I'm glad to go and get this cleared up. I'll be home tomorrow, honey." But *I* was worried, having been through the horrible crisis of Jim going to prison. I knew that most of the time, truth has nothing to do with this kind of situation. I have absolutely no faith in our justice system. I know that you can have proof right in front of you, and if they are out to get you, your proof does absolutely no good. I was more than worried. However, the next evening Roe got home and did not seem at all upset; he said he had answered everything to their satisfaction. So I relaxed.

Then, to my horror, we were informed that Roe had been indicted. It was almost more than my heart could take. Roe was stunned. But once again, when the time came for him to go to Wichita and have his day in court, Roe was peaceful and full of optimism.

To make a long story short, however, he was found guilty by a panel of jurors.

Roe's lawyer, Steve Joseph, had not allowed Roe to testify at his trial because he was sure that Roe had already won. To their astonishment, they found out that Roe had lost. Roe was sentenced to twenty-seven months in jail. At the time of this writing, he is free on bond. He and Steve Joseph are appealing the case.

If those judges do put Roe in jail, I wonder what criminal element they will have to set free to make room for him. Murderers? Rapists? They told Roe that the prisons were so overcrowded he would have to wait until they could find room for him in one of them. How awful to release men who are dangerous to society so that they can make room for someone who has never hurt anyone, who has been a pillar of his community for forty years! It does not make any sense to me.

The week after Roe was convicted, Randy Rathbun resigned from his post to run for Congress. He had just landed the biggest fish of his career: Tammy Faye's husband. It seems he needed the publicity that Roe's high-profile case provided, and he got it. I watched him on TV, grinning from ear to ear over Roe's conviction. It made me sick to my stomach. I feel like Rathbun used Roe to climb the ladder. I would never vote for a man like that to be a dogcatcher, much less to help run our country.

In any event, I don't think Roe ever officially proposed to me. I just remember that one day the phone rang. It was Roe, and he was in Wichita. "Honey," he said, "my divorce is final. You need to set a wedding date."

I don't know if I was in shock or what but I told him, "Roe, I don't know how to set a wedding date. How do you do that?"

Roe laughed and said, "Well, honey, I think setting a wedding date has something to do with your time of the month." We both laughed and decided on October 3, 1993. I will always be thankful to God for a new beginning and a second chance.

Our wedding was a small affair held at the clubhouse at our subdivision. The children weren't there. We purposely didn't invite them. We didn't want his kids hurting their mom, or my kids hurting their dad. Jamie took my marriage pretty hard, although Tammy Sue, being older and married herself, understood. She handled my divorce and remarriage wonderfully well. Roe and I went to Hawaii on our honeymoon.

So here we were: two hurt and lonely people starting over again, both of us over fifty and still suffering over what we had been through, both of us having survived some very traumatic experiences. We were two lucky people who had arrived at the same point in life and found each other. The news media crowed over and over that I had married Roe for his money, that he was a multimillionaire. Well, we would both laugh so hard whenever we read that or saw it on TV.

Death Comes in the Night

After I went away to Bible college and married Jim, many years passed before I was close to Mom again. Although I always promptly remembered all the special times with presents and cards, I was never to be home again on a regular basis. For as soon as we got married, Jim and I were constantly on the road, and the years just went by so fast.

After Jerry Falwell fired Mom from PTL, my sister Debbie Ball and her two little boys moved in with her. Debbie worked at the 7-Eleven, and Mom took care of her two children. Those darling little boys filled some of the void in Mom's life. My dad had stayed on with her for a while, but their problems became worse and worse. Eventually they separated and he went back to International Falls.

She had some girlfriends who lived close by, and once in a while Mom would go out to supper with them. But most of all she loved to play the piano and sing with her grandchildren. I have a tape of her teaching the little boys a song, and it is my dearest treasure. Mom's once neat house was now filled with toys and playpens, while the couches and chairs were covered with throws so they

316 Tammy Faye Messner

would not get soiled. Mom was back to where she had started all over again. She had come full circle.

The thing I loved the most in the whole world was cuddling up on Mom's couch and just talking and laughing with her. We became very close after the loss of PTL and even more so after my divorce. Mom understood the divorce and was very supportive of me.

Mom had high blood pressure but was keeping it under control with medication. In addition, she gave herself daily shots of insulin to control her diabetes. But you would never have known she suffered with any of these ailments. She never complained. Everyone loved visiting Rachel. They would come away rejuvenated and encouraged. I never dreamed she could die.

But she did, all alone in her cute little house, sitting in her favorite chair. That will haunt me as long as I live— Mom dying alone. But it would have been far worse had the two boys she so adored been there when it happened. One of Mom's close friends told me that she had been out to supper with a couple of her friends. They said that for a week she had been concerned about her chest fluttering. Mom had even gone to the doctor saying that her medicine must not be working right. The doctor assured her all was well, but I think Mom knew by then that it wasn't.

Mom and her friends had had a good meal and had been laughing and talking. As Mom got out of the car, she said she had an upset stomach and was going to have a glass of 7UP to see if that would settle it. She hugged her girlfriends and said goodbye. The next morning the neighbors noticed that Rachel's front door was still open and it was a chilly morning. They called to her, but she didn't answer. Looking in through the locked screen door they saw Mom lying perfectly still in her chair. Immediately they called security, who then came and got the door open. But it was too late. Mom had already gone to be with the Lord sometime that night. She had suffered a massive heart attack.

It was early in the morning in Palm Springs. I had taken a friend to the airport early and come home and climbed back into bed. The phone rang, waking me from a deep sleep. I glanced over at the clock. It was 8:00 A.M. Wearily I picked up the phone, never realizing I was about to receive the worst message of my life. "Is this Tammy Faye?"

"Yes," I answered, still groggy.

"This is the county morgue. We have some bad news for you." I went numb. I started to panic. Was it Tammy Sue? Was it Jamie Charles? Was it my grandsons James or Jonothan? "Your mother is lying here in a chair dead. What do you want us to do with her?"

The words slowly sunk in, and I started to sob. "I don't know, sir, what do they do with people who die?" I couldn't think. I couldn't remember anything. I couldn't even remember that Mom lived at Heritage! I didn't know what to do. I was paralyzed by grief.

"Look, we're going to take care of it," said the voice at other end, probably realizing that I was in a state of shock. "We're going to take her down to the local hospital. When you're able to focus, call us about the final arrangements. Sorry for the news. Bye."

I put down the phone and started to scream, "Oh God, why? Why? I'm the oldest, I should know what to do—but I can't even think of anyone's name!"

For an hour I paced the house crying, asking God to help me. Finally my Aunt Gin's name sprang into my head. My mom's sister lived in International Falls. With trembling hands I picked up the phone and dialed her number. My voice was so choked up that she had a hard time understanding what I was saying. But in her matter-of-fact way, she calmed me down with her presence of mind. "First of all," she told me, "check and make sure it wasn't a trick, some kind of a crank call."

Then she instructed me to phone Tammy Sue and have her go to the hospital and check to make sure that it was

Mom. In my grief I had totally forgotten that Tammy Sue lived only a couple of miles from her grandmother. So I did as Aunt Gin said. Like a little child, I followed her orders. "Sissy, this is Mom," I sobbed into the phone. I told Tammy Sue what had happened and asked her to go to the hospital. Then I sat by the phone begging God that it was a prank call. In a few minutes, the phone rang. It was Tammy Sue. She was crying. "Yes, Mom, it's Grandma. But she looks good, Mom." And then through her tears, she added, "Mom, they put bright pink lipstick on Grandma before they would let me in to see her."

With that we both started to laugh hysterically. We had never seen Mom in any kind of makeup. I bet you anything Mom would have been laughing too.

That bit of frivolity brought me back to life. I was able to call my brother, and together we made the funeral arrangements. I would have loved to have had Mom buried at Heritage USA, but they would not even consider permitting that. Not knowing what else to do, we had her body taken by plane back to International Falls. Mom had always been afraid of flying. In death she had her first trip in an airplane.

I called Roe in Wichita, and he immediately got on a plane and headed to California to be with me. I wandered around the house all day, tears streaming down my face, remembering my precious little mom; trying to hear her voice in my mind, trying to picture what had happened. I prayed till there were no more prayers to pray and cried until there were no more tears to cry.

I had to get out of the house. I was suffocating. I got in my car and drove to the mall and began to walk. I walked and walked, not seeing anything, wanting to shout at the top of my lungs, "Doesn't anybody care? I don't have a mom anymore! What does a girl do without her mom? I want my mom!" But finally I tired out and went back home to find my friend Emma Howard waiting for me.

She had moved in bag and baggage to stay with me until I left for the funeral. Emma held me and rocked me as I sobbed and shook. She had lost her mom and knew what it was like. As if I were a small child again, she cradled me in her kindness, helping me pack and encouraging me to at least try to eat something. Emma was an angel. She let me talk and cry and cry and talk, even though I was hardly making sense.

It was the only time since I was a young girl that I didn't put any makeup on—and I didn't care. I didn't even try to put any on. For the first time in my life I didn't care how I looked or who saw me that way. I was a little girl again without a mother. This was the first time I actually felt my own mortality. I wanted to die too. I wanted to go to heaven where Mom was. I wanted to see her one last time. I wanted to hear her voice just once more. God, please let me die, I prayed. I guess it's a good thing God does not choose to answer all of our prayers.

Roe finally arrived, and we boarded a plane for International Falls. I had on a dress I had bought a few days before. I never knew I would be wearing it to my mother's funeral. We drove to the funeral home that was located right next to the church I had attended every Sunday and every Tuesday night while growing up. We had known Mr. Cudmore, the owner of the funeral home, all of our lives. The second I got out of the car I dashed inside. "Mr. Cudmore, where's my mom?"

He put his arm gently around me and said softly, "In here, honey." Then with tears running down his face he walked away.

I tiptoed up to that casket and looked down at the woman who had brought me into the world. She had carried me inside her for nine months. She had diapered me, bathed me, fed me, comforted me, made me laugh. She looked as if she were just sleeping. She was so beautiful and looked so peaceful in her lavender turtleneck sweater.

I was glad she had on that sweater. It was cold and rainy outside, and she would be cozy and warm. That reassured me. Isn't it funny, the things that go through your mind when you are hurting so bad?

I touched her hair, I touched her beautiful hands. Mom had the most beautiful hands and fingernails. I looked at my own hands and realized they were hers. I have my mom's hands! I kissed her and told her how much I loved her and how much I was going to miss her. My brothers and sisters had lined her casket with little notes and pictures. A banner on the casket read "Going Home!" I asked for a lock of her hair and for her glasses. Mr. Cudmore saw to it that I had both before the casket was closed. I brought a camera and was standing there debating whether to take pictures of her.

I needed to be able to look at her when I got home. I felt a tap on my shoulder, and there stood one of my former classmates, a man named Larry. He said, "Do what you have to do, Tammy." So I snapped the photos, and I am so glad I did. For when I take them out, whether it's in the quiet of the afternoon or late at night, they bring me peace and contentment. She gave me so much of what I am today. It's unbelievable. I look in the mirror, and there's my mom.

On the day of the funeral everybody was there, with our family occupying the two front pews of the church. I sat next to Dad. My sister Debbie, along with her two little boys, sat directly behind me. All of a sudden I heard one of them, little Jakie, say, "Mom, where's Grandma? You said she would be here." I lost it when I heard their little voices. "Please, Mom, we want to sit with Grandma." They didn't understand death. I wept unashamed.

The casket was closed, and we walked down the aisle holding on to Dad. It was the first time in many years that all eight of us kids had been together. Why did we have to wait until a funeral? We hugged one another and cried and vowed we would get together more often and share memories of Mom. Then came the part I dreaded the most. It was time to go to the cemetery. Outside it was cold and raining hard. The cemetery looked so bare and lonely. I looked over and saw the graves of Grandma and Grandpa Fairchild and my Uncle Rod, and then I focused my eyes on the fresh mound of earth that would be my mother's grave.

I wanted to run screaming and throw myself on Mom's casket. I couldn't leave her there alone. I wanted to join her in that cozy-looking box lined in cream-colored satin. I wanted to say to her all the things I had not had a chance to say. Then I felt a tug. It was Roe urging me back to the car. I walked away not looking back. "Good-bye, Mom. I'll see you in heaven!" I was clutching Mom's glasses and a lock of her beautiful hair.

A photographer, sent by one of the tabloids, was hiding in the bushes trying to get pictures of me in my grief. A couple of wonderful policemen, who were so kind to help out at the funeral, went into the bushes and came out with a roll of film. I will forever be grateful to them for that. I have not been back to International Falls since then.

After my mom died, Debbie sent me Mom's pajamas—I told her not to wash them. As soon as they arrived, I held them up to my nose and hugged them to me, trying to somehow get a smell of my mom. I needed that closeness with her, and I could smell her Estée Lauder perfume just faintly on her pajamas.

I hung her pajamas on the back of my bedroom door, like I knew she used to do. And every time I'd go by I would reach for them, grab rolls of the fabric in my fists, and then just clutch them to me. The tears would stream down my face as I would try to get another smell of Mom. But after a few short weeks the smell was almost gone.

I remember when I first told my mom about Roe. She was delighted. She said, "Honey, I always loved that Roe Messner." She even thought we looked "cute" together.

That's my only true regret. Mom never lived long enough to see us married. But I know she wished us every happiness.

One day the *Jerry Springer* show called and asked me to be on. But Springer said they wanted to do something different than I had done on other shows, and he asked if I had any suggestions. I had a wonderful suggestion. I had always thought I would love to meet my natural dad's— Carl LaValley's—other kids, as they were really my brothers and sisters too. But I could never figure out how to do it. There were eight of them.

So I told them of my dream, and they loved it. They immediately arranged to fly as many of them who could manage it to Chicago, where they would meet me for the very first time on TV. Everyone came except two of the girls and Carl himself, who was suffering from kidney failure and had to be on a dialysis machine. Still, it turned out to be one of the most exciting moments of my entire life. Since the first moment I met them, it was as if we had always been together. We still keep in touch.

It was my sister Penny who called one day and said, "Tammy, if you want to see Daddy alive, you need to fly to Minnesota as soon as you can. He is very sick." Part of me wanted to leave that day on the next plane, but another part of me wished that they had not called me with that sad news.

After a week of sleepless nights, I finally made my decision. I chose not to go—not even to his funeral. Not because I didn't want to, but because I wanted to more than anything else. I didn't want to get to know my real daddy, fall in love with him, and then see him die. I couldn't stand another loss in my life. And I knew if I saw him, I would love him like any girl would love her father, and I couldn't be put through that torture. After my mom's death, I couldn't open up another raw spot in my heart.

Life is strange. Sometimes you don't realize you miss somebody until they die. And then it's too late. I believe so much petty bickering could be overcome if people only realized how mortal they are. When someone dies, it's too late. Following the death of Carl LaValley, I called to order some flowers on 1-800-FLOWERS. And when I did, the woman at the other end said, "Well, where did you find out about us?" With this I started sobbing.

"Lady, listen, I'm ordering flowers for my father who just died, and you're wanting to know where I found out about you. I don't think that's important, you know!" I found myself out of control, jumping all over the poor woman. I was crying so hard I couldn't even order the flowers. When I finally was able to stop my tears, they were able to process my order with a card that read: "Daddy, I always loved you. Your daughter, Tammy Faye."

Strangely enough, death is not frightening to me. Like the Bible says, "Death, where is your sting?" Death is a part of life, and I'm not afraid. I'm probably more afraid of the way I might die. I don't want to suffer. But I'm not afraid of dying itself. After all, I want to see my mother again real bad, so I will be excited about seeing her and about seeing God and about seeing my Grandma Fairchild and the people I know are waiting for me.

Life Begins at Fifty

*T*oday Roe and I are deeply in love and have a wonderful marriage. Roe understands my need to speak about the old days once in a while. After all, he was there too. But he also gently reminds me that what's past is past and that we must move on beyond the grief of yesterday. Roe lost over $15 million when Heritage USA went down. "That's over, that's done, there's nothing you can do about it," he says. And we move on. That's the kind of person he is.

Roe has helped me to heal. For the first time in so many years, under his gentle, constant prodding, my heart has become willing to trust again. Things are totally different with him. Roe is nurturing, and I needed nurturing so bad. He believes that you must smell the roses every day. Before I almost never stopped to smell the roses. I rarely had the chance to even notice they were there! Every day Roe makes sure that we take the time to stop and enjoy what the Lord has provided for us. "Honey," he says, "out of every day, we're going to take time to stop and enjoy today as a day." And that's what we do, whether it's as simple as watching a sunset over the mountains or as complex as the two of us trying to figure out how to make the perfect spaghetti sauce.

Every morning Roe goes out to the golf course and hits balls. The man is as thin as a rail, with the muscular body of a superbly conditioned athlete, so you can see I'm fortunate in many respects. Thanks to my husband, today I am a lot more playful, I kid around a lot more, I take a lot more chances.

I let myself fail, because I realize failure is no big deal. You've got to allow yourself to fail, because without failure there's never any success. Nine times out of ten, what you think is wrong with you nobody else notices; or if they do, it's not that important to them, because they've got their own insecurities. You're your own worst critic. Even God isn't as hard on you as you are on yourself. So let yourself be real, let yourself be vulnerable, let yourself fall flat on your face.

Roe is inquisitive, interested in everything and anything. Being with him makes me feel like a child again, picking up every single rock to examine what's underneath. With Roe I discovered that my creativity was still alive. The feeling and the sensitivity I was born with, and which was repressed for so many years, has blossomed once more.

My husband should have been a psychologist. He has taught me how to shatter those self-defeating myths about myself, how to cast them forever out of my life. Love is the greatest healer of all. It can overcome any traumas. I know that now for a fact. Years ago I lost everything. But I've learned you can always regain anything you lost. It's just stuff. Everywhere you look there's more stuff. You can replace jewelry. You can replace cars. You can replace houses. The only thing you can't replace is each other.

When Roe and I got married, he told me that if I ever wanted to go back into television, he would be there to support me 100 percent. And when I said that I *did* want to do TV again, it came as no surprise to him. I felt that I had something valuable to share with hurting people. I had been to the depths of despair and made it back. I wanted to share this message: "God is who He says He is, and He will not and does not fail."

I knew TV forward and backward, and I felt as comfortable on TV as I did in my own living room. I loved Christian television and felt there must be a place for me in it. After all, we knew the entire Christian TV world, we had helped almost all of them at one time or another with large financial gifts, or by doing telethons, or by having them on our TV network. Surely someone would help me find a place to minister again.

But I didn't know where to start, so I started by writing a long letter to Paul and Jan Crouch of Trinity Broadcasting. As you remember, we helped them start Trinity many years ago. I begged them for help. I have never begged anyone for anything in my whole life.

I received a call from Jan's secretary saying that she had personally handed Jan the letter from me and had also hand-delivered a copy to Paul. When I did not hear back from them, I followed up with phone calls both to their home and office. Neither Jan nor Paul ever answered my letter or returned my calls. I finally gave up.

Next I called Richard Roberts, Oral's son. I got his wife, Lindsey, on the phone. I will never forget Lindsey's kindness to me. She told me that she would talk to Oral and Richard but she was positive they wouldn't do anything for us. I thought of the thousands of dollars Jim had given to their ministry when they were in financial difficulties. I thought of how Jim had taken Richard in and had him on television when no one else would have him, after his much publicized divorce from his wife, Patty Roberts.

Jim built up people's trust in Richard again by supporting him on our TV program. The show that Richard has today is a direct result of Jim's constant urging back then, plus the free airtime he gave Richard to get started. Richard's show was on our network for years because Jim bothered to care. But Lindsey was right. I never heard from Richard or Oral, ever!

Then I was going to try Pat Robertson. I even went as far as to call Pat's secretary, who was a friend of ours. She let me know very quickly that I was on the wrong track thinking that Pat would ever help us in any way. In Robertson's caste system, I was not intellectually, socially, or financially up to the minimum standards of acceptability. Pat always felt that way about Jim and me and made no secret about it.

By the way, soon after that call I found out the government was planning to give Jim an early parole and that it was Robertson, who had a lot of clout in Washington, who appealed to them not to release Jim. Pat told them he felt Jim should be made to serve out his full sentence.

I kept trying, but to no avail. Every ministry I called claimed they could not help me in any way. I felt totally discouraged. I didn't know what I was going to do with my life. I knew I had so much to share with hurting people, but no way to do it. I didn't know where to turn except to the Christians, and they wouldn't help me. But Roe gave me courage. He told me that neither Paul Crouch, Pat Robertson, Oral Roberts, nor Richard Roberts was my source. He said, "Tammy, *God* is your source. You have preached that for years, honey. Now believe it."

"I'm trying, Roe," I said, "I really am. But my heart is so full of misery I don't know what to do. Why won't somebody help me?"

A few days later I was sitting on my bed crying my heart out. "God, what am I going to do? No one will help me!" Tears of dejection streamed down my face.

Then suddenly I heard a voice in my heart say to me, "Tammy, you don't need their help. I can do it for you all by Myself. Just give it to Me and let Me do it."

Beyond a shadow of a doubt, I knew that it was God

talking to my heart. I never worried about my situation again after that day. I just simply put my trust in God, not people. Because people will fail you. God never will. That's a fact of life. Sure enough, two weeks later, something unbelievable started happening for me.

Out of the clear blue the Sally Jessy Raphael show was calling, *Good Morning America* was calling, and so were Tom Snyder, *A Current Affair,* and John and Leeza. I was scared to death. Secular television!

A new world was beginning to open up for me. As a result I met a young man by the name of John Redman. He was convinced that I needed my own show and decided to go to bat for me. He began to introduce me to producers, one of them being Dan Weaver.

Unknown to me, Dan had watched me on *PTL* for years and had been a fan of my daily show, *Tammy's House Party.* Dan liked the format of that program and discussed doing something similar. He began to speak to the executives at the Fox network about me and just wouldn't give up. One day he called very excited and said, "Tammy, one of our executives in charge of new programming would like to speak to you. Can you come in?"

Before I knew it, Roe and I were in Los Angeles getting ready to drive over to the Fox studios to meet with Dan Weaver. We were going to discuss producing a new talk-variety show. My heart was about to explode. God really *could* do it by Himself. Roe's words came back to me: "Tammy, *God* is your source."

Dan Weaver was waiting for us at the building entrance and ushered us up to the office of Brian Graden, who was in charge of new show contracts. The moment I walked into his office was the first time I could really admit to myself that something might actually happen. And it did! As I signed my name to a seven-year contract with the Fox Television Network, a prayer of thanksgiving went from my heart to God: "Thank you, God, for taking such good care of me." A dream had just come true.

Originally, Dan wanted me to do the show by myself. But I was gun-shy, not having been on television for so many years. The thought of doing it all by myself was more than my mind could comprehend. So I asked Dan if he could get together a group of potential cohosts for me. He did, and it was during those interviews that I met Jim J. Bullock. Now, the other nine interviews I conducted were calm, and I had actually made up my mind, even before I met Jim, on a young black man I had felt comfortable with and with whom I felt I could work well. But the minute Jim J. and I met, it was like an explosion of magic. Everyone felt it!

I guess "explosion" is the key word in describing him. Jim J. seemed to be everywhere at once. He was funny and crazy and full of boundless energy. We were in the middle of talking about something and he jumped up and ran— no, I should say *bounded*—off the set. I was worn out by the time the interview was over. Later, when I talked to Dan Weaver about it, I said, "I really like Jim J., but I don't know if I can work with all that energy day after day. He wore me out." But Dan, too, had felt the magic between us, and felt that magic would be contagious to a TV audience.

One of the first things Jim J. said to me when we met was "Tammy, I'm gay. Do you find that offensive? I know that you're a Christian."

This was my answer: "Jim J., when I look at people, I do not see gay or straight; all I see is the person. And I see a person that God loves, and that His son Jesus died on the cross for. So who am I to judge? I do not judge anyone anymore. I have been misjudged so many times—by people who either didn't understand or didn't *want* to understand the things that happened in my life. I know how it hurts to be judged. I don't want to be a courtroom. I want to be a hospital."

Jim J. Bullock was hired, and we were on our way. Dan decided that the program would be called *The Jim J. and Tammy Faye Show*. He laughed and proclaimed that now Jim and Tammy were back together again. They even used that phrase in some of the subsequent advertising. I didn't mind.

We began to do test shows—practice shows, as we called them. We worked for many months perfecting them. But early on we all realized that we saw the show a little differently. I saw it as a clean, all-American show. Jim J. saw it more like *Saturday Night Live*, with lots of comedy and energy, and a bit risqué. I think that Dan saw it somewhere in the middle. However, I told Dan that I would not do anything to compromise my Christian testimony. I was first a Christian and only second a talk-show host. He agreed.

Finally, we started our on-the-air programming. The fan mail was pouring in, and Jim and I were on top of the world. We had a great staff of people working with us. We became family and really cared about each other.

Then something exciting happened. We heard that we were going to NATPE, the annual convention of producers and distributors of TV shows, where new shows are bought and sold. The time came to go. Our wardrobe lady handed us our clothes (all color-coordinated, so that we wouldn't clash). Off we went to Las Vegas, where we were given a beautiful suite at Caesars Palace.

The convention proved to be a great success for our show. Hundreds of people came by our beautiful booth. One of them was Rosie O'Donnell, whom I'd always wanted to meet. She told us that she loved our show and thought it had great potential and that she wanted to be a guest sometime. We were thrilled! Rosie's name and picture were pasted all over Vegas, and we couldn't believe that she would take the time to come and see us. In fact, she surprised me by saying that she watched the *PTL* show. She knew the entire theme song and then sang it to me. Even *I* had forgotten the words, but Rosie remembered.

It was one exciting thing after another. *Good Morning America* asked Jim and me to do a chat with them concerning the convention. When it was time to leave, we were exhausted, but we were certainly happy that things had gone so great.

When we got back to L.A., there were numerous messages on our answering machine. One of them was from David Letterman's show, asking me to be a guest. I accepted, even though I was scared to death. However, David was very kind to me and it turned out well. Then the *Phil Donahue* show asked Jim J. and me to appear. We were receiving unbelievable publicity, and our show was getting an excellent response everywhere they were showing it.

I will never forget that wonderful time in my life. Jim J. and I did sixty fun-filled shows together.

Then, terribly, I found out that I had cancer of the colon and would have to leave the show. I had been bleeding for a year. When I started doing the TV show, the bleeding got worse. I would not go to a man doctor and waited until I could find a woman. By then it was too late. That day I received the medical news will always be clear in my memory. Our house has three bedrooms: one for us, one for guests, and one that my husband has made into a special closet for me. I was nervously working in that closet, waiting for the phone to ring. When it did, I nearly jumped out of my skin. Roe, in the other room, answered it with his usual soft hello. Then there was complete silence. I ran out of the closet to him. Roe was sitting at his desk, quietly listening.

"Honey," I said, "is it the doctor?"

He nodded his head yes.

"I don't have cancer, do I?"

With that, a look of sadness passed over my husband's face. I knew the answer before he even answered me.

"Yes, you have cancer, Tammy. Here, honey, take the phone. The doctor wants to talk to you."

I put the phone to my ear and heard her say, "Tammy, I have some bad news for you. Your tests came back positive. You have a large tumor, and it is cancerous." I talked with her calmly, making arrangements for the next steps I had to take. Roe sat there, listening to our conversation. I knew he was preparing himself for the storm that must surely be coming when I hung up the phone: the crying, the denial, the "Why me?"

I hung up the phone as he threw his arms around me, tears in his eyes. "Oh, honey," he said. "I am so sorry. It's going to be all right, Tammy, it's going to be all right."

My very first words to him were "Well, God is the God of cancer too. He was the God of cancer yesterday when I thought things were fine. He is still the God of cancer today. He hasn't changed just because I have it." There were no tears, no saying "Why me?" There was only a deep peace that I felt going all over me. I never felt even the first tinge of fear.

Roe and I sat and quietly discussed what we must do next. "Do you think I should call Jamie and Tammy Sue?" I wondered. "I don't want to worry them. I don't think I'll let them know until it's all over."

With that, Roe handed me the phone. "You must call them, honey. It wouldn't be fair to them if you didn't." For the first time, fear struck my heart. How would my kids react? Hadn't they been through enough? How much more could they take? Would Jamie freak out? I was most worried about him. I knew that Tammy Sue was tough like me, but Jamie was a worrier. He takes everything so hard. He was in Atlanta, at school, and I just didn't want to upset him. But Roe insisted and took the phone and dialed the number.

"Hi, Jay," he said, "this is Roe. Your mom wants to talk to you." He handed me the phone.

"Mom, what's wrong?" Jamie asked. I could hear the fear in his voice.

"Now, honey," I said, "it's nothing to worry about. I'm not worried and I am not afraid."

"Okay, Mom, but what is it?"

"Jamie, I went to the doctor, and I have colon cancer. They're going to operate on me. They said that if I was going to get cancer, colon cancer is the easiest to cure." I could hear Jamie breathing hard. "Jamie," I added, "now is the time we have to put our trust in God."

"Yes, Mom, I know," he said.

Then, to my horror, I started to cry.

"Please, Mom, don't cry. I'll get all the people here to pray for you, Mom."

I quickly regained my control and made a joke of some kind and we said good-bye and hung up. Jamie handled it much better than I ever thought possible. I was grateful to God. Jamie and I are real pals. We were together by ourselves for such a long time while Jim was in prison and Jamie was the man of the house, taking care of Mom.

Next it was time to call Tammy Sue. She took the news calmly, but she firmly stated that she was going to come to California and spend a couple of weeks with me. She arrived March fifth, and my operation was March sixth. The night before the operation, we stayed up talking and laughing, and by the time we got to bed it was nearly 5:00 A.M. and time to get up.

My best girlfriend, Debra Keener, came all the way from Los Angeles with a limousine and a driver so that I could be driven to the hospital in style. She has always been there for me. Roe, Tammy Sue, Debra, my next-door neighbor Sigrid, Vi Azvedo, Emma, and many of the people from our church gathered in the hospital waiting room to pray for me during my surgery. I was never afraid. As they put the IV tube in my arm, the nurse and I were laughing and talking, and I don't even remember going to sleep.

I do recall waking up and seeing the dear faces of my husband, my daughter, and my best friends, all smiling at me and telling me that everything went fine and that they had gotten all the cancer and that Doctor Michael Last had been able to reattach my colon. I did not need a colostomy, thanks to the skill of that wonderful surgeon. That is what the fear is with colon cancer, that you will have to be attached to a bag the rest of your life. I will always be grateful to God for that, as that would have been very hard for me to face.

Thanks to Dr. Marvin Brooks, I was given a beautiful two-room suite at the Eisenhower Hospital. That made it possible for Tammy Sue, Roe, or Sigrid to stay with me at night. I don't know who was responsible for allowing me to leave my makeup and eyelashes on during surgery. Whoever it was probably felt it wouldn't matter, that my head and my you-know-what were a long ways away from each other.

The next few days were pain-filled as I recovered and the nine-inch incision in my tummy began to heal. But it was a time filled with love, flowers, and lots of presents. Both of my hospital rooms were filled with flowers. Everyone said it was like walking into a huge flower garden. Two life-size teddy bears and dozens of other gifts filled every corner of the room, and get-well cards were arriving from people all over the country. I will always be grateful to the marvelous people who stood with me and showed me they cared about me.

My daughter stayed with me for three weeks. It was a very special time for us. We became not only mother and daughter but best friends. It was worth getting cancer to be able to spend three weeks with my daughter.

As of this writing I am still debating on whether or not to go through chemotherapy and radiation. My doctors have strongly advised me to do both. It is a very difficult decision to make. Half the people you talk to and half the books you read say that chemo is a killer to the immune system, that you should never do it. The other half say exactly the opposite: that you must do it if you want to be a cancer survivor.

I am praying that I will make the decision that is right for my body. I never dreamed I would have cancer. I always thought cancer is something that happens to someone else. I have always been so healthy and so full of energy. Cancer showed me that I am not invincible, that I need to take better care of myself, and that the things that happen to other people can happen to me. It makes you feel very vulnerable.

But with all the pain and disappointment, other positive things began to happen as well. I was contacted to do an infomercial, and guess what they wanted me to talk about? How I made it through all the things that had happened in my life. I was going to get a chance to help hurting people. And to put the frosting on the cake, they paid for me to make a new singing album to be sold as part of the infomercial.

But God did not stop there. Villard Books has made it possible for me to write this book. And recently I signed a contract with a wig company called HairArt. The Tammy Faye Wig Collection will be out by the time you read this. Plus, I have also been offered a part in a sitcom that I am thinking about.

The other day I was sitting in a restaurant and I saw a young man with a T-shirt that read DON'T EVER, EVER, EVER, EVER GIVE UP. I'm so glad that I didn't.

Roe and I have a wonderful marriage. Even with the troubles we have had to face, our relationship is filled with love, peace, and much joy. We allow each other room to be who we are. We are two separate people, not appendages of each other. We respect each other in every way. We have been married now for three years, and Roe still opens the car door for me. He never forgets to be a gentleman. That is rare among men in this day and age. He makes me feel special, every day. We always make time for each other. And when I forget, he gently reminds me to slow down and smell the roses.

We laugh a lot.

He was raised to always turn the lights out when you leave a room. I love light, so I turn all the lights on, and he follows me around turning them all off.

He loves quiet. I love noise, and I always have a TV blaring away in one or maybe two rooms of the house.

He loves health food and vitamins. I am a junk-food junkie!

Roe loves to golf; I think golf is a little slow. I love to shop. So he golfs while I shop. Now, *that* works!

He thinks a man can live the rest of his life if he owns one good suit, four or five pairs of slacks, a few golf shirts, and a pair of shoes. I'm always sneaking something into his wardrobe. He has two small hanging rods full of clothes. I have an entire small bedroom full of clothes, *plus* all the spare closets in the house. He just looks at all my stuff and laughs. One of his favorite lines when he walks into my closet is "Honey, aren't you running short on shoes?"

The secret to our happy marriage is, first of all, that we love each other, that we have magic, and that we both love God. He is first in our lives. Second, we don't take life too seriously. We have learned to laugh at our problems. Third, we are always there for each other, no matter what. We hug and kiss all the time, and it doesn't always have to lead to sex. I think that is important in a marriage. A wife doesn't want to feel pressured every time she gets a hug or a kiss from her husband. That has ruined many marriages. We accept each other just the way we are, and we don't try to change each other.

We still flirt with each other and say "I love you" several

times a day. We share housework and cooking. And we both give. I found out that when you give, you get back much more than you have given to your mate. We have a marvelous marriage. I thank God for second chances.

People ask me what my feelings are when I see people who have disappointed or hurt me. Am I still angry at them? The answer is no. Being angry is a choice. I have chosen to forgive and move on with my life. People ask me if I ever still think about the past. Of course I do! Life would be so much easier if God had provided our brains with an ERASE button. Whenever thoughts of yesterday come, I think of the story about the bird. "You cannot stop a bird from flying over your head, but you need not let it build a nest in your hair."

Then what do I think about Jerry Falwell today, you may ask. God demands that we forgive, and for many years now I have been working on forgiving Jerry. I feel in my heart that I have. You may say, Well, if you've forgiven him, then why are you writing those things about him in this book? That is a good question, and I will answer it for you. I believe that truth is truth. What happened happened and is now history. I just want history to be told correctly for my children's sake and for the sake of my grandchildren and generations to come. They may read many different accounts of what happened, but they will know that Mom, or Grandma, did not lie. You believe what you want to believe. For some people I could write my heart out all day, and they still wouldn't believe what I say.

One thing I have learned in life is that some questions have no answers. I have learned to quit looking for those answers and get on with my life. Remember that yesterday is gone. There is nothing we can do to change yesterday. We must live today fully, as today is all we have. It is called the "present" because it is a gift from God to us. Of course we must plan for tomorrow, but we must not worry about tomorrow because it may not come. Not one of us has a guarantee that tomorrow will come. I have learned to live for today, and I trust God with all my tomorrows.

Recently, Blair Bycura, our next-door neighbor in Charlotte, died in a plane crash. It was a terribly sad time for all of us. Jim Bakker was asked to preach Blair's funeral, and Jamie was asked to be one of the pallbearers. After the funeral service, caught in the throes of reminiscing, Jim decided that all the old gang, he and Blair's wife, Judy, and her two boys, Darin and Ryan, plus Jamie and Tammy Sue, should all go back to Tega Cay, where our houses were in the PTL days, for one last look at the past.

Blair and Judy's place was still sitting there, but our former house had burned down and was just a huge black hole in the ground surrounded by the beautiful trees and the lake. Tammy Sue and Jamie could still see the outline of where their bedrooms used to be. They saw where the kitchen was and remembered all the wonderful times we had there, Mom making fudge and Dad doing his beer-battered shrimp. It was a time for memories. The tree house was still there, but seemed much smaller to the kids than it had been so many years before. How did four of us ever sleep in there?

Then they all walked back to where the garage used to be. There in the cement you could still see the outlines of several pairs of hands. The words written in the cement next to those handprints said "We are all going out to eat at the fish camp tonight." Everyone started to cry.

After getting back to Judy Bycura's house, Jim told her, "I would like to buy the property and rebuild the house."

But Judy's response was quick and to the point. She looked him straight in the eye. "No, Jim. You can't bring back what's all over now."

Jim, if you're reading this, here's my advice: Get on with your life, and don't worry what people think. Hold your head up high. Both Roe and I want to see you make it again. Continue to preach the gospel of Jesus Christ, and let the chips fall where they may. Those who know know, and those who don't know we're never going to convince anyway. So don't waste your time trying to prove your innocence. You're the father of my children, the man who changed my life, and more than anything I want you to succeed. I hope everything you touch prospers and that you can finally find the happiness you deserve.

Today Tammy Sue is preaching around the country. She's singing, and she's with her dad as of this writing. Jim recently preached and Tammy Sue sang at the big Azusa Street conference in front of thousands of people there. And so they're doing that together, which I just think is so wonderful—like mother, like daughter! I feel God has been good to me. Tammy Sue's two little boys, James and Jonothan, are delightful. James looks just like his grandpa.

My son, Jamie Charles, now better known as Jay, is busy learning how to be a youth minister and is doing quite well. He is totally free of cigarettes, alcohol, and drugs. There's not very much any young person could tell Jamie that he doesn't already know. As a result of that, he can really be an incredible help to teenagers trying to straighten out their lives. Jay is strong and tall, a very good-looking boy indeed.

Yes, thanks to my children, my grandchildren, my wonderful marriage, and all the people who have shown me their support through the years, I truly believe in miracles. Of course, if you had led my life and were still around to write about it, you'd believe in miracles too.